AAY-9333

CHILDREN OF POVERTY

Studies on the Effects of Single Parenthood, the Feminization of Poverty, and Homelessness

edited by

STUART BRUCHEY
University of Maine

A GARLAND SERIES

AFRICAN AMERICAN MEN IN CRISIS

Proactive Strategies for Urban Youth

Wesley E. Pullman

GARLAND PUBLISHING, Inc.
New York & London / 1995

Library of Congress Cataloging-in-Publication Data

Pullman, Wesley E., 1949–
    African American men in crisis : proactive strategies for
urban youth / Wesley E. Pullman.
        p.   cm. — (Children of poverty)
    Includes bibliographical references (p. 262) and index.
    ISBN 0-8153-2141-4 (acid-free paper)
    1. Social work with Afro-Americans—Case studies. 2. Afro-
American boys—Services for—Case studies. 3. Social work with
youth—United States—Case studies. I. Title. II. Series.
HV3181.P85 1995   95-9660
362.84'96073—dc20

Printed on acid-free, 250-year-life paper
Manufactured in the United States of America

Dedication

This work is dedicated to my wife and best friend Happy, who supported and endured the entire process with grace and beauty. The research was conducted in memory of Bumps, the Prince of Diamond Hill, and Richie, the Boxing Champion of Mudtown. May God bless them, wherever they may be.

Contents

List of Figures

African American Men
in Crisis

Chapter 1: Fallen Heroes or Forgotten Victims

The challenges and obstacles to full participation of African American men in the mainstream economic and social structure of American life is rapidly becoming an area of public debate. Amidst record breaking homicide rates, media sensationalism and popular stereotypes, people are inclined to forget that the most frequent victims of urban violence are young black men. The scholarly works of modern pioneers such as Gary (1981), Staples (1982), and Gibbs (1988) reflect an emerging focus on this fact. By labeling black males in America as an endangered species, Gibbs (1988) creates a graphic metaphor for a social crisis of major proportions. Nevertheless, little has been written about projects programs or strategies designed to address identified problems such as high rates of incarceration, homicide victimization, unemployment, and educational disruption among black males in American society.

This critical condition has been the subject of profound philosophical debate among a small community of scholars whose concerns reflect a mutual commitment to the political and socioeconomic empowerment of African American people, in general, and black men in particular (Bowser 1990; Gary 1981; Gibbs 1988; Madhubuti 1990; Staples 1982; Wilson 1991). The combined perspective can be described as occurring within the context of racial discrimination and focusing on the adaptive responses incorporated by minority people in an ethnically stratified society (DeVore and Schlesinger 1987; Gordon 1978). If the quantity of academic publication is any indicator of official interests, this small community of scholars is more closely likened to a voice crying in the wilderness than to the harbinger of a new age. Little has been done to address the critical needs of black men or the concerns expressed by this group. As rates of crime, incarceration and violence continue to soar, it appears that amelioriative strategies, exclusive of get tough law enforcement policies, have been left to the devices of local grass roots organizations and private voluntary agencies (Jeter 1993; Seigel 1993; Wilson 1991).

Efforts to address the crisis of violence, unemployment, and incarceration (Gary 1990; Gibbs 1990; McGhee 1984) affecting black men in America have resulted in local initiatives to create specialized programs in churches, neighborhoods, communities and some schools (Wilson 1991). Concerns about lost cultural heritage compel some academics to call for a return to systematic efforts in the socialization processes for African American youth by suggesting a renaissance of knowledge about traditional African rites and ceremonies (Karenga 1977; Kilson and Rotberg 1976; Nobles 1974b; Vizedom 1976; Warfield-Coppock 1990).

Identifying and recognizing African traditions in American culture has been a continuing source of controversy (Frazier 1939; Herskovitz 1958; Hollaway 1993) which reflect some of the underlying racial tensions which comprise American culture (Myrdal 1944; Reuter 1927; Wacker 1983). Efforts to create culture specific manhood training, male socialization and rites of passage for young black men have generated some controversy in academic and political circles. An example of this controversy can be seen in the discontinuation and subsequent conflict over a Milwaukee school-based program designed specifically for black males (Leake and Leake 1992; Toch 1991). In spite of the tension, however, similar programs continue to operate in other localities (Collison 1991).

Community organizers, group counselors and school social workers all have a vested interest in this subject because specialized efforts are being developed in each of these venues (Asante1991; Frye 1990; Lee 1987; Wilson 1991). Whereas sociological studies and explanations of the issues are important, implementation of proposed solutions based on scientific inquiry place the burden on policy makers, social workers, educators and other helping professionals to apply new knowledge in meaningful ways.

The study utilizes a constructivist research strategy based on the "naturalistic" model developed by Lincoln and Guba (1985) and elaborated upon in later works (Guba and Lincoln 1989). The research goal is to discover and articulate common themes based upon the claims, concerns and issues voiced by people who are actively involved in developing programs for young black men. Constructivist inquiry is uniquely appropriate for this policy research approach (Majchrzak 1984) because the issues and concerns have yet to be fully defined by the available academic literature.

Multiple data collection strategies include participant observation, structured interviews and collection of physical documentation from program sites located in three mid-Atlantic coastal cities. Case study comparisons of programs were used to identify conceptual similarities and differences. The end result is intended to provide readers with a conceptual framework for understanding the operating principles behind specialized programs designed to facilitate positive social adjustment for young black men in urban settings. The study findings provide an empirically based body of knowledge, offering a comprehensive description of the claims, concerns and issues (Guba and Lincoln 1989) as presented by people active in the field.

Statement of Purpose

The essential rationale for this work is that there is a need to clarify the basic issues and to achieve a better understanding of the obstacles facing young black men in our society. This subject is important to social workers and social scientists alike, because it strikes at the heart of contemporary concerns about ethnic sensitivity and human need in a pluralistic society (Carter and McGoldrick 1988; DeVore and Schlesinger 1987; Pinderhughes 1988; Schaefer, 1990). Secondly, there is a need to develop a broader consensus on policy development surrounding these concerns. Finally, there is a need to provide more academic resources with which to inform social work practice as it pertains to addressing the problems of at risk urban youth.

This study is designed to enhance current knowledge and understanding of how different people in urban communities are attempting to address the needs of young black men. Its purpose is to further academic understanding and knowledge about community based male socialization programs for black inner city youth. Precious little research has been devoted to problems experienced by black males, in general, and male socialization programs, in particular. Although some information is available through the popular media, the issue is too important to allow newspapers, magazines and television journalism to have control over knowledge of the subject. Too many children are growing up in fatherless households, dropping out of school or being shot by their peers in the streets (Gibbs 1988; Madhubuti 1991). Too much fear and not enough understanding already exists between the different factions which make up American society (Kotlowitz 1991). Negative stereotypes abound and solutions still seem scarce.

Projects focusing on the needs and concerns of young black men currently operate in a variety of settings throughout the country (Gary and Pullman 1993) and have been reported on in the popular media (Jeter 1993; Siegel 1993). Although these enterprises may represent only partial solutions to a very complex set of social problems, they have taken place on a grass roots level by people in cities as far apart as Milwaukee, Washington, Chicago, and Philadelphia (Jeter 1993; Wilson 1991). Scholars have just begun to identify and report on these efforts, but a great deal more information is needed in order to develop informed interventions, programs and policies.

The goal of this study is one of discovery. Its purpose is to identify and articulate the essential issues, program philosophies and practical strategies adhered to by people actively involved in specialized programs for young black men in high risk urban communities. This goal was accomplished through extensive observation and interviewing at three separate research sites. Transferability of the findings to other settings is a task the readers must undertake based on their own determination of whether the circumstances described in the case studies fit or apply to them. The intent of this research is not to represent a general condition or create a stereotypical picture of all such programs, and the findings should not be construed in that way.

One criticism of the constructivist orientation is in the degree to which inductive processes of analysis can be judiciously applied as general principles. Guba and Lincoln (1989) however, quote Cronbach (1975) in the assertion that generalizations decay over time regardless of the research paradigm and are therefore context bound. For these reasons, constructivist approaches do not encourage theory building or grounded theoretical statements (Glaser and Strauss 1967). Instead, they recognize that all social observations occur within an ever changing context (Guba and Lincoln 1989, 95). Instead of generalizability, constructivists emphasize transferability and the tentative application of findings to other settings (Chambers, Wedel and Rodwell 1992). Given this notion of a dynamic social world in which hard and fast general laws rarely apply, constructivists maintain that transferability of findings is a better measure of utility in research. Guba and Lincoln (1989) describe transferability as a function of relevance. Ultimately, the concept of transferability asserts that it is for the reader, or the receiver of the message, to determine its relevance. Rather than make lawlike claims or assertions, constructivists are content to provide idiographic interpretations (Chambers, Wedel and Rodwel, 1992) designed to inform but not control general conceptions. It is the job of the researcher to provide sufficient information about the context and details of the setting, a thick description (Geertz 1973). The reader's job is to make an informed decision about the applicability of the findings to his or her own experiences (Lincoln and Guba 1985; Skritic 1985).

It is the author's intent to accurately reflect the experiences and perspectives of people who participated in the study and in so doing to provide some practical examples for people interested in this subject. The desired outcome is to provide an enlightened understanding of how people construct and respond to the social realities of their world (Guba and Lincoln 1989, 60-61). If general guidelines can be inferred by the reader and productively applied to another social setting, then a further purpose will have been served. Ideally the presentations here will inform the process of needs assessment, policy analysis and program development through the enhancement of human understanding. If this end can be achieved, then a valuable contribution to social science knowledge, social policy formation, and social work practice will have been made.

Foreshadowed Research Questions

This research project explores three basic questions. The first question asks what are the fundamental issues, needs and concerns of people involved in specialized programs targetting young black men?

The second question pursues underlying philosophies. What are the theoretical assumptions and driving principles affecting the development and operation of these programs? The third question emphasizes implementation, by asking how are these assumptions and principles put into practice? The findings presented here provide three case studies along with an examination of common themes. Implications for social policy are discussed, with the goal of enhancing future efforts in program planning by conveying the experiences of people who are actively confronting the problem in the field.

Chapter 2: The Scope of the Problem

Since the subject of program development for young black men is not abundantly available in the academic literature, this overview of previous research is designed to provide a broad base of information in order to facilitate a better understanding of what was encountered during field observations. The intent is to educate the reader with regard to the overall social and intellectual context within which the three programs, about to be discussed, take place.

The multitude of issues confronting young black men in contemporary American culture are best recognized as problems in which the whole of society has a vested interest. Describing young black men as a population at risk is a documentable observation. Explaining how or why this situation came to be is an entirely debatable matter. The current crisis among black men is reflective of historical, political and social patterns which have emerged out of the actions and interactions of the whole and not any single faction (Wilson 1991). It is truly an American dilemma because racial conflict is ingrained in American history. All are victims, and all are responsible. The importance of this distinction should not be underestimated because the solutions will most likely require prolonged cooperation and collective efforts.

Gunnar Myrdal (1944) asserted that the problem of racial discrimination is a problem for white people in America because only white people have the power to change it. While Malcolm X echoed these sentiments (Haley 1964), the philosophical orientation of this study is that inequality is a problem for people of all races, and that, only by working together will it be resolved. Almost fifty years have passed since Myrdal, a Swedish anthropologist, first referred to the "American dilemma" of race, yet deep seeded patterns of economic and political inequality persist (Pinderhughes 1988 ; Schaefer 1991). In many ways subsequent social scientists has failed to pick up the gauntlet thrown down by this definitive statement.

Past research on social problems confronting African American people has tended to emphasize three basic themes, biological deficits, cultural deficits or racial oppression (Oliver 1989). A persistent focus on alleged shortcomings, particularly as they relate to family (Allen 1981; Auletta 1983; Moynihan 1965), has been thorough if not misguided, according to Oliver (1989). Family inadequacies and cultural deprivation theories have been sharply criticized for lacking a comprehensive theoretical context of analysis; using faulty, over simplified, and monolithic conceptual models; ignoring intraracial variation; and fixating on low income or pathological populations (Peters 1974; Staples 1985; Staples and Johnson 1993). Van Dijk (1993) also suggests that analysis of research discourse is essential to weeding out prejudice and racial bias in social scientific inquiry. Such analysis includes not only how problems are initially defined but also the language used to describe the social context in which they occur.

In pointing out the inherent inadequacies of the dominant theoretical perspectives, Oliver (1989, 17) calls for a structural-cultural focus. This approach, as he defines it, recognizes institutional factors such as racism, capitalistic exploitation, family patterns, and other structural influences without ignoring the ability of people and communities to exercise self-determination over how they adapt environmental pressures. The structural-cultural perspective maintains that people are both shaped by and shape their social world. Oliver (1989, 17) describes this process as an "interrelationship between structural pressures and cultural adaptations."

Cornel West (1993) also argues that the failure of civil rights reforms and growing frustration within the African American community have resulted in what he calls a nihilistic response characterized by a widespread "sense of psychological depression, personal worthlessness and social despair (pp.12-13)." By denouncing both "liberal-structuralists" and "conservative-behaviorists," West (1993, 11-20) urges scholars to recognize and confront the nihilistic malaise which he believes is a pervasive social influence crippling black communities. Although the threat of nihilism is not new, West (1993) maintains that in recent years it has taken on a more powerful stature. He attributes this change to the effects of "market forces and market moralities" on black social life and to a perceived failure of black leadership (West 1993, 16).

The pervasiveness of materialistic market influences results in a philosophical ethic of pleasure seeking, according to West. The subsequent effects of this moral philosophy are the perception and treatment of fellow human beings as objects of pleasure. The resulting behavior is that people are treated as means rather than ends unto themselves. West (1993) contends that rabid materialism constitutes a moral bankruptcy that is promoted and sustained through marketing strategies of corporate institutions. These strategies have an aberrant effect on people "living in poverty ridden conditions with a limited capacity to ward off self contempt and self hatred" (West 1993, 17). Market-promoted values in turn replace non-market values through a seductive process of media bombardment and glamorization. The end results, according to West (1993), are that values such as love, caring, and service to others are replaced by emphases on pleasure characterized by prioritizing such things as comfort, convenience, machismo, violence, femininity and sexual stimulation. Wilson's (1991) explanation of black adolescent male violence seems to parallel the observations and assertions made by West (1993), when he describes fatalism and comsumer orientedness as two of the "psychosocial aftereffects of white racism" (Wilson 1992, 11-16).

In terms of community leadership West (1993, 40-46) calls for a return to "race transcendent moral leadership." He defines this concept in contrast to what he calls both "race-effacing managerial leaders" and "race identifying protest leaders (West 1993, 39)." West contends that both overly accommodating establishment oriented black politicians and overly confrontational black activists are ineffective in addressing the needs of the black community within the context of present day American culture.

West (1993) presents a powerful political and philosophical argument. One weakness in this discussion, however, seems to be in providing examples of his ideal style of leadership. Aside from providing a few sparse examples, such as Dr. Martin Luther King Jr. and Chicago's ex-mayor Harold Washington, West (1993) does not fully develop a prescription for how race transcendent leadership can be cultivated. He does, however, recognize the existence of such leaders operating in black communities on the local level.

Both West (1993) and Oliver (1989) argue that the combination of external social forces and adaptive responses must be examined in order to arrive at a better understanding of African American culture. Both authors also recognize the limitations of previous research and call for breaking down of the barriers established by entrenched liberal, conservative, and radical philosophies. Their respective solutions to the social problems confronting many black Americans, especially males, are Afrocentric socialization (Oliver, 1989) and "race transcendent psychic conversion" (West 1993, 100). These solutions are compatible, if not identical, and reflect a progressive discourse on race relations in American society.

Addressing the Crisis

Sociologists have identified a close relationship between crime and poverty. The F.B.I. Uniform Crime Reports consistently show the highest rates of violence and property crime in low income neighborhoods (Curran and Renzetti 1990; Kornblum and Julian 1992), while public welfare investment has been found to be inversely related to criminal violence (Heffernan, Shuttlesworth and Ambrosino 1992). Although social programs developed in the 1960's reduced the number of officially poor people by almost 50% from 1961 to 1972, in subsequent years these gains were undermined by conservative law and order political philosophies (Heffernan, Shuttlesworth and Ambrosino 1992). As a result, the number of American children under the age of six living in poverty climbed from 15% in 1972 to 25% in 1982 and currently lingers well above the 20% level (Kornblum and Julian 1992). Over the past three decades President Johnson's war on poverty evolved into President Reagan's war on drugs (Curran and Renzetti 1990), and the dream of a Great Society metamorphosed into the welfare swap (Heffernan, Shuttlesworth and Ambrosino 1992). During the same period, violent juvenile crime rose relentlessly with the conservative law enforcement strategies of the 1980's resulting in a 10%

rise in felonious crime in less than five years (Federal Bureau of Investigation 1990).

These social realities disproportionately affect black children growing up in low income communities. They are at greater risk for inadequate housing, disease, violence in their neighborhoods, and educational failure by virtue of their being poor (Kornblum and Julian, 1992). They attend schools that are poorly financed and are less likely to be able to afford post secondary education. A report by the Children's Defense Fund (1987) correlated poor academic achievement and limited school resources with low income populations. Families living in poverty in our nation are disproportionately black and female headed (Kornblum and Julian, 1992).

The problems faced by young black men in urban settings are directly related to these social conditions. Socialization in an environment characterized by economic deprivation, physical deterioration, racial discrimination and family instability could create hardships for anyone. Yet, this is the environment into which many urban children are born during this last decade of the 20th century. Some of the primary agents of socialization for urban males are experiencing extreme stress. These include families without fathers, schools without funds, and peers without supervision. Kotlowitiz (1991) in his description of the life of two young boys growing up in the housing projects of Chicago quotes their mother as saying "There are no children here, they have seen too much to be children (p.x)." This quote better than any statistic depicts the difficulties of growing up amidst urban poverty and despair.

Black children presently have a greater likelihood of living in low income, fatherless homes than at any other time in our nations history (Kornblum and Julian 1992). The end result is that men and boys, alike, are deprived of the joys of vital paternal relationships. Today, black males are less likely to complete high school and are more likely to become wards of the state, or victims of homicide than at any other time in recent history (Gibbs 1988; Wilson 1991). If these problems are to be adequately resolved, policy makers must be mindful of past failures while simultaneously providing the basic skills and opportunities necessary for economic and social success among African American males. The fundamental institutions society depends upon for teaching values, providing leadership and preparing youth for economic participation seem to have inadequately served the needs of young black men.

Homicide is currently recognized as a leading cause of death among black males between the age of 15 and 25. In 1990, the *New York Times* reported that in some areas of the country it is "now more likely for a young Black male to die from homicide than it was for a U.S. soldier to be killed during a tour of duty in Vietnam" (Wilson 1991, 9). Educational inadequacies, substance abuse, teenage parenthood, and high rates of incarceration are destroying this important and potentially valuable segment of our population (Gary 1981; Gibbs 1988). Unemployment is a pervasive concern, whereas enforcement tactics for equal opportunity in the work place have suffered major setbacks resulting from recent the Supreme Court decisions (Kornblum and Julian 1992).

These developments are indicative of persistent economic and political inequality and increasing social problems affecting minority communities. Concerned scholars have demonstrated that adolescent African American males are a population at risk and that there is a need for new approaches to address maladies and social problems affecting this group (Gibbs 1988; Staples 1982; Gary 1981). The consensus is that something more needs to be done. Specialized programs designed to address the needs of adolescent black males represent but one attempt to discover a solution to these problems (Lee 1987; Wilson 1992; Jeter 1993). Do these types of programs provide viable solutions to real problems or are they better conceptualized as first aid efforts to stop the bleeding? If so, what can be done? Do they represent promising innovations or are they old formulas bent on blaming victims (Ryan 1971) without incorporating real structural change? These are questions that beg to be answered, because they address a problem that cries out to be solved. Too many young black men are dying, killing and falling through the cracks.

Compounding these observations is the fact that many traditional male role expectations have been challenged in recent years. Perhaps a rethinking of male socialization would be desirable for the whole of American society (Clatterbaugh 1990). With this possibility in mind, many of the issues, ideas, and practice principles discovered during the inquiry might be applied to white majority males as well. That determination will be left for the reader to decide.

Theories of Socialization

Socialization is the process whereby people learn that which they must know in order to survive and function in society (Farley 1992). It can also be described as the process of social interaction through which people acquire personality traits and learn the ways of their society or group (Popenoe 1993). Talcott Parsons' (1951) social action theory defines socialization as a process whereby the human actor learns to make choices in the social setting that are compatible with the immediate social control mechanisms that apply.

Socialization is complete when a person consistently chooses to behave in ways that comply with the normative orientations of the larger community to which he belongs. Choices which fulfill human needs and incur minimal social sanctions are sustained while social control mechanisms intervene to prevent persistent violations of socially accepted behavior (Parsons and Bales 1955).

This functionalist perspective seeks to describe the structural mechanisms which influence and control human behavior or fulfill human need, both individually and collectively. Within this framework aberrant or nonconforming behavior will frequently be described as pathological or dysfunctional (Little 1989; Pfohl 1985). Functionalist explanations for such deviance often emphasize alternative means for needs fulfillment given existing structural barriers (Merton 1968).

Interactionist theories of socialization can be found in the works of sociologists such as Charles Horton Cooley and George Herbert Mead. Cooley (1902) described the social processes which affect a person's perception of self. He depicts the development of self identity through a three step process of perceiving first how one's behavior is received by others. Secondly the person becomes aware of the judgments placed upon him or herself by others, and thirdly, a person evaluates his or her own behavior via the responses of others. Cooley (1902) referred to this process of identification as "the looking glass self" as an analogy for the social interaction in which a person defines him or herself in relation to others in the social setting (Manis and Meltzer 1972, 231). Primary social groups, such as the family or other people with whom a person comes into close contact, have been described as the most important agents of socialization (Popenoe 1993; Farley 1992; Goslin 1969). The socialization process begins at infancy and continues throughout life.

Mead (1934) in his lectures at the University of Chicago and in the subsequent publications of his students elaborated on a similar theme. Mead divided the notion of self into two parts, the I and the me. The I represents the spontaneous sense of self unfettered by social convention. In contrast, the me was defined as that sense of self which develops in response to other people in the environment. As a person becomes more aware of the people around him or her the sense of me begins to take shape. Socialization occurs as a person's sense of me progresses through three stages. For Mead, these include the imitative, the play and the game stage (Popenoe 1993).

These three stages depict ever more increasing levels of self awareness through interaction with others in response to societal rules, obligations and expectations. The roles that people assume as they become increasingly aware of significant "others" (Mead 1934) in their social world eventually lead them to internalizing cultural and societal norms. This "taking on the role of the generalized other" then becomes the guiding force governing social behavior (Manis and Meltzer 1972, 155).

Psychologists also contributed to theories of socialization via such people as Sigmund Freud, Erik Erikson and Jean Piaget. Psychological theories of personality development parallel and complement interactionist sociological theories. Freud's theories on personality are similar, in some respects, to those of Cooley and Mead but stress basic conflicts between a person's natural tendencies or desires and the constraints applied by society (Freud 1930). Freud emphasized the unconscious aspects of personality and the repression of biological desires resulting from societal demands. He emphasized the potential negative effects of repressed desires and depicted five psychosexual stages of personality in which specific conflicts must be resolved before emotional growth could occur. Freud used a psychological focus to recognize the importance of early childhood events and the influence of family relations on social adjustment.

Erikson (1963) expanded on Freud's concept of developmental stages by hypothesizing the existence of eight psycho-social stages of personality development. These progressive stages were characterized by the resolution of conflicting emotional concerns which were defined by an identity crisis requiring resolution as emotional maturity developed. Each of these crises correspond to stages of physiological maturity so that a person's psycho-social development parallels his or her physical growth. When these identity crises remain unresolved, emotional problems are thought to occur (Monte 1987).

The reknown psychologists, Jean Piaget (1932) and Lawrence Kohlberg (1969), also developed theories about developmental processes in children which add to this discussion of socialization. Piaget's (1932) theory of cognitive development describes the processes by which children learn to make moral judgment in the social setting. He identifies two moral dimensions, constraint and cooperation, in the mental processes of children.

According to Piaget (1932), mental awareness and judgment in children occurs in stages. In the early stages good and bad are defined on the basis of consequences. The constraints placed upon a child within the social setting serve to shape his or her perceptions of right and wrong. As the child grows older, he or she begins to distinguish between good and evil according to what Gilligan (1982) describes as an ethic of cooperation. At this stage intentions as well as consequences affect the child's perceptions of morality. Social interaction based on the effects of social constraint and the benefits of cooperation thereby influence not only cognitive but also moral development (Farley 1992). Accordingly, social interactions simultaneously constrain and shape the child's gradual adjustment into his or her social world.

Lawrence Kohlberg (1969) explained moral development as occurring in relation to cognitive skills. He described three levels consisting of two separate stages. Preconventional moral development includes needs satisfaction and punishment avoidance. These two stages require the least sophisticated reasoning abilities. The conventional level, according to Kohlberg (1969), includes the social approval and law and order stages. These require cognitive skills which account for the perception of others and understanding of societal rules. The most highly developed sense of morality for Kohlberg involves an awareness of abstract notions of social contracts and universal ethics. Many people progress to one of the middle stages and remain there, while a rare few reach the highest, or postconventional stage of moral development (Kohlberg 1969; Popenoe 1993).

Kohlberg's (1969) theory reflects the influence of Mead and Cooley as well as his predecessors in the field of psychology by emphasizing social interaction in the development of self concept. Cooley's (1902) looking glass self, and Mead's (1934) generalized other, both emphasize the effects of other people in the social environment on the perceptions and behaviors of a person in society. This process of social interaction can also be seen to occur during Kohlberg's conventional and postconventional stages of moral development.

There are a variety of ways these social interactions take place. Traditional institutions such as the family, the school, and church have been described as socializing agents (Farley 1992; Popenoe 1993). Additional influences include the media (Bierm, 1990), peers, and individual role models (Bandura 1969). Farley (1992) defines socializing agents as "people and institutions that...act as important influences on the individual's attitudes, beliefs, self-image, and behavior" (p.145). Though the processes may be similar for most people, the impact and effects of these various agents may differ based upon structural factors such as age, class or race (McNeil 1969).

Minority Socialization

The differential effects of social institutions and socialization processes on black Americans is stressed by McNeil (1969) who maintains that being both poor and black in American society disenfranchises a person from full participation in the socioeconomic opportunities available to the majority. Young (1969) also maintains that an ascribed inferior status for minorities profoundly affects socialization processes. He refers to significant differences in background and social environment, as well as differences in group influences on personality and behavioral expectations. Even the basic institutions, which serve as agents of socialization, such as family and church, differ significantly from corresponding dominant group institutions due to varying ethnic traditions and the effects of subordinate power relationships (Young 1969).

McNeil (1969) emphasizes an ever widening gap between black professionals and the urban poor. He echoes Merton's (1968) theory of anomie when he states that the middle class formula for success seems alien to many black Americans. McNeil (1969) also asserts that school curricula tend to overlook or ignore the historical contributions and the social experiences of African American people. These observations can also be found in the writings of later scholars such as Gary (1981), Staples (1982) and others.

In a somewhat different vein, Allen (1981) maintains that socialization processes within black families, particularly as they pertain to fathers and sons, are frequently misunderstood. He finds little evidence to support the notion of pathological socialization patterns among black families when controlling for class, and maintains that research bias towards studying only impoverished families resulted in inaccurate representations of black family life. Allen (1981, 111) contend that black families "represent a distinct cultural form in this society and, as such, the definitions responsibilities and roles of their members differ from those of whites." He confirms the idea that black mothers are the "central adults" in their sons lives but that black fathers "retain warm personal relations with their sons and are active in the child rearing process" (Allen 1981, 112).

In a study of middle class black fathers, John McAdoo (1981) found no significant differences in the observed patterns of interaction between his sample and the white middle class fathers and children from a previous study (Radin 1972). McAdoo (1981) described certain patterns of parent/child interaction which he felt could have long term negative effects. These involved highly restrictive parenting practices such as focusing on negative while ignoring positive behavior.

McAdoo's findings led to the discovery that the majority of middle class black fathers expressed the same "range of attitudes, beliefs and behaviors as did fathers from other ethnic groups"(p.129). The findings also suggested a need for mental health practitioners to find ways to assist the overly restrictive father in becoming more "nurturing toward himself, his wife and his children," regardless of race and ethnic background (McAdoo 1981, 129).

Warfield-Coppock (1990) maintains that traditional African socialization processes were disrupted among people of African American heritage due to the experiences of slavery and ongoing racial oppression. She calls for an organized community based approach to restoring the socialization processes whereby young people attain adult social identity through the restoration of rites of passage ceremonies consistent with African philosophies and world views. According to Warfield-Coppock (1990), the young person's world view is shaped by what might be described as a concentric circle of influences consisting of the mother, the family, the extended family, the immediate community, the larger community, society and the world. She describes the African child as being surrounded by his or her family and community and removed from the outer world's values and influence until such time as he is ready for exposure. The African child is then "guided by the ways of his/her people-ideology, values and customs" (p.59). Courtland Lee (1987) echoes these sentiments when he calls for the development of black manhood training in schools. Afrocentric rites of passage programs have also been proposed by Asante (1991), Kunjufu (1993), and Oliver (1989).

The Importance of Self Esteem

For many Americans ethnic identity is seen as an important component of self esteem and social identity according to Baruth and Manning (1991). The social identity of a black child constitutes the people with whom he or she interacts throughout life, including parents, peers, friends, teachers, the police, and all those people found within his or her immediate community. Although previous literature has alluded to low self esteem and alleged self hatred among black youth (Clark and Clark 1947), more recent research contradicts these findings by discovering high levels of self esteem among black, school-age children (Allen 1985; Gibbs 1988; Richman 1984; Taylor 1989).

Erikson (1964) describes the achievement of personal identity as the fundamental task of adolescent development. His theory of adolescent identity formation provides a useful framework for analyzing issues relating to emotional stability and self esteem among young black men. Taylor (1989) builds on Erikson's ideas by focusing on the complex nature and multiple determinants of personality growth and stressing the importance of role models for black youth. According to Taylor (1989), the process of social and emotional maturation in minority youth is inextricably linked with the racially determined social structure of our society.

Phinney and Rotheram (1986) assert that the ethnic aspect of identity formation has been largely ignored. Like Erikson (1964), they suggest that identity formation proceeds by crises involving the exploration of alternatives. These experiences are followed by commitment to an identity, a social self which involves the development of ethnic, racial and gender awareness. The process of personality development is most intense during the teenage years with positive self concepts being closely related to ethnic identity for minority youth (Phinney 1991). Baruth and Manning (1991) support this position by emphasizing the importance of ethnic identity during psychotherapy.

Spencer (1985) borrowed from DuBois' (1903) notion of dual consciousness when he stressed that black adolescents must learn two culturally derived means of coping with societal expectations in order to be psychologically healthy. Spencer (1985) emphasizes the influences of the larger society, the African American community, and race relations as conditioning forces shaping black adolescent self esteem and behavior. These findings and theoretical observations suggest the need for reassessing the various factors that influence self esteem as it relates to black children, and the role that self esteem plays in influencing social behavior.

Manhood and Minority Status

In his classic study on suicide, Emile Durkheim (1897) found support for the argument that social structures influence suicide rates in different religious communities. When societal institutions maintained clear and concise boundaries, suicide rates were found to be lower. When clear social boundaries were not maintained, a crisis of societal norms was said to occur resulting in increased suicide rates. Robert Merton (1968) expanded Durkheim's idea of anomie to include normlessness resulting from persistent inability to achieve societal goals due to unequal opportunities. Some typical behavioral responses, according to Merton (1968), include the rejection of conventional goals or the finding of alternative means for achieving them.

Similar arguments have been made relating to social attitudes and behaviors of African American males (Majors and Billson 1992; Wilson 1991). Taylor, Bogart, Leashore and Toliver (1988) and Hendricks (1981) shed light on this theory with regard to black fathers and their provider role expectations. Cross (1991) also looks at the influence of reference group orientation on personal identity. Differential access to resources, such as jobs education and privileged networks, are seen as influencing male aspirations and role expectations. Hence, a black man faced with lack of employment opportunities as a result of geographic isolation or racial discrimination might tend to devalue employment as a symbol of manhood and may stress ingenuity or stoic endurance as more highly valued personal characteristics. These guiding principles for masculine ideals have been described as being represented in the mythical archetypes of such folklore figures as Shine, the trickster, Stagalee, the outlaw and John Henry, the strong silent type (Asante 1987).

Leland Hall (1981) maintains that the developmental processes for black men in American society are essentially the same as those for all other members, but that the social circumstances require unique adaptations. Minority male status, according to Hall (1981), places black men in a threatening position, relative to majority white males. This social reality is a fundamental influence in the socialization of black adolescent males (Hudson, 1990).

Gary and Pullman (1993) found that more frequent experiences of perceived racial discrimination were reported by young, highly educated, black men, than by any other African American group. Significantly, black men with highly masculine sex role identities also reported higher levels of racial discrimination. These findings tend to support Hall's argument that black men, especially young, intelligent, virile black men are perceived as threatening to the larger white community.

The possibility that different gender related value orientations may be operating in ethnic communities is supported by the popular notion of Latin machismo, Majors and Billson's (1991) reference to coolpose, and Clatterbaugh's (1990) reference to the group specific, gender identity. In his typology of contemporary perspectives on masculinity Clatterbaugh emphasizes the importance of minority group membership in the development of sex role orientations. He defines five basic orientations to gender identity among American men. These different perspectives include traditional, profeminist, men's rights, spiritual and group specific role orientations. Although there appears to be some overlap among gender identity types, the essential position made by Clatterbaugh (1990) is that male gender identity is complex, varied and multidimensional. This important point should be kept in mind when studying, evaluating and or developing programs to facilitate positive social adjustment in adolescent males.

Academic Achievement

Both families and schools have been described as primary agents of socialization (Farley 1992). However, McNeil (1969) maintains that in many respects the schools have usurped some of the essential socialization tasks traditionally assigned to parents, thus implying that these two important social institutions are in some ways operating at cross purposes. One of the school's essential functions is to transmit the technical and intellectual skills necessary for a person to become a contributing and valuable member of society. As evidenced by high drop out rates and other previously mentioned social indicators, this does not seem to be happening for a significant portion of young black men (Gibbs 1988). Three of the five essential factors placing children at risk for school failure reported by the National Commission on Children's Final Report (1991), include living in poverty, belonging to a racial or ethnic minority and growing up in a single parent home.

Patton (1981) described the educational system as the primary socializing agent in our society and emphasized the negative outcome of white middle class, female dominated elementary education on black male students. Though our educational institutions have not adequately addressed the needs of black children as a whole, these negative outcomes seem to have more profoundly affected males than females (Hare 1979).

Statistics on academic attainment levels effectively demonstrate problems surrounding the educational needs of black male children in elementary and secondary education. In 1991, the percentage of persons 25 years and over, who completed less than five years of elementary education, was five times greater for black males and females, than it was for their white counterparts (U.S. Department of Education, 1993). Similarly less than 70% of black people, aged 25 and over, had finished four years of high school, whereas, over 85% of white people in the same age group had done so (U.S. Department of Education 1993).

Drop out rates, compiled by race and gender, are consistently higher for black males than they are for white males and show dramatic increases between the ages of 14 and 19 years (U.S. Department of Education 1993). The most dramatic leap in dropout rates seems to occur between the ages of 15 and 16 where, in 1991, the rates for black males leaped from less than one percent, for the 14 to 15 year olds, to more than eight percent, for 16 and 17 year olds. Although the situation has improved significantly over the last thirty years, dropout rates for black and hispanic students, remain considerably above the rates for the white majority.

Research has shown that black students are disciplined in school more often and more severely than are their white counterparts (Carnegie Corporation of New York 1984; Irvine 1990). Disciplinary problems and general alienation from the educational system have lead to alarming disparities in rates of student attendance by race. Taylor and Foster (1986) found that one southeastern U.S. school district during the 1983-84 school year reported African American males to have missed an average of 159 school days compared to 62 days for white males, 32 days for black females and 4 days for white females.

Marked deficiencies can be observed in the educational proficiency levels recorded by black students when compared to the overall population at 9, 13 and 17 years of age. The percentage of children achieving proficiency in basic educational skills, such as mathmatics, science, history, reading and writing is consistently lower for black children than it is for white children, albeit higher than for Hispanic children (U.S. Department of Education 1993).

Academic achievement levels among black males and corresponding discrepancies in their educational outcomes have fostered theories hypothesizing deliberate attempts on the part of predominantly white institutions to perpetuate inequalities in education (Kunjufu 1983, 1986; Woodson 1934). Conspiracy and cultural conflict theories regarding the education of African American children have resulted in the a call for a greater awareness of cultural differences and the implementation of multicultural curricula in public schools (Dodson 1983; Fordham 1988; Kunjufu 1993).

The Miseducation of African American Children

There has been extensive research on the factors that affect academic achievement among black children (Boykin 1984; Epps 1987; Fordham and Ogbu 1986; Hare 1979; Hare 1985). Patton (1993, 204-210) advocates that educational assessment strategies incorporate a basic awareness of fundamental African American philosophical orientations and world view. He offers several methodological approaches for assessing and identifying gifted African American students. These suggestions include the use of multiple criteria for selection and evaluating students; use of an action oriented, or dynamic, assessment methodology; and use of "test, teach, retest, teach curriculum based assessment approaches" (Patton 1993, 208).

Clark (1983) compared academic achievement for black children from low income homes. He identified seventeen ways in which home life differed between high and low academic achievers. Six of the seventeen factors related to parental involvement in school or achievement related activities such as frequent interaction with school personnel and display of goal oriented norms. Four variables differentiating high and low achievers involved parental disciplinary practices. The provision of liberal nurturance, the establishment of clear role boundaries, and status structures all significantly correlated to academic achievement. Other important variables included the student's role in his/her own education, frequency of family conflict, and support from the child's teacher.

Additional variables associated with academic achievement are related to socioeconomic status (Children's Defense Fund 1987). Poor academic outcomes are also related to the limitations on resources within school systems attended by lower income populations in the United States. Adding to this inequity is the frequent tracking of minority and low-income students into non-academic curricula (Oakes 1985). Additional social science research concerning academic achievement centers on psychosocial elements such as self concept, self esteem and ethnic identity (Phinney 1988; Phinney 1991; Spencer 1982; Taylor 1976). One ramification of these psychosocial elements is what Irvine (1990) calls a lack of cultural synchronization. He describes a pervasive clash or dissonance between the cultural experiences of the black student and those legitimized in the educational system by teachers, administrators and policy makers. He notes that culture conflict arises when teachers misinterpret language differences, dismiss nonverbal cues or misunderstand differences in learning styles and world view.

Perceived cultural differences between African American culture and the dominant Anglo American culture lay at the heart of the call for Afrocentric education (Asante 1987). Many of these African cultural traits are found in oral traditions such as folk tales, language and religious practices (Dillard 1975; Holloway and Vass 1993; Mintz and Price 1976).

A controversy over what role vernacular and language differences play in the shaping and maintaining of African American culture persists (Stoller 1975). Some educators and scholars have advocated for the recognition of a vernacular Black English as a stigmatized language variety while others have perceived of it as an outgrowth of inadequate cultural and social conditions (Stoller 1975). In either case the existence of language patterns that differ from standard American English has been the subject of debate in academic communities over several decades.

Recognizing that language patterns differ from place to place for any group of people, Halloway and Vass (1993) document a host of African based linguistic and cultural characteristics which persist in many African American communities today. These include commonly used words of Bantu derivation such as boo boo, bozo, jamboree and kook.

Smitherman (1986) stresses the over arching significance of Black English use in educational systems serving African Americans. Middle-class black students who are generally better able to alternate the use of standard American English and Black English, a practice referred to as code switching, do not suffer as much from rigid control of vernacular in educational systems. Recent research indicates that there is a linguistic divergence currently separating Black English even more from mainstream American English. African American linguists such as Smitherman (1986) call for an upgrading of Black English to an equal status with the language of instruction. It is argued that recognizing the legitimacy of black vernacular will serve as an instructional bridge, particularly for African American under-class populations whom Smitherman (1986) maintains reject standardized American English in varying degrees.

Short of legitimizing slang and bad grammar as alternative means of communication, Orr (1987) calls for the recognition of standard American English as a second language for some minority youth. She suggests that teachers and school administrators need to be educated as to how home and community based language differences influence students' perceptions of mathematical concepts especially when expressed in word problems or other language based format. Orr (1987) stresses the point that educators need to focus on language differences rather than language deficiencies and promotes educating the educators in order to better meet the needs of the students. Smitherman (1991), Orr (1987) and Irvine (1990) are not alone in their insistence that African American culture in the form of language, arts music and history, be incorporated into the classroom (Boykin 1984; Hale-Bebson 1986; Shade 1982).

Additional studies have concluded that black adolescents' opposition to various aspects of what is perceived as white culture have resulted in their alienation from the educational system. Weis (1985) found contradictions between aspirations and behaviors in a sample of black high school students whose stated desires were to attend college, but who were often absent and lagging in their homework. She speculated that these contradictions were a result of resistance to dominant culture expectations.

Fordham and Ogbu (1986) also found that peer pressure seemed to retard educational achievement among black students who were deterred from their studies by a fear of "acting white" (p.176). Kunjufu (1988) reached similar conclusions in his study of peer group influences based on case studies. Fordham (1988) concluded from a survey of 600 Washington D.C. high school students that high achievers tended to identify more with values of the dominant society adopting a "raceless" personality in order to achieve academic success (p.54).

Body language is also considered to be an area which is particularly vulnerable to miscommunication cross culturally and between different societal groups. Particular variants of kinesics (body motion), facial expression, eye movements, touching actions, speech tone, pitch, postures, proxemics and other nonverbal modes of communication are unique to black Americans. Majors and Billson (1991) conclude that school administrators, teachers, and other educational personnel often misinterpret eye behavior. The culturally based tendency to look away when listening to a teacher may be interpreted as communicating dishonesty, lack of respect, or poor concentration when this may not be the case. From the opposite point of view, a black person may read a deliberate gaze or intense eye contact as a disrespectful stare and react with hostility. Gouldner (1978) found, in a study of 242 predominantly black elementary classrooms, that teachers commonly misinterpreted behavior in black students. Actual behavior was found on the whole to be markedly less menacing than that which was perceived by the teachers.

As American society enters into the 21st century there is a clear danger that the educational status of black students will slip further behind. Irvine (1990) points out that the rote learning techniques used among lower-income and other disadvantaged student populations are increasingly ill suited for the work world of the future. He maintains that students must have critical thinking skills to be adequately prepared for the world of work. Irvine (1990) maintains that "the skills necessary for survival in the twenty-first century should include problem solving, creativity and above all, the capacity to be introspective, self-directed, adaptive, open-minded, and tolerant of change and ambiguity" (p.15). He asserts that the present educational structure falls short of the goal of capturing the imagination and mobilizing the capabilities of many African American youth. It consistently fails to recognize the unique African American cultural heritage and corresponding lifestyle patterns of black students. The solution, according to Irvine (1990), lies in the positive incorporation of African American values, communication patterns and other cultural determinants into the academic setting.

Asante (1987) describes his approach to this problem as an Afrocentric focus, one which recognizes the diversity in a complex cultural framework and attributes full value and worth to a variety of cultural traditions. Institutionally this translates into greater flexibility in school curriculum and changing the western European cultural focus currently in place. These changes would necessarily require cultural literacy and education of majority faculty and school administrators, sensitivity to conflict arising from cultural dissonance and realignment of educational policy to foster an inclusive as opposed to an exclusive values orientation.

Concern over educational disparities has reached a point where some black educators have advocated all black male classes and/or Afrocentric private schools as a solution to educational inequities (Ascher 1992; Chiles 1991). Key to these educational experiments is the belief that the presence of strong black male role models in the form of teachers, administrators, and staff within the context of an Afrocentric learning environment will facilitate better academic achievement among young black men (Kunjufu 1985).

African Heritage and Afrocentric Philosophy

Melville J. Herskovitz (1958) maintains that the influences of African culture on the historical and social development of African American people have long been neglected. He contends that 19th century anthropologists not only misunderstood and misrepresented African social institutions, but they also perpetuated these mistakes in their conclusions regarding New World African people. These erroneous assumptions stem from incorrect presuppositions about the nature of "Africanisms" among Black Americans (pp. 143-260).

The first widely accepted proposition attacked by Herskovitz (1958) is the assumption that African cultural forms are not a functioning reality and have not been retained in the nature of Black American traditions. He refutes this position by examining commonalities of culture found in West African societies from slaving regions, and comparing them with similarities manifested in black people in the Americas. Herskovitz illustrates broad based religious, artistic, and linguistic patterns which he equates with an African cultural heritage. Although it is generally recognized that few physical artifacts remain with which to verify the retention of African cultural traits in the New World (Mintz and Price, 1976), Herskovitz (1958) points to oral traditions, religious ritual and ethnomusicological evidence to support his position.

The second pervasive misconception identified by Herskovitz regarding African culture is the selective nature with which cultural traits were identified and used to perpetuate racial stereotypes of black people in America. Here the author asserts that the misuse of African derived mythology, and failed understanding of symbolism fostered prejudices while simultaneously disregarding deeper intellectual meaning. The denial of African cultural heritage or the branding of the African character as primitive and savage has played no small part in the devaluation of African Americans as a people, according to Herskovitz (1958). Rethinking and recognizing western European prejudices against African cultural forms and exploring the possibilities of surviving cultural patterns in the Americas is an area of academic interest in need of further reflection.

The identification by Mintz and Price (1976) of a unique African American heritage among slaves and their descendants on the American continent provides fertile soil for a discussion of black traditions in American society. These authors assert that the brutalities associated with the American tradition of marketing and enslaving Africans tended to equalize the victims regardless of previous status or rank, thereby facilitating and necessitating the forging of new social bonds in a strange world.

The identification of strong dyadic social bonds between shipmates of the same sex during the middle passage was described by Mintz and Price (1976) as a "major principle of social organization which continued for decades or even centuries" among people of African heritage (p. 43). The intense relationships established during the experiences and mutual suffering of the middle passage were described as having a kinship quality such that "shipmates were said to look upon each other's children as mutually their own" (Mintz and Price, 1976, p. 43). Out of these bonds and common experiences emerged a generalized African American heritage characterized by patterns of culture emerging from shared oral traditions such as language, music, arts and mythology. Strong bonds stemming from the common experiences of African heritage, slavery, segregation and white oppression also serve to explain how kinship and parenting practices evolved into what Mitchell (1990) calls "community co-parenting (pp. 160-182)."

Herskovitz (1958) describes West African kinship patterns and the traditional honoring of ancestors as influential processes affecting the development of an African American cultural heritage. Approaches to spirituality were also described by Mintz and Price (1976) as stemming from the African tradition of ritual knowledge being "owned" by select people and/or cults and passed on from one generation to the next within families or through initiations ceremonies (p. 45). In the absence of specific tribal holy persons different ethnic groups shared or exchanged "ritual assistance" in times of spiritual need (Mintz and Price 1976, 46). This process, and similar patterns of inclusive cultural borrowing, served to establish bonds and foster collectively held cultural traditions between people of otherwise diverse backgrounds.

The observations forwarded by Herskovitz (1958) and Mintz and Price (1976) are supported in the writings of subsequent black scholars who have also focused on oral and philosophical traditions to advance this perspective. Asante (1980) compares what he describes as competing world views based on an Afrocentric, Eurocentric and Asiocentric models. The Afrocentric world view is described as personalistic. It embodies a continuity between the spiritual and the material world, in which there is no separation between the sacred and the profane. The Eurocentric world view, according to Asante is essentially materialistic. This perspective tends to deny the spiritual as unreal or intangible and hence inconsequential. The Asiocentric world view maintains that the material world is an illusion and that spiritual issues are dominant.

Nobles (1980) also contrasts the African world view with that of European cultural traditions. He maintains that Eurocentric understandings emphasize individuality, uniqueness and differences, while Afrocentric perspectives are described as stressing group identity, sameness and commonality. In the area of values, African traditions value cooperation over competition and collective responsibility over individual rights. Finally, the ethical orientation of African cultures is toward survival of the tribe and maintaining a oneness with nature. European world views are seen as emphasizing survival of the fittest and control over nature. The individual emphasis of western cultures versus the group identity of African culture is an important distinction which lays the foundation for values and related behavior (Warfield-Coppock 1990).

Decades of social research have alternatively supported and refuted the concept of distinct subcultures within complex societies such as the United States (Harrington 1962; Leibow 1967; Miller 1958). The issue of African American cultural heritage has not escaped this controversy, and the debate is ongoing. Warfield-Coppock (1990) describes Frazier (1939) and Myrdal (1944) as proponents of the notion that African traditions were essentially lost to African American people. Other scholars (Herskovitz, 1958; Mintz and Price,1976; Nobles, 1974a) rebut this assumption with compelling arguments about oral traditions, religious beliefs and folklore. In a more recent account Petrie (1991) presents interviews with eight leading black scholars whose comments typify the diversity of opinions about the role of African culture and its effect on the lives of African American people. The debate ranges from healthy skepticism to a resounding endorsement of Afrocentrism as a guiding principal for philosophical discourse. Some social science researchers have maintained that socioeconomic similarities can be controlled to explain for differences in values and attitudes and that intra group diversity is more a reflection of intercultural variation than existing subculture theories can support (Leacock 1971; Valentine 1968). Others insist that intergenerational patterns, traditions, and rules for behavior in ethnic communities merit recognition as distinct cultural traditions (Lewis 1961b). This recognition, however, is a sword that cuts both ways when it comes to contemplating social policy. In an interview with Petrie (1991), Wilson J. Moses cautions uncritical proponents of Afrocentric education against white racists paying lip service to the cause, thereby promoting their own segregationist agenda. Moses warns against an overly romantic embracing of Afrocentric ideal while appreciating the scholarly contribution of African based knowledge (Petrie 1991).

The presence of diverse customs and attitudes within our society is seen by some some social scientist as representing variation within a larger complex whole (Ellison 1989; Valentine 1968). Others describe American culture as a polyglot of interdependent cultural communities (Pinderhughes 1988). A particularly relevant problem for this study is that of the persistent refusal of many social scientists to acknowledge identifiable patterns of culture in African American communities. This controversy is viewed by many black scholars as institutionalized resistance to an inevitable break with traditionally Eurocentric paradigms in social science knowledge building (Asante 1987; Freire 1973; Kuhn, 1970; Lum 1986; Moses 1991). These inherent biases lend themselves to hypothesis testing and theory development with built in assumptions that tend to blame the victims while simultaneously upholding long standing negative stereotypes of racial and ethnic minorities (Ryan 1971; Valentine 1968).

The purpose of this discussion is not to discover the origins of African American culture but rather to provide information that will establish a backdrop for developing an understanding of the theoretical arguments we are likely to encounter in the field observations about to be undertaken. If African culture is seen as relevant to understanding the present social situation of African American people, as is proposed by many black scholars, then it becomes a salient political as well as a philosophical issue.

What makes recent arguments over Afrocentrism different from previous advocates of subculture theories is the perspective from which the argument is generated. It is one thing for an outside observer to label a pattern of behavior as cultural, based upon time bounded, narrow and limited understandings. It is quite another thing for members of a specific group or community to decry that cultural patterns within their own community are going unrecognized and that the integrity of their traditions are thereby being trivialized and undervalued (L.E.Gary, personal communication, April 1992). To ignore such a criticism would be to ignore potentially damaging bias in the process of scientific inquiry.

Serving the Need

Urban professionals have made efforts to recognize and serve the needs of young black men on the local level. These efforts have resulted in the development of specialized programs for minority males in schools, youth centers, churches and other institutions. Wilson (1991) describes these projects as organizational strategies and activities for preventing black adolescent violence. He identifies and divides currently operating programs into both educational and environmental approaches. Educational strategies include activities such as mentoring, conflict resolution, training in life skills, firearms safety and recreation. Environmental strategies include activities relating to work opportunities and therapeutic activities (Wilson 1991).

The concept of black manhood training is further elaborated in the development of a model for group counseling by Courtland Lee (1987). Lee's intended counseling experiences include three outcomes. The first objective is for group members to increase their awareness of themselves as strong black men. The clear implication here is that there are issues germane to black males that differ from those for other members of society. The message is that these issues should be more thoroughly explored and understood. The second objective for black manhood training, according to Lee, is to reinforce appreciation for the strength and uniqueness of black men. Here again the theme of uniqueness is established and coupled with recognition of that uniqueness as a strength. The third objective is to enhance a sense of brotherhood among group members and to create a common bond as strong black men (Lee 1987). The emphasis for this final objective seems to be on mutual support, ethnic pride and emotional strength.

Asante (1991) calls for the development of Afrocentric school curricula in which traditional ethnocentric biases in education will be offset by a more culturally sensitive curriculum. Majors and Billson (1991), Wilson (1991), and Franklin (1984) describe perceptions of masculinity among black young men in urban settings as contributing to anti-social or self destructive behaviors. These attitudes are further described as reactive responses to conditions of poverty, unemployment, hopelessness and urban stress resulting from persistent inequality and racial discrimination. If these observations hold true, then the development of male oriented programs providing structured approaches to defining role identity, values clarification and relationship building based on African traditions may be an effective prevention strategy.

The goals of positive group identity, strong social support and enhanced self esteem are common themes that can be found in counseling literature as well. Baruth and Manning (1991) recommend that social workers and counselors working with African American adolescents should be aware of unique problems that may create unnecessary barriers if not properly identified. Self concept stemming from the adverse effects of negative stereotypes and racism is a constant concern. Problems relating to conflicting pressures for socialization outside of the black community is another. Class differences and father absence in the home are two more frequently encountered issues (Baruth and Manning 1991) that must be sensitively addressed.

Cultural differences regarding language, family relations and values can result in differing perceptions about what is important and valued when compared to majority opinions. This can be particularly problematic when black teens conflict with authority figures at school or in the community. Baruth and Manning (1991) recommend promoting a self identity among black adolescents which embodies both African American cultural values and those characteristics unique to the individual.

Summary

The primary a priori assumption of this study is the identification of young black men in American society as a population at risk. Past literature and recent statistics have demonstrated the extent to which young black males are more likely to experience jail, school failure, violence and the like. Whether one chooses to define these circumstances as creations of the social structure or self inflicted consequences of life choices depends largely on one's perspective, political orientation and personal experiences.

The preceding review of relevant literature has attempted to provide an overview of some of the salient issues that impact the lives of young black men in our society. Together, the author and the reader have examined socialization processes, the influence of social institutions, historical trends and the emotional effects of minority status in a racially stratified society. Education, cultural influences and developmental issues have all been explored. The debate over which of these factors bring the most to bear in resolving the problems of social inequality, racism and violence in our cities will continue well beyond the duration of this study. The intent of this review is to illustrate the view that people are born into and shaped by their social environment. It shapes them before they can begin to shape it.

It should also be stressed that the problems of black men affect all of society in subtle and not so subtle ways. Some would say that these problems are the result of our inability as a nation to come to grips with the two long standing moral dilemmas of inequality and discrimination (Harrington 1962; Madhabuti 1990; Myrdal 1944; Ryan 1971; Wilson 1992). Each of the authors mentioned add to an overall picture of the social environment within which young black men come of age in American society. Their works embody the bulk of the scholarly literature currently available on the subject.

This literature review focuses on selected areas which are intended to inform a reader's working knowledge of the subject. The basic processes of socialization have been described with an eye towards demonstrating how they are influenced by a variety of psychological, interpersonal and environmental factors. Institutions such as the family, the school, the community, and the church play key roles. Informal networks such as peers, friends and the media also have profound impact.

Some concerned professionals support a more structured approach for influencing positive growth and social development among young black men in urban communities. These efforts are based on the assumption that many African American, adolescent males are, simultaneously, at risk and in need. This account of the debate is intended to help the reader shape his or her own understanding of the problem and apply his or her own critical judgment regarding possible solutions.

Just as previous research has postulated variations of the deficit theme (Auletta 1983; Moynihan 1965), there has also been a tendency to overlook the continuing effects of racism (Wilson 1978). Stanfield and Dennis (1993) examine some of the historical pitfalls associated with studying race and ethnicity and discuss methodological options for overcoming these historical obstacles. Dennis (1993) suggests advantages in the use of participant observation while Anderson (1993) suggests that researchers enter the field with a sense of humility, rather than emphasizing their own expertise.

In examining the pitfalls of conducting research across racial, ethnic and class differences, Andersen (1993) discusses the difficulties and importance of developing trust and accountability between a dominant group researcher and minority group subjects. Even in the best of situations, limits on research objectivity are imposed by the relative social positions of the researcher and the people who are the primary focus of the study. Race, gender, class and outsider status can all impair the collection and reflection processes.

Franklin (1986) describes what he sees as chronic negative biases in research on black males. He maintains that the persistent use of pathological populations, random sampling and official statistics has resulted in the misrespresentation of black men in social science research (Franklin, 1986). In response to these criticisms a strategy of inquiry has been selected which attempts to maximize the input of community leaders, young black men, parents and other directly affected by the problems described in the study. The research strategy is designed with the intention of maximizing the practical participation of study respondents in ways that will assist in the minimization of bias and enhance a credibile representation of the issues. In this manner, it is hoped that the project's goal of accurately representing the philosophies and program strategies designed to meet the needs of young black men in high risk urban communities, can be realized .

Chapter 3: Constructivist Inquiry

Overview

In response to the pitfalls of conducting research across ethnic differences, Andersen (1993) suggests that majority scholars "develop and utilize tensions in their own cultural identities to enable them to see different aspects of minority group experiences and to examine critically majority experiences and beliefs" (p.42). With these concerns in mind, constructivist inquiry has been selected as a research strategy because of its unique approach to power sharing throughout the research process (Guba and Lincoln 1989).

Given Dennis' (1993) recommendations for participant observation, the constructivist approach provides a valuable alternative to more conventional survey research. Rigorous guidelines have been established which are conducive to avoiding majority bias because they maximize the ability of study participants to define important issues. Participants play an active role in reviewing the findings and provided input at strategic points during the research (Guba and Lincoln 1989; Chambers, Wedel, and Rodwell 1992). Trustworthiness, or research accountability, is achieved and documented in a variety of other ways, as well.

Achieving authenticity is the second criterion for measuring rigor in constructivist knowledge building. It recognizes research as an intervention process and requires that fairness and mutual benefits are derived from the inquiry (Guba and Lincoln 1989). These ethical considerations are relevant to all research but are especially important when conducting inquiry across cultural or ethnic differences (Andersen 1993). For this reason, constructivist safeguards of trustworthiness and authenticity became an integral part of the research design (Guba and Lincoln 1989).

The criteria of trustworthiness and authenticity are established to insure credibility via grounded interpretations of the data. Procedural requirements are designed to limit arbitrary bias and promote logical accountability for the research findings (Glaser and Strauss 1968). An in-depth discussion of the requirements for trustworthiness will be provided in more detail later in this chapter. The point, however, is that these criteria support and uphold the already stated advantages of participant observation conveyed by Dennis (1993). When implemented with appropriate levels of rigor and discipline, constructivist strategies, and their emphasis on mutual discovery and power sharing, provide opportunities for interpretive balance and fairness. Efforts to document both authenticity and trustworthiness have been made through the selective identification of related comments and observations taken from the field.

Sampling was purposive (Glaser and Strauss 1968; Patton 1980), both with respect to site selection and interview participants. Data collection took place at each of three selected field sites. The mode of information collection was participatory, interactive and empirically based. Recording information involved multiple means including hand written field notes, tape-recorded interviews, photographs and collecting documents . Data analysis was subjected to disciplined rigor, including the process of respondent feedback known as member checking (Lincoln and Guba 1989). This research strategy is intended to protect against misinterpretating respondents' ideas, statements or points of view (Chambers, Wedel and Rodwell 1993). Additional dependability and confirmation for the findings included peer debriefing and review, creation of an audit trail, and a certified audit performed by an independent professional auditor (Guba and Lincoln 1989).

Constructivist Inquiry

Constructivist strategies for research are well suited to achieve a participatory or negotiated outcome in social science research (Chambers,Wedel and Rodwell 1992; Guba and Lincoln 1989). They require that researchers enter into the field with a minimum of a priori questions and assumptions. Hypothesis testing and theory formation is not a central goal of the research. Instead, the goal of the research is to provide a voice and vehicle by which people who have intimate knowledge of the problem can present their case. The purpose of the research is to build an informed understanding of the social realities encountered during the inquiry.

The constructivist model for research is one of mutual empowerment through shared experiences and understanding. This is frequently but not exclusively accomplished through case studies (Chambers, Wedel and Rodwell 1992, 303-304). Researchers typically take on the role of an informed but naive student. Their job is to facilitate discovery (Glaser and Strauss 1968) by providing detailed descriptions that enhance the reader's understanding of the people and the social realities of their world, which he or she has vicariously encountered. The ethical responsibility of the researcher is to strive for a rigorous, trustworthy and authentic reconstructions (Guba 1991).

The constructivist approach differs from positivist and many other philosophies of science in three fundamental ways. From an ontological viewpoint, constructivists assert that reality is by nature relative rather than absolute. Epistemologically, the constructivist scholar maintains a subjective posture based upon the assumption that the enhancement of understanding and knowledge depends on multiple perspectives.

Methodologically, constructivists emphasize a dialogue between the researcher and the person or phenomenon being studied. The dialogue is designed to lead to a cooperative and emergent construction of a case, resulting in the best attainable representation of the reality experienced by those people who participate in the study (Guba and Lincoln 1989).

Guba and Lincoln (1989) maintain that social realities are human constructions "ungoverned by natural laws, causal or otherwise" (p.88). While conventional scientific belief systems assume a fixed objective truth arrived at through unbiased observations and reporting facts (Wallace, 1972), constructivists define truth "simply as the most informed and sophisticated construction about which there is a consensus" (Guba and Lincoln 1989, 86). This philosophical position represents a recognition of the limits of scientific facts while simultaneously placing knowledge in the context of human activity. Knowledge and scientific facts exist in relation to what people remember, say and do, not independently of them. Science, thereby, becomes a product of human understanding with all its limits and potential, not a body of undiscovered natural laws.

The difference between the realist ontology and a relativist or interpretive ontology can be found in the way one attempts to answer the question of what is knowable (Guba 1990). Realist approaches and assumptions point to a singular reality, independent of the observer's interest and subject to immutable laws (Guba and Lincoln, 1989). In contrast, the relativist alternative asserts that a reality can only be understood in relation to the observer. The nature of reality, therefore, depends upon a consensus of multiple shared perspectives and interpretations of meaning. For the realist, truth is singular and final, for the relativist truth is plural and emergent (Chambers, Wedel and Rodwell 1992; Guba 1990; Guba and Lincoln 1986).

Because of these fundamental distinctions the epistemological response to the question of "How do we know anything?" is answered differently for both paradigms (Guba and Lincoln 1989; Kuhn 1970). Whereas positivism and other realistic ontologies attempt to retain unbiased or objective orientations (Wallace 1972), constructivism maintains that the observer can never truly detach himself or herself from the observed (Guba 1990). Another way of expressing this is to say that interaction between the studier and the studied, however great or small, can never be absolutely controlled for and will inevitably affect the outcome. To contend that interaction can be eliminated is to deny a necessary component of any research project.

Scientific inquiry demands interaction so that empirical observation can take place. Without such interaction there would be no findings. The contention that interactivity does not exist or that its effects can be eliminated is illusory. To say that the effects are insignificant is merely to say that they are small and one doesn't think they should matter. This contention is in itself based upon a subjective value orientation.   Furthermore, basic assumptions about the measurability of phenomena, the value of objectivity and what Guba (1990) calls the "subject/object duality" created during detached observation are fundamental prejudices that predispose results (p.66).

The biases of realistic methodologies, correspondingly, are not eliminated but are simply implemented at a different time or place and on a different level. The time is usually a priori; the place is frequently in the office or boardroom; and the level is often subliminal. The constructivist paradigm offers an alternative to this philosophical paradox of objectivity by recognizing the subjective nature of human inquiry. Constructivist research attempts to address the problem of interaction and that of subject/object dualism by presenting an understanding of realities as outgrowths of the combined efforts and perceptions of both the inquirer and that which is being studied (Guba and Lincoln 1989). No attempt is made to eliminate or control for values but rather to illuminate them in the inquiry process, to illustrate them sufficiently so as to understand their impact on our perceptions and the social reality of those whom we study.

Methodologically, constructivist research is logically driven by these two previous assumptions into a strategy which emphasizes maximum feasible participation of the respondents. Since reality and, hence, "Truth" is relative, each person's arrival at his or her own perception of truth has value and merit for his or her own world. To utterly dismiss somone's perception of reality would be unethical because it would defy the legitimacy of diverse perspectives; immoral, because it would devalue a fellow human being's perception of his world; and ignorant, because it would lead to divergent rather than convergent perceptions of reality (M.K. Rodwell personal communication, 4/93). It therefore follows that the best possible level of understanding, according to the constructivist paradigm, is through a synthesis of collective perceptions and subjective realities.

This empowerment model consists of what Guba and Lincoln (1989) refer to as a "hermeneutic dialectic process" between the researcher and the researched. In order for this to take place, six basic criteria must be met (p.149). There should be a commitment on the part of researchers and respondents to ethical integrity, honesty and accuracy; competent communication; a willingness to share power; an openness to change; a willingness to critically reconsider values; and a commitment of time and energy necessary to complete the study (Guba and Lincoln 1989, 191). Once these preconditions are met, a process of inquiry develops that accommodates a variety of perceptions by depicting the diversity as well as the unity of opinions, beliefs and understandings.

Chambers, Wedel and Rodwell (1993) define three distinct phases of research in the constructivist paradigm which they call "orientation and overview", "focused exploration" and "comprehensive member check" (pp.308-310). The orientation phase includes the traditional review of literature, preparation for and the initial introduction into the field setting. Initial site visits and exploratory questions should be designed help the study participants shape for the investigator an initial understanding of the phenomena being observed.

Phase two of the research involves a period of focused exploration in which a more targeted probing of observed data occurs. As common themes emerge they may require more in-depth inquiry and verification. The investigator may attempt to identify relationships or develop a more sophisticated level of understanding for some observed situation. He/she might compare and contrast conflicting perceptions among different participants or test assumptions drawn from previous observations. He/she might engage in triangulation alternative data collection techniques in order to cross check findings (Chambers, Wedel and Rodwell 1992). Each of these processes occurs during the second phase of research. This phase is characterized by an increasing involvement with participants and a testing of ideas developed from observed data.

The final phase of a study involves comprehensive member checking to obtain credibility with regard to the reported findings and to assure disciplined accountability. Memberchecking is a process of participant feedback in which the object is to "obtain confirmation that the report has captured the data as constructed by the informants, or to correct, amend or extend it..." (Lincoln and Guba 1985, 236). Once the goal of confirmation has been achieved and differences reconciled, either through consensus or contrasting representations, then the final report can be presented. Memberchecking and ultimate agreement on the accuracy of the final report are essential to the integrity of the research project because the goal of the study is to convey the social reality of the participants, not the generalizations construed by the researcher.

Sampling

Sampling strategies for site selection and interviews were based on the purposive sampling model described by Patton (1980). Purposive sampling is a process used when one wants to learn something about select groups possessing skills or attributes important to the study question. It is described as "the strategy of choice when one wants to learn something and come to understand something about certain select cases without needing to generalize to all such cases (Patton 1980, 107)." People or sites with identified attributes, histories, or experiences are purposefully chosen for observation based upon these characteristics.

Because there is so little published information on the research subject it was assumed that a study providing descriptive information from multiple sites would have the greatest likelihood of providing a broad foundation for knowledge building. With this goal in mind an effort was made to achieve diversity in the site selection.

Methods of identifying appropriate study sites included a variety of selection criteria. Programs under consideration had to be located in or serve low income urban communities and they had to have a component that specifically addressed the needs of young black men. Site selection was determined in part by accessibility, both in terms of the program director's willingness to participate, and the convenience of site locations.

Through the use of academic and popular literature, word of mouth and chance encounter, nine potential sites in four mid-Atlantic cities were identified. Efforts to secure participation involved letter writing, phone calls, and interviews with program directors. Three study sites located in separate urban communities were selected based upon their efforts to provide structured programs for young black men. Two sites were church affiliated and are comparable in design, although this was not readily apparent at the time of the time of initial selection. The third site was a private secular, non profit organization with a relatively large full time staff. The purpose for selecting an alternative program design was to examine the range of possible approaches for confronting similar issues.

The researcher had some previous knowledge and was familiar with the program and personnel at one site but, prior to the research process, had no experience with the other two. Characteristics common to all three of the programs selected for the study were their joint orientation to meeting the needs of young black males, their use of community based resources, and their urban setting.

Once study sites were established individual "stakeholders" (Guba and Lincoln 1989, 51) were identified based upon their status as program administrators, staff, youth participants, and related people such as parents or boardmembers. Stakeholders are defined by Chambers, Wedel and Rodwell (1992) as those various parties who are involved in or affected by the program in identifiable ways . A modified form of Patton's (1980) preferred method of serial nomination governed the selection of candidates for formal tape recorded interviews (Lincoln and Guba 1985; Rodwell 1989; Skritic 1985). This networking procedure, referred to by Guba and Lincoln (1989) as the "hermeneutic process" was a conscious attempt to maximize diversity in the collection of information. An effort was made to provide every staff member or program participant who wished to be interviewed, the opportunity to be heard (p.72). This goal was essentially accomplished at two of the three sites. Time and resource limits did not permit a comprehensive sampling from the third site. Nevertheless, more people were interviewed, including a majority of the staff. Informed consent forms were signed and a written abstract describing the nature of the research were provided to participants at each site.

Patton (1980) describes some basic guidelines for purposive sampling. Extreme case sampling is used when people who are believed to comprise unusual examples are sought. Typical case criteria include those people thought to represent commonly held attributes or experiences. Youth who appeared to be typical or average members of the programs being studied were selected as interview subjects. Sampling for maximum variation involved efforts designed to elicit a wide range of possible cases so as to insure a diversity of perspectives. The investigator on one occasion interviewed respondents with recognized leadership skills and then other people who appeared to be followers or new members. Alternatively respondents were both brand new members and seasoned veterans. Critical case sampling involved the selection of people who had an unusual or essentially demonstrative point of view, such as program directors or people with specialized knowledge. Politically important cases was another approach to choosing respondents. Board of directors and other community members were sometimes strategically or politically important. The researcher was mindful of each of these selection models when choosing interview candidates. Each of these basic sampling techniques was used to secure various pieces of information during the course of the fieldwork. In addition openness and flexibility were maintained in utilizing the various sampling possibilities so as to allow for adjustments in the inquiry as themes and awareness of salient issues developed (Chambers, Wedel and Rodwell 1992).

Guba and Lincoln (1989) emphasize the value of maximum variation as a sampling strategy of choice in order to obtain the broadest scope of information. They further recommend that sample "elements" be selected both "serially" and "contingently" (Guba and Lincoln 1989, 178). These distinctions refer to the idea that each sample element, whether it be a person or an additional site, be chosen after data collection from the preceding element, or case, has been largely completed. Furthermore cases should be selected contingent upon achieving maximum variation or in ways that "best serve the particular needs of the inquiry at the moment" (Guba and Lincoln 1989, 178).

Participants initially selected for formal interviews were chosen based on identified roles and responsibilities. Program directors, professional or volunteer staff members, and program participants were the most frequently interviewed people. On site observation by the researcher also helped to identify potential sources of valuable information. Depending on the site, formal interview candidates also included available volunteers, parents, board members and the like. Table1 shows the different stakeholder groups that participated in the formal, tape recorded, interviews at each research site.

Table 1
Stakeholder groups / participants in tape recorded interviews

	Site 1	Site 2	Site 3
Program directors	1	2	4
Staff & volunteers	3	3	12
Boardmembers	2	1	0
Youth participants	8	5	9
Parents &			
significant others	0	3	0
Summer interns	0	0	5

Participant observation and informal contacts with program participants and other stakeholders also provided valuable information. The informal interviews and discussions that took place during the course of regular daily interactions with youth, program staff and volunteers, helped to provide direct experience and guidance for sampling decisions about selecting formal interview candidates. These contacts contributed to on-site memberchecking by providing opportunities for triangulation and verification of emerging themes during data collection (Webb, Campbell, Schwartz, and Sechrest 1965). Informal discussions were recorded in handwritten field notes which were then entered into an expanded field note book in accordance with data collection strategies about to be described.

Instrumentation

Constructivist inquiry emphasizes flexibility in its approach to data collection and the superiority of human beings as the primary data collection instrument (Chambers, Wedel and Rodwell 1992, 296). Collection strategies must retain the ability to adjust to the changing conditions and information found in the field. For this reason preferred instruments of data gathering are not standardized tests, structured questionnaires or other quantitative data collection tools, but the human being in the context of interpersonal communication (Chambers, Wedel and Rodwell 1992). The human instrument provides the degree of adaptability necessary to take full advantage of the range of ideas sought in the constructivist model for research.

Polyani (1966) emphasizes a distinction between propositional and tacit knowledge. Propositional knowledge is that which can be deduced and stated verbally. Tacit knowledge on the other hand, is arrived at intuitively, the origin of which "cannot be stated verbally but is somehow known to the subject" (Chambers, Wedel and Rodwell 1992, 282). Tacit knowledge implies an intrinsically based understanding derived from a host of experiences manifesting themselves in feelings, senses, and other inductive processes or characteristics unique to the human being as a data collection instrument. Constructivist research upholds the legitimacy of tacit knowledge, especially as supportive confirmation of propositional conclusions, but also as a factor in its own right (Chambers, Wedel and Rodwell 1992). Social work also recognizes the value of tacit knowledge in such concepts as empathic understanding and practice wisdom (Bloom 1990; Johnson 1992; Monte 1987).

The primary researcher in this endeavor was the primary instrument for data collection. The researcher was trained in constructivist and other qualitative data collection strategies, having completed doctoral level graduate courses in both qualitative and quantitative research methods. He served as a peer reviewer for analysis of open ended questions in a study of social work doctoral program graduate's research productivity (Rodwell and Pullman 1991) and conducted field based ethnographic interviews (Pullman 1993;

Spradley 1979). In addition, he has provided interview training and research strategy consultation on a variety of research oriented projects.

Data Collection

Multiple data collection strategies were used. Although the primary emphasis was placed on semi-structured interviews with identified stakeholders, alternative data collection strategies included informal discussions, direct field observation, documents and records, photographs and other unobtrusive measures.

Study participants were provided with written information explaining the nature of the research, followed by a verbal explanation of the research aims prior to each interview. Signed releases were obtained at each site. Documentation of knowledgeable participation through recorded statements was also sought whenever feasible. Confidentiality was maintained by eliminating surnames from recorded data, using fictitious names in the final reports and nondisclosure of the study site locations. Subsequent to transcribing the recorded interviews tapes were destroyed in order to prevent electronic voice pattern identification.

Although a minimum of forty hours of participant observation per site was scheduled, an average of sixty hours was actually conducted and documented in a calendar notebook. Between 14 and 25 tape recorded interviews were conducted at each site (see Table 1). The researcher involved himself in the daily activities of each program as a volunteer participant, answering telephones, tutoring school children and occasionally participating in group discussions. This aspect of the data collection was designed to facilitate informal communication and overcome initial distrust or resistance. The goal of these strategies was to remain unobtrusive during observation and to provide experiential insights for comparing and contrasting emerging themes developed from the formal interviews (Chambers,Wedel and Rodwell 1992).

Information was collected by on site note taking, tape recording, photographs, collected documents and expanded field notes. Abbreviated field notes were recorded at the time of observations and later entered into an expanded field journal thereby providing elaboration and detail from the original notes. A daily record or chronology served to document data collection activities and time spent on site or in the field. Low inference observations such as direct quotes, recorded statements, and other means of direct documentation were emphasized during note taking (Spradley 1979; Strauss 1987). Once a representative group of stakeholders occupying similar positions with regard to the organization was identified and interviewed, recurrent themes began to emerge. Such "claims, concerns and issues" were seen as those matters most frequently referred to by the respondents based on the commonality of their experiences (Guba and Lincoln 1989, 40). They represent the relevant interests common to most people engaged in the problem on that particular level, such as staff, youth participants, and others. When repetition or redundancy in observation and data collection began to occur, or when the available number of respondents for a particular status group was exhausted, then data collection from that group or site was concluded. Additional stakeholders representing another related group were then sought until work at that site was completed. Data collection efforts were designed to attain a wide range of diversity in opinions, attitudes or points of view at each site. In order to avoid confusing observations at one site with those from another, data collection was completed at one site before activities began at the next.

Several interview strategies were used based upon Spradley's (1979) ethnographic interviewing model and similar techniques promoted by Lincoln and Guba (1989). Filling in patterns of seemingly absent information refers to investigating the gaps in data as collected and initially analyzed (Lincoln and Guba 1985). Such gaps in the data can be identified when anomalies (Kuhn 1970), or logical inconsistencies, seem to occur or when seemingly critical pieces of information are missing. The researcher deliberately attempts to extend knowledge into unknown or under explored areas by seeking either confirmation or contradiction of hypothetical connections.

Filling in gaps might be required when a person implies, through innuendo or inflection, a certain idea without stating it clearly or plainly. The researcher, in order to attain clarity, might then ask specifically about that idea. One example of this technique occurred when an interviewee indicated his belief regarding a conspiracy in education to keep black males from achieving academically. Familiarity with educational theories allowed the researcher to recognize the statement as an implied fact and inquire about it. Confirmation of that belief as an existing perspective was achieved and the existing gap was filled.

Chambers, Wedel and Rodwell (1992) divide the idea of filling in patterns into extension, bridging and surfacing. Extension is defined as the technique of building on pre-existing knowledge. It can be referred to as a process of fanning the flames of knowledge. Seeking the experience of participating directly in activities rather than just watching them is one example of extending knowledge. By learning the insider's point of view the participant gains a different kind of information and a different perspective than the nonparticipant observer.

Bridging refers to the attempt to link apparently related pieces of information through substantive confirmation or observation. Asking about apparent linkages or predicting possible outcomes is one way of bridging. When two things occur simultaneously a researcher might want to determine whether people see a connection between the two events. At one research site reduced crime in the community was related in the minds of apartment residents to the opening of the community center. Confirmation of this impression as commonly held understanding in the community was obtained during interviews with non residents, such as police and the apartment manager. By linking the experiences of the police and the manager to the opinions of the residents, it could be reasonably confirmed that the center's presence significantly impacts on crime in the neighborhood.

Surfacing is a third aspect of discovery in which the researcher attempts to expose or discover factors that logic or experience indicate should be present, yet have not been found (Chambers, Wedel and Rodwell 1992). This can be accomplished by asking direct questions when something that would be presumed to be present is missing, or by asking for elaboration of specific pieces of information already provided (Spradley 1979). Allegorically speaking, if extension is fanning the flames, surfacing involves the researcher's attempt to find the fire, or at least the glowing embers, after having witnessed an abundance of smoke. Asking about the extent of drug activity or criminal violence is one example. Whereas most reputable researchers may not want to extend their knowledge in these areas through participation, as in the case of extension, discreet and unobtrusive questions leading into a general discussion of such topics could occur under the right circumstances.

Surfacing can be described as an attempt to carefully draw out information that might be difficult to get to, even under favorable circumstances. Information that is of a personal nature requiring high levels of trust and sensitivity may be involved. Ethics demand, when approaching sensitive issues such as the death of a family member or something that requires a high level of personal disclosure, that the researcher convey a willingness to allow the interviewee to change the subject or terminate the discussion at will and without prejudice.

The data collection and data analysis in constructivist inquiry often merge into a cyclical pattern. During data collection, the researcher was constantly comparing new findings with old information. The researcher inquired about seeming anomalies or discrepancies and attempted to find consensus or distinct differences where they occurred (Glaser and Strauss 1967). This effort included attempts to confirm observations or identify contradictions based upon a cyclical pattern of data collection, analysis, hypothesis testing, recollection, and further reflection. The term "recollection" is especially important because it implies both the mental process of recalling and recorded information as well as the physical process of going back out into the field to re-collect data in order to verify hunches, test ideas and fill in gaps. As ideas and discoveries emerged, relevant information was identified and placed in meaningful groups and categories. Lincoln and Guba (1985) refer to a four-step process in the analysis of data. These steps include unitizing, categorizing, filling in patterns and member checking.

Data Analysis

Data analysis techniques included the use of *The Ethnograph*, a software program developed by Seidel, Kjolseth, and Seymour (1988). This computerized text analysis program which allows for labeling, categorizing and selection of designated text segments for the purpose of combining them into separate documents. Field notes and transcriptions of recorded interviews were analyzed utilizing these computerized data analysis procedures (Tesch 1990). The software program has the capacity for identifying individual labels assigned to various text segments, counting the number of labels assigned to a document and combining selected labels into groups for the purpose of creating topic specific documents. By using this program the researcher was able to compile and display desired information from the field notes. The various codes assigned to pieces of information were mapped according to established code labels and are traceable to their original source. A code auditing process was established to verify accountability and insure that any final report reflects observations grounded in the original data.

The Ethnograph is best described as an "interactive menu driven program designed to assist the qualitative researcher in some of the mechanical aspects of data analysis" (Seidel, Kjolseth and Seymour 1988, 1-1). It can provide an overview of how many different types of issues were presented during the collection of information and has the capacity for reviewing pieces of information related to those entered into the final report but not themselves included. It also allows for the establishment of documents based upon categorical issues and enhances the analysis process by eliminating time consuming manual procedures.

Unitizing involves the breaking down of collected data into meaningful units or pieces of information. Similarly Seidel, Kjolseth, and Seymour (1988) refer to these units as text segments. The researcher identified pieces of information that are relevant to the three main areas of research interest; *issues*; *philosophy*; and *program*. Data units are defined as pieces of information that stand alone, requiring little or no explanation for understanding by an uninformed reader (Chambers, Wedel and Rodwell 1992, 319). A data unit can include a single word or phrase. It can be a sentence or a whole speech. It can also be an artifact, a picture or a document. After being identified as such, text segments were then labeled for future reference. *The Ethnograph* (Seidel, Kjolseth and Seymour 1988; Tesch 1990) computer software program allowed for the coded segments to then be selected from the body of the transcripts individually or collectively.

This technology provided for a quick and easy way to create a separate document according to common themes, and specific areas of interest. The next step in the data analysis process involved the categorization of data units. Constant comparison and contrasting of code labels resulted in the grouping of various ideas into meaningful categories. This procedure included the creation of basic decision rules for separating data units and grouping them into related themes. Clearly articulated decision rules provided the rationale for consistent grouping and categorization. The decision rules were specifically stated, recorded and documented in the appendices. General coding procedures and guidelines can be found in Appendix 1. Specific code rules and definitions can be found in Appendix 2.

A master code list was compiled by identifying all of the coded labels assigned to statements or portions of statements made by interview subjects. A relatively small portion of the code labels used to define text information did not readily fit into either of the primary code categories of *issues, philosophy* and *program*. These anomalous code segments consisted of less than 5 % of the data and were, in most cases, identifiable as smaller segments of text contained in larger, more relevant pieces of information. A fourth category for coding relates to descriptive codes, which were maintained in order to assist in providing independent verification of the setting, time, and place. Codes that did not seem to fit under any of the major categories, were set aside for future reference.

Issues are defined by the researcher as those concerns and interests reflected by statements that inform the reader's understanding of the influences shaping the lives and experiences of young men participating in the programs being described. A broad range of important issues was identified relating to the needs and concerns of young black men in urban communities. Frequently discussed subjects included the need for leadership, role models, concerns about school and schoolwork, drugs, violence and values. A closer examination of issues revealed that areas of concern were often reflected in the idiosyncrasies of the community being studied. Initially coded text segments were grouped into common themes reflecting broad issues such as employment, relationships, community concerns, education, and race relations.

The code category for *philosophies* consists of labels that identify statements of fact, faith or belief which depict the interviewee's understanding or perception of a given situation. Interview comments relating to philosophical orientations include a wide variety of interests ranging from the mundane to the ideological. Philosophies are identified through the use of program mottos and slogans, professions of belief and faith, and articulations of ideological or strategic focus. Values such as trust, respect or discipline were often related as a need or an activity goal from which a guiding principle or program philosophy was inferred. In most cases an effort was made by the interviewer to draw out philosophical orientations by encouraging respondents to elaborate on program goals or ideological rationale.

The code category for *program*s refers to strategies and/or specific activities conducted at each site. This category includes the different types of activities, goals, strategies, and evaluation criteria. Program codes also include guiding principles such as constructive criticism, peer support, discipline and caring. In this way many of the guiding principles for program activity overlap with the philosophies for program design. Some program code labels are direct references to different activities or programs at each site. These codes include names, or abbreviations for program names, such as Rites of Passage, Real Men, Black History, and others. Additional code labels represent more informal activities such as basketball, dance, cookouts and trips. Issues relating specifically to program development were also frequently double coded. These items included codes reflecting references to parental involvement, youth and adult leadership, building trust and developing a model for future programs.

These central areas of interest having to do with basic social *issues, philosophical* perspectives and *program* design were found to be broad enough to subsume the vast majority of codes at each of the three sites. Descriptive information was coded separately and included comments about neighborhood, the community setting and other statements providing physical description of people, places or things. Those coded segments which did not seem to fit into one of these main categories were labeled as other.

Code labels were originally entered into the computer program as eight character acronyms and then expanded into intelligible terms the code group lists presented in Appendix 3. An attempt was made to minimize duplication of code labels on the code lists by combining similar acronyms into one code. The rationale for these changes is to enhance the readers' understanding of how the labels reflect people's experiences in their social world without the encumbrance of computer generated limits on labeling.

The master code list for the Diamond Hill Development Center consisted of 267 code labels depicting information collected during interviews with staff, volunteers, board members and youth. This information derives from thirteen (13) recorded interviews and is supplemented by field notes taken during direct on-site observation, informal interviews and casual discussions. There were twenty (20) miscellaneous related documents collected on site during 60 hours of field observations.

The representations reflected in the code category and code grouping diagrams are intended to demonstrate the range and depth of information related during the interviews. They are not intended to suggest relative importance based only as a function of frequency tallies. Constructivist research encourages the inclusion of unique or singular perspectives when meaningful information is coneyed by a solitary source or response.

Figure 1 illustrates the relative frequency with which different code labels were assigned from interviews at Diamond Hill Development Center. The pie chart reflects the researcher's assignment of topical codes that identify segments of text taken from transcriptions of tape recorded interviews conducted at the Diamond Hill Development Center. This process resulted in the creation of three major coded categories depicting different aspects of research interest. Code categories were established based on labels reflecting important *issues, philosophy* and *program* structure. In addition, descriptive information about the center and the local community was compiled into a fourth category.

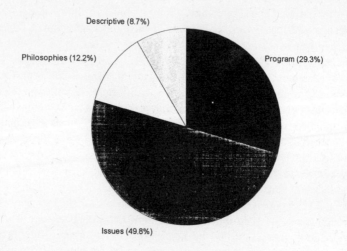

Figure 1. Diamond Hill Development Center - Code Categories
Issues n=114; Philosophies n=28; Program n=67; Descriptive n=20

At the Bunker Hill Community Outreach Center sixteen (16) tape recorded interviews were conducted. Content analysis of these interviews resulted in the assignment of 350 different code labels to text segments taken from sixteen tape recorded interview transcripts. More than sixty hours of on-site participant observation was conducted, and a separate file of documents collected at the site was maintained. These observations are similarly illustrated in Figure 2.

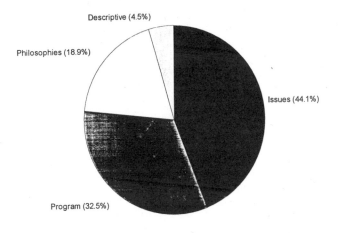

Figure 2. Bunker Hill Community Outreach Center - Code Categories

Issues n=168; Philosophies n=72; Program n=124; Descriptive n=17

Data collection and recording procedures at the Comprehensive Youth Services Center were the same as at the two previous sites. From sixteen recorded interviews with administrators and staff, 603 different labels were assigned to text segments and grouped according to common themes. Taped interviews with summer interns and youth participants were entered into a reflexive journal containing reconstructed interviews. Field notes recorded sixty hours of on site participation. An overview of the main topics of research interest reveals that interview codes at this center emphasize program over issues and philosophy (See Fig. 3).

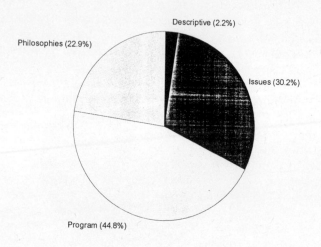

Figure 3. Comprehensive Youth Services Center - Code Categories
Issues n=182; Philosophies n=138; Program n=270; Descriptive n=17

The observed shift of emphasis in favor of program at the Comprehensive Youth Services Center reflects significant differences in program design, when compared to youth related activities at the other sites. These results are influenced by the fact that the Youth Services Center provides services to adolescents and young adults throughout the metropolitan area, thereby making physical descriptions of the immediate neighborhood less relevant to discussions of issues, philosophy or program.

Trustworthiness

Scientific rigor and accurate representation of empirical evidence is developed in constructivist inquiry by adherence to principles of trustworthiness and authenticity (Guba and Lincoln 1989). Trustworthiness is an approach to investigative rigor that closely parallels conventional concepts of validity and reliability. The concept of authenticity, however, is unique to constructivist inquiry. Authenticity looks at the quality of the interactive research process by addressing ethical issues such as fairness, mutual benefits for both researchers and respondents, and empowerment on a variety of levels (Chambers, Wedel and Rodwell 1992; Guba 1990).

Trustworthiness in constructivist research depends upon four basic criteria which are designed to insure valid, reliable and relatively objective findings. Because of the unique philosophical and methodological orientations of constructivist inquiry it would be a mistake to assume that the terms as used in the constructivist paradigm are synonymous with those used in neo-positivist research. The types of questions being asked and the types of methods to get at the information being sought are fundamentally different.

For this reason it is advantageous to use a slightly different set of terms in order to understand the nature of scientific discipline being used. Credibility, the first of four criteria used to establish trustworthiness (Guba and Lincoln 1989), includes all of those activities designed to increase the likelihood of credible findings (Chambers, Wedel, and Rodwell 1992). It is established through the implementation of prolonged engagement, persistent observation, triangulation, peer debriefing and member checking (Chambers, Wedel and Rodwell 1992; Eisner 1979; Guba and Lincoln 1989; Lincoln and Guba 1985).

Prolonged engagement emphasizes time spent in the natural setting collecting information, interacting with stakeholders and building trust. This extended process theoretically places the researcher in a position to facilitate discussion, observe relationships and reduce reactivity to the presence of an inquisitive stranger in the midst. It also enables the researcher to attain a better understanding of the "larger picture," the total social milieu in which activities take place

(Chambers, Wedel and Rodwell 1992). This process of prolonged engagement was achieved during the study by means of extended on-site visits, interviewing and participant observation. An average of 60 hours was spent at each site. During that time the researcher collected information and documented experiences by participating in or observing program activities and interviewing people at each site. Additional time was spent touring the neighborhood and communities in which programs are located.

Persistent observation can be defined as the act of "noting, watching and taking into account the physical and psychosocial dynamics of the time and place" (Chambers, Wedel and Rodwell 1992, 314). This task was accomplished through abbreviated note taking during direct field observations. These brief notes were then expanded upon and entered into a larger field journal. The field journal contains additions to the notes, based on unrecorded, remembered observations, in accordance with the parameters for field observation described by Spradley (1979). Field and journal notes emphasize the use of low inference observations in order to minimize interpretive bias in the data collection process.

Triangulation is a process of verification through the constant comparison and cross checking of data collected and data analyzed (Glaser and Strauss 1967; Guba and Lincoln 1989). Examples of triangulation include interviewing more than one person on the same subject, verifying information given through documented evidence or other means of obtaining multiple sources for data collected. It can be a useful check on stakeholder manipulation and helps to prevent research bias from developing by ensuring the acquisition of multiple perspectives (Chambers, Wedel and Rodwell 1992). Triangulation techniques used in the study included multiple interviews in identified stakeholder groups, such as talking to several youth or several staff members. Documenting information by obtaining program descriptions from brochures or other written handouts was another means of triangulating data.

Peer Debriefing

Peer debriefing is defined by Guba and Lincoln (1989) as the "process of engaging with a disinterested peer in extended and extensive discussions of one's finding conclusions and tentative analyses, and, occasionally, field stresses (p. 237)." An independent expert is enlisted to listen to and talk about the inquiry process, and to provide advice and reflection about possible avenues for future inquiry. He or she is debriefed by the researcher and helps to review the data. Throughout the research process the debriefer helps to formulate and reflect on ideas deriving from the inquiry. The researcher shares the study design and initial impressions from the field with the debriefer who then attempts to help him or her discover possible new avenues of investigation.

Peer debriefing and reviewing was conducted on two levels. Two separate peer scholars, each with a different areas of expertise, were involved. The task of the peer debriefer was to insure rigor. He examined coding procedures, such as grouping strategies, for logical consistency and provided consultation with regard to the technical aspects of data collection and analysis. The emphasis for this debriefer was on helping to insure grounded findings (Glaser and Strauss 1967) and logical consistency in the code groupings. The peer debriefer in this study was a doctoral student experienced in the use of constructivist research design. He has extensive professional experience in counseling with adolescents and their families and demonstrated familiarity with social policies affecting the needs of troubled youth (Pullman 1994).

Peer Review

Peer reviewing is more closely related to the analysis process and involves critical evaluation of how and why the researcher shapes the information for the final report. These techniques involve the use of a professional peer evaluator who is intimate with the research question and who oversees the data collection, recording and analysis processes. The purpose of peer review is to encourage the asking of poignant or difficult questions, to examine methodological steps with a disinterested observer and to provide sympathetic professional support (Lincoln and Guba 1985). Peer review occurs during both the data collection and analysis process. The reviewer helps to determine whether data units are understandable as defined, are relevant to the subject and capable of standing alone as independent bits of information (Chambers, Wedel and Rodwell 1992).

A peer reviewer with an established expertise relating to issues facing young black men, and community based youth programs, provided consultation and expert advice during data collection, analysis and the final compilation of the findings (Pullman 1994). The primary emphasis for this consultation was in the area of content credibility. The goal for the peer reviewer was to insure that interpretive processes did not lead to premature conclusions or misunderstandings. The peer reviewer examined the data collection strategies, the field notes and the case study reports. He provided reflection and feedback as he deemed appropriate, insured cultural sensitivity and provided guidance for further inquiry. The goal of peer review was to minimize majority based, interpretive bias on the part of the primary researcher during the collection, reflection and reporting phases of the study.

Periodic conferences with both the peer debriefer and the peer reviewer were scheduled and research notes examined throughout the data collection and analysis process. Records of peer debriefing and peer reviewing schedules were kept in a calendar note book and entered into the research strategies journal. In addition, a third journal was kept to record the researcher's opinions, thoughts and other reflections. This reflexive journal serves to provide an account of the reflective processes that occurred during the study while simultaneously keeping them separate from the observations themselves. It is designed to assist in clearly distinguishing researcher based subjective comments from more inference-free observations (Taylor and Bogdan 1984). Both journals were made available for an independent audit to be discussed later in this report.

Memberchecking

The final criteria for credibility is memberchecking (Lincoln and Guba 1985). This activity can be described on two levels. It involves both a formal and an informal process in which collected and analyzed data are continuously tested for accuracy or clarity of understanding. The process took place informally by seeking direct verification from informants during data collection and recording. Accuracy and clarity were maintained by asking for elaboration; following up responses; and asking for verification of summary questions when the interview was ending (Spradley 1979).

During the member check the researcher actively sought input from study participants and their guidance with respect to how he should interpret and/or summarize information. Memberchecking was designed to achieve agreement as to the representative quality of the results. It took place both during the data collection and after data analysis.

Informal member checks took place during the interviewing and during the field observations at each of the three sites. During data collection the researcher attempted to seek verification or confirmation of ideas generated from statements or observations in the field. Memberchecking was an ongoing activity involving observation, idea formation, reflection and confirmation. It was an effort to achieve a progressive depth of knowledge on the part of the researchers through the mutual interaction and reflection process. Responses to inquiries directed by previous observations helped to determine additional areas of inquiry. The researcher continuously sought feedback in the form of confirmation or contradiction from study participants during the inquiry. The primary objective of member checking is for interpretations to accurately represent the social reality being studied based upon the mutual understandings of all the parties involved.

Memberchecking also took place on a more formal level prior to the completion of the final summary report. During this stage the researcher provided study participants with transcribed copies of their tape recorded interviews and requested feedback or elaboration in writing or by telephone. This additional information was incorporated into the data analysis. Finally, three study participants from each site were provided a rough draft of the final case study for their program. These people acted as representatives who then evaluated the document for accuracy of meaning by providing critical assessment in order to bring the representation in line with their own perceptions of the phenomena being described. Suggested changes, such as rephrasing certain comments or adding additional information, were included in the final reports.

Audit Trail

Dependability and confirmability in this study were achieved by establishing an audit trail (Lincoln and Guba 1985). The audit trail consisted of establishing meticulous records of data collected and analyzed, as well as decision rules for sampling and codification. A separate journal depicting research strategies and plans was maintained in order to sustain and demonstrate an organized methodological approach to collecting information. The purpose of this record was to document and plan out strategies for data collection as the situations and circumstances changed from site to site, or from person to person. Decisions about who needed to be interviewed, how questions should be structured and other deliberate efforts to collect and make sense of information were recorded in this methodological journal.

In addition an audit trail allows an outside observer to see how interpretations or conclusions made in the final report are directly supported by observations in the field. This process is accomplished through maintenance of field notes, a journal of expanded field notes, a reflective journal as described earlier and a file of written documents or records obtained during the study.

Confirmability and dependability were assessed by the hiring of an independent auditor, with recognized expertise in constructivist research strategies, who examined the findings by tracing selected segments of the final report through the interpretive, analysis, collection and recording stages. This accounting process determines the degree to which summary statements in the final report are traceable to the actual observations made on site (Chambers, Wedel and Rodwell 1992).

An extensive audit and confirmability assessment was conducted on the field notes, the interview recording and other collected data by a disinterested professional auditor. This data was cross referenced with the coding procedures and the final report in order to make an objective evaluation of the rigor and dependability of the findings. This independent procedure is an accepted part of constructivist research and can be described as a self-study which is designed to validate the grounded nature of the findings (Glaser and Strauss 1967).

The auditing process lasted for two consecutive days during which time the auditor was provided full access to research notes, computer information and all other related data. The auditor's assignment was to ascertain and document the degree to which research procedures were consistent with constructivist criteria for trustworthiness (Guba and Lincoln 1989). A report of the auditor's findings was subsequently submitted to a committee of five social science professionals for final approval and verification (Pullman 1994).

Authenticity

As a concept relating to discipline and rigor in constructivist research authenticity is still in its evolutionary stages (Guba 1990). In recognition of the proactive approach to social science research implied by constructivist theory, authenticity was developed as a principle for study which stresses the philosophical ideal of empowerment. Authenticity recognizes research to be an intervention as well as a scientific pursuit, and stresses outcome over methodology (Guba and Lincoln 1989).

Authenticity refers to the nature of the investigative process and implies a values orientation compatible with social work ethics. Similar to the physicians' credo to do no harm, authenticity implies fairness, ontological growth, educative effects, and tactical results (Chambers, Wedel and Rodwell 1992; Guba and Lincoln 1989). It requires that reports derived from the investigation be subjected to prior critical analysis by study participants as well as an independent peer reviewer (Guba and Lincoln 1989). Fairness involves adherence to the principle of evenhanded representation. This involves fully informed participation, eschewing hidden agendas, and negotiating outcomes. In practice this means that people will, in so far as they are capable, be fully informed of the intent of the research and the inquiry process. Informed consent was achieved by having respondents read a brief abstract explaining the nature of the study and signing written consent forms. Additional questions about the research were answered in informal discussions. Documentation of such inquiries was maintained in the field notes for future verification. Final reports also include participatory critique as described in the member checking procedures.

Ontological authenticity is defined as the "increased awareness of the complexity of the program's social environment" (Chambers, Wedel and Rodwell 1992, 326). This involves the ideal of assisting the respondent to enhance his or her awareness and appreciation of the intricate relationships taking place in his/her world. Ontological authenticity strives for the outcome of improved self awareness as a by-product of the research product. Participation should promote consciousness raising by enhancing their awareness of and relation to their world.

This research goal was approached in a variety of ways. Interviewing efforts included deliberate attempts to stimulate an informed dialogue and concentrated reflection on basic issues, rationale and program strategies for activities at each of the sites. One goal of the reporting process was for study participants to improve their self awareness by seeing themselves as other people see them. Reading the rough drafts and final reports also was designed to provide opportunities for reflection, discussion and information about other programs addressing similar problems.

Indications of ontological growth occurred during the research when one program director said he intended to use the final report to provide support for the research requirement in a grant application. The same director stated that he was planning to share the report with his executive board at their next meeting. Another director expressed the desire to dispense with the use of a pseudonym and was hopeful that the study would help with fund raising efforts. Each of these occurrences suggest perceptions of utility with regard to the findings, on the part of study participants. They also suggest an interactive process implying growth in awareness and deliberate intentions to apply the research experience.

The educative function of constructive inquiry is designed to assist participants in developing an understanding of and appreciation for the diverse value systems affecting their world. It is not intended to dissuade or persuade but rather to inform and improve the participants' understanding of alternative points of view (Chambers, Wedel and Rodwell 1992; M.K. Rodwell, personal communication, April 1993). Educative and similar functions take place when the participants are exposed to the diversity and range of opinions reflected by the inquiry process. They also take place as a result of the inquiry procedures when questions are asked in an attempt to compare or contrast differing perspectives. Incidences of educative authenticity have been observed in comments reflecting the influence of the research on program planning, during participant observation, and during the final member check phase. Observations and indications of possible ontological, educative or catalytic outcomes were documented by recording them in the expanded field notes and the methodological journal, which became a part of the audit trail.

Catalytic authenticity emphasizes the ideal of providing impetus for social action (Guba 1990). The inquiry process should stimulate and facilitate change where the participants determine action is needed. Maximum feasible participation is one means of achieving catalytic authenticity. Sharing preliminary findings with study participants, encouraging them to critically analyze the findings, and negotiating the outcome for the final report, were the strategies used to help participants achieve critical insights into their own program development. By engaging participants as equal partners in the reflective process, practical problem solving was initiated while tactical authenticity was simultaneously enhanced (Guba and Lincoln 1989).

Related to the notion of catalytic authenticity, tactical authenticity emphasizes the goal of empowerment by asking to what extent the study has provided participants with a means for action (Guba 1990). To make people aware of a need for change, and then provide no viable vehicle for accomplishing change would exacerbate a problem. It is morally and ethically incumbent upon the researcher to employ methods that empower people to arrive at solutions when problems are identified. Although it may be difficult to determine whether this has occurred, at the very least it implies enhancing possibilities. This was accomplished by providing practical suggestions and policy related information in the site summaries and final chapter. Tactical authenticity might also be determined subsequent to the final report with follow-up inquiries.

Both tactical and catalytic authenticity can be observed in respondents' comments about wanting to follow through on certain ideas developed during the research interaction. One respondent, in this study suggested enthusiasm over using the research code categories as a framework with which to develop new program ideas. Another participant suggested that he had been working on an activity in anticipation of the researcher's visit. A third participant expressed enthusiasm over using the final report as a help with funding requirements. These comments are indicators of both catalytic and tactical authenticity.

Presenting the Findings

The Relationship among Issues, Philosophies and Programs

One important focus for this inquiry is the identification of important issues in the lives of young, black, inner-city males. Issues have been defined by the author as those topics or concerns emerging from site observations that have importance to people in the study. They are those factors which seem to either negatively or positively affect the quality of people's lives.

Issues were distinct from philosophies or guiding principles in that they did not convey a sense of moral obligation or ethical action, nor did they pragmatically direct program. Instead of directing activities, issues were defined as the structure of social concerns upon which philosophies, guiding principles and programs depend. They are the foundations upon which the latter are built.

Philosophies and guiding principles are defined as moral, spiritual and political perspectives participants used to understand their world. A philosophy might provide a way of seeing the world which dictates how a participant or group of participants perceives a certain problem. A religious philosophy, for example, might explain an issue in terms of divine retribution or divine command. An ethical philosophy might define the same problem differently, by excluding the influence of spiritual or religious criteria.   In this way philosophies shape participants' perceptions of issues and their strategies for social change. Those who arrive at a general agreement on identifying basic issues can, and frequently did, disagree as to the causes and the nature of the problem.

If one perceives of issues as the building blocks for social action, then philosophies and guiding principles are the perspectives brought by a participant to that pile of bricks.   This perspective determined both that participant's perception of what was encountered, and his or her response. One participant may have seen a pile of bricks as an obstacle in the road, while another may have seen them as material for building a shelter. Each of these outlooks depend on the perspective brought to the problem. Following this metaphor one step further, program design can be seen as the practical strategy applied to the problem. Program designs, in this inquiry, depend on the material participants have at hand and the perspectives brought to the problem.

Kornblum and Julian (1992) maintain that social status and life experiences effect a person's perceptions of and prescriptions for social problems. For these reasons it is important to know what informed people believe to be the major problems facing young black men, why these problems exist, and what specifically should be done about them.

The findings presented here include individual reconstructions of the information   collected from each of three research sites. Reconstructions are derived from the stated issues and concerns related by people seen and interviewed at each site.   A description of identifiable common themes, across sites, is also provided.   The significance of an issue, philosophy or program related observation is inferred by the researcher, not only as a function of how frequently a topic is mentioned, but also by how passionate the informant is and how poignant the message seems to be. This is a reflective, interpretive process, resulting in tentative conclusions which are subsequently confirmed or challenged further inquiry.

Three separate case studies, derived from interviews and experiences in the field, illustrate the perceptions, philosophies and rationale that lead people in different settings to varying courses of action. These site reconstructions are intended to provide a thick description that will allow the reader to have both a vicarious experience of the social setting described, and enough information to assess similarities between his or her own situation and the experiences of those people described in the report (Geertz 1973). Transferability of the findings from one social setting to another, therefore, depends upon the similarities and differences to be found among the sending and the receiving agents (Guba 1985, 316).

In the course of reflecting on and judging the case studies that follow, the reader must determine whether there is a relationship between what is presented and the assumptions underpinning the inquiry. Are multiple perspectives presented? Is the interaction between the participants and the researcher apparent? Are the case studies good stories? Can the reader get a sense of what it would be like to be in the programs? Do the stories have a common theme? By keeping these questions in mind, the reader will be better prepared to assess the utility of the finding for his or her own purposes.

Transferability: Interpreting and Applying the Findings

Transferability of findings is defined as the extent to which the case study allows for inferences to be made by the reader which may apply to his or her own context or situation (Guba and Lincoln 1989). The means for achieving a high degree of transferability entail the use of detailed and thick description (Geertz 1973). The depth and breadth of the description is intended to promote in the reader a vicarious understanding of the reality being described. The reader who feels that observations reported in the findings are relevant to his or her own experience and wants to apply this knowledge to another setting, should do so with full awareness that success or failure at one site does not guarantee success or failure somewhere else.

The findings from this study should be approached with several important points in mind. These qualifying points may be considered limitations by conventional research standards, but are logical consequences of the assumptions undergriding constructivist inquiry. First and foremost, they are intended to represent experiences of people, in a specific time and place, whose ideas and impressions derive from that setting. These experiences may provide valuable information for people in different but similar settings, but are not to be understood as general rules or statements of fact outside of their own social context.

Secondly, the information contained in these case studies is designed to increase the readers depth of knowledge and enhance his or her understanding of the rationale for and strategies used in each of the programs described. Site selections were made with the intentions of describing several approaches used by people who have the common interest of providing services for young black men. These sites are intended to be seen as examples of what some people say and do without claiming to be transferable models for intervention everywhere.

Thirdly, the case studies are intended to depict the real life drama and character of human experiences without romanticizing or embellishing the realities that have been shared. Other communities and other programs with similar concerns may have different experiences. The transferability of these experiences depends to a great extent upon the reader's ability to determine how and when certain aspects of the case studies apply to his or her own needs.

The researcher has attempted to enhance the transferability of these findings by selecting multiple sites. The rationale for this decision is based on the assumption that what is lost in the details presented at each site is balanced out by the ability to compare and contrast observations across sites. The end product will, hopefully, allow for a higher degree of transferability by identifying common themes without sacrificing a rich idiographic description of the individual programs.

Ultimately, the burden of proof regarding transferability of the findings to other settings is on the receiver of the message (Guba and Lincoln 1989). the researcher has, by design, avoided sweeping generalizations or theoretical claims. If such claims are made by people who read this report, it is the responsibility of the claimant to substantiate them by providing additional support for whatever conclusions they may draw.

Chapter 4: *The Diamond Hill Development Center*

History and Mission

The Diamond Hill Development Center is a small, privately run agency operating out of St. Augustine's Episcopal Church in the Diamond Hill section of town. In spite of its laconic name, Diamond Hill is known locally for its high crime rates, public housing projects and predominantly low income African American population.

The primary mission of the development center is to serve the needs of the urban community in which it is located. At the time of the field observations and interviews the center employed one full time director, four part time employees, and utilized volunteers to operate three basic programs. These programs included a socialization and recreation for senior citizens; a resource and referral program designed to link needy people with appropriate community resources, and an after school youth program. The Rites of Passage program for boys was a part of the overall youth project and is of particular interest to this study.

Brother John, the center's first director and founder, established the program in the mid 1970's as an outreach ministry for St. Augustine's Church. His original goal was to provide constructive after-school opportunities for area youth. Brother John was a short , somewhat rotund man with a dynamic and enthusiastic style of speaking, and is still remembered fondly by many of older members of the church and community. He was referred to by one interviewee as a "trained lay worker" and, under his leadership, the center's activities grew to include the activities for the elderly and referral services. Brother John's sudden and unexpected death in 1988 resulted in the near demise of center activities and a time of reorganization around new leadership that adversely affected its growth and operation.

The current director is a fulltime, paid employee who has been with the center for almost two years. Reverend William Carter is an ordained Baptist minister and a college graduate. He is a African American man in his early forties who has worked professionally in other human services agencies. He is referred to by both staff and program participants as Mr. Carter. More informally he goes by the nickname "W.C."

Neighborhood

The immediate neighborhood in which the Diamond Hill Development Center is located can be described as urban, low income and working class. This general description, however, does not accurately depict the diversity and depth of human resources described by those interviewed during the course of the fieldwork. In order to fully understand the characteristics of the community it is useful to examine both the physical and the human aspects of life in the community.

The part of Diamond Hill where the center is located consists of approximately ten square blocks. The church building is located on a corner lot with the parish hall adjoining the church on the same piece of property. A sign for the center is in front of the parish hall which faces a side street. There is a city transit bus stop in front of the entrance and a small grocery store across the street. The remainder of the neighborhood consists of residential housing.

Three basic modes of architecture comprise the community which, in turn, reflect the social stature of community residents according to descriptions provided by center staff and volunteers. These housing forms consist of single-family, bungalow style homes; multi-family converted apartments; and public housing projects.

On the street immediately facing St. Augustine's Church and for several city blocks in either direction are wood framed row houses with flat roofs, clapboard siding, and small fenced-in yards. Several of these building within sight of the church have boarded windows and doors. Others have broken windows covered with cardboard or appear to be in need of repair in various ways. There is little or no space between buildings and while some are in apparently distressed condition, others show signs of occupancy and regular maintenance. One home located nearby had burned down and remained a burned-out shell, from February, when the field visits to the center began, until May. That following September the debris was finally removed. No new construction has been initiated as of the date of this writing.

The street directly behind the church consists of several blocks of small one and two story suburban style homes with small front, side and backyards. Many of the homes have hedges and bushes. These homes were described by one long term resident as "bungalows" and they give the appearance of financial stability, if not affluence. These same houses were described as being owned by people who have lived in the neighborhood for many years, and who are largely retired or working older citizens.

The third dominant architectural influence can be found at the several housing projects within a two or three block radius. The projects, as they are frequently referred to, consist of row upon row of two-story, cinder block and brick units connected by sidewalks and joined by a central courtyard. Approximately 3000 people live in the nearest project, which was built about 25 years ago. All apartments in the projects are owned by the metropolitan housing authority. The issue of ownership has been depicted by the current director of the center as a central influence on the values or mind set distinguishing people who live in different parts of the community. Those people who live in public housing, and those who own their homes were depicted as having differing attitudes towards work and community.

> "... first of all, the individuals that own their homes
> ...have lived in the neighborhood for well over 10 years.
> When they grew up, they grew up with the attitude
> of understanding that they had to work twice as hard to
> make it. It's like everything they had, they really worked
> hard. They earned, and their whole hope was to acquire
> a home and live there comfortably ever after...
> and when they bought their homes...not that this is a bad
> neighborhood, because this is not a bad neighborhood...
> but this was a real black middle class neighborhood.
> So that the attitude of the individuals was to get a part

of the American dream. They worked hard, because
many of the homeowners are in their 50's and 60's and
so on."

With respect to the public housing and the value of ownership,
the director said the following...

"There is no real ownership there because they belong
to the housing authority. The thought of ownership
does not exist, and when you don't claim ownership
of what you have, you have less respect for it. That
lack of respect trickles down into other areas of a
person's life. So there is a real difference in the
mentality, when there is not ownership."

One long term neighborhood resident and board member at the
development center described a similar impression of human
characteristics in the community. With regard to the homeowners he
depicts a "working to middle class" group which represents "a
tremendous resource" for positive change in the community. In contrast
to what he sees as a stable and silent population the same board member
states...

"What this neighborhood is most known for is that it is
surrounded by at least three or four public housing
developments and that's what gets the notice in terms
of the numbers of people that live here. There is an
instability in terms of families, crime. Most of the notice
is for this area of the city."

A third human faction in this predominantly black community
consists of people who occupy what was previously referred to as the
row houses. These homes are usually not owner occupied and in many
cases are large older two story houses that have been broken up into
smaller rental units. Frequently they are "badly in need of repair."
Further social and economic diversity within the Diamond Hill
community was illustrated in the following summary.

"So we have really quite a mix of people here and if you drive through, within a block or two, you can go from what looks like a very stable clean quiet neighborhood to one in which the older two story homes look like they are badly in need of repair and with the fellow standing on the corner, drinking and with the nip joints and little convenience stores, where people have been shot and killed two blocks from here. So it's very diverse neighborhood and the first group I mentioned (the homeowners) is the one that is never seen."

Issues

Four major themes were identified under the code category of *issues*. Although each of the people interviewed had different things to say about what factors significantly impacted the lives of young people in the Diamond Hill area. Figure 4 illustrates the relative frequency with which issues relating to these code groups were brought up during interviews.

A general consensus seemed to emerge over the problem of drugs and, by implication, crime and violence in the community. This assertion is illustrated by statements from youth relating to the research question about things in their lives that bother them the most. Typical responses referred to crack cocaine, murderers and drugs in the community. Contrary to popular stereotypes about inner city life, however, these were not the primary issues discussed in the taped conversations.

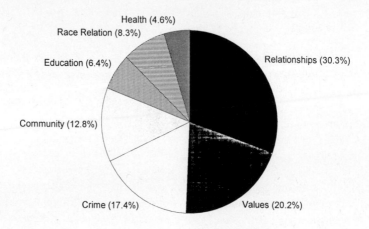

Figure 4. Diamond Hill Development Center - Issues Code Groups

The single most frequently identified theme relating to issues was the subject of relationships. Thirty three different code labels could be logically categorized as having to do with relationships. These code labels referred to a wide range of relationships having to do with family, friends and a variety of significant others.

The next most frequently mentioned the issue was the subject of values (n=22). As an issue values is important for a variety of reasons. Having well defined values, and whether or not they conflict with those of others, is certainly important to determining the quality of a person's life. However, values are also philosophical in nature and make up an important part of the thought processes which influence behavior. For this reason the subject of values is thought of as both a social issue and a philosophical perspective.

Two additional major code grouping have been developed around issues having to do with problems of crime and violence (n=19), and race and ethnicity (n=7). Less frequently mentioned issues include community concerns (n=4), health (n=5) and education (n=4).

Relationships

Relationships and the influence of relationships on the life choices that young people make during their teenage years was a matter of central concern at the Development Center and was represented by the largest portion of code labels. A wide range of relationships was discussed during the interviews. Considerable discussion was devoted to different types of relationships and how they influenced the lives of youth in general and young men at the center, in particular.

Three major types of relationships seem to apply. These are family relationships, male/female relationships, and role models. Throughout the research these varying but related themes emerged as important issues. Among the young men at the Development Center the importance and influence of family members was typified in responses to two interview questions about who are the people in their lives that help them and the people whom they admire the most.

The teenage boys who responded to this question at the Development Center referred to parents, aunts, and mothers as people who help them in their lives. Similarly discussions with staff reflected the high level of regard placed upon family relations, especially mother/son relations.

The prevalence of children being raised in single parent homes or in homes with absent fathers was an issue presented frequently by staff members. This issue becomes even more complicated when mothers of young men begin to date or develop romantic interests. The conflict which occurs as a result of such occurrences was depicted in a quote by Mr. Carter, the executive director.

> "...I have a strong sense that these young men feel that
> all they have is their mother. When there is no father
> around, all they have is their mother, and she is someone
> they treasure. Even when they have problems with

> their mother, she is their most valued treasure, and
> nobody wants to share their treasure. Nobody wants to
> lose their treasure."

Independent observations by the researcher support this assumption. On one occasion a young man was heard discussing with the male group leader how he didn't want his mother "bringing home no man" stating that he would "contract out on him."

One area of special consideration was the issue of positive male role models. Because most of the boys and girls attending the center did not have a father in the home, a primary need for many of the young men at the center was that of seeking out the attention of an adult male. The following quotations express the extent to which this need is perceived as an issue.

> "..and many of the (young) men bond to me because
> I am a male and they know that I care even when I have
> to be authoritative. Its not so bad because they know
> I care."

> "...they want a male in their life and sometimes they grab
> for the wrong thing. Basically they take what they can get."

Ms.Cheryl Green is an adult staff member in the after school program. She works with all of the children at the center. Her duties include driving the van, tutoring and group leadership. She is frequently referred to as "Ms. Cheryl" by the youth and she leads the Girl Talk activities on Wednesdays while Mr. Ronnie Jones works with the boys on Rites of Passage activities.

Ms. Cheryl describes what she felt was a need for "strong supportive","Black male", role models, and depicts the ideal qualities of such men. These characteristics include some one who is educated but whose education does not put him..."far above people's heads" and who "is still able to relate." Similarly a positive role model would have a "presentable appearance," be able to "interact" with children, "show them a lot of love and compassion," and be willing to "push them to achieve."

Ms. Molly, an older lady who drives one of the sixteen passenger vans operated by the center also oversees the younger children's activities. She talks about the need for male role models as well. The issue is personified by her discussion of a group of primary school age boys from the housing projects. She are describes this "little gang of boys" as being "highly at risk," yet , they are unable to attend the center due to space limitations.

> "Well what I just said is the most crucial need. People
> from outside the community, mostly men, relating ,
> who can offer activities that are wholesome as the
> relationship develops of trust..."

> "...that's the worst thing, that's the worst problem.......
> is the relationship with other men, father figures,
> big brother figures, that they can trust."

The idea of role models, especially as they relate to young men, was consistently linked with the subject of meaningful relationships with fathers and other responsible adult men by center staff and board members alike. The need for positive male role models extends to girls as well as boys. Many girls, according to Ms. Green, look for and need someone...

> "... to comfort them, someone to be over them. When
> they are not getting that strong support from a father,
> they go to any male because they want that attention.
> They want that love."

Father Andrews, who is a board member and is also the rector of St. Augustine's Church where the center is housed, is a white Episcopal priest who has lived in the Diamond Hill community for 11 years. While talking about the rites of passage program and the problems of teenage boys becoming men on Diamond Hill he stated...

> "I think that particularly in terms of some of the families
> of our youngsters. If there is not a father in the home

regularly, and a strong positive male influence in their
life, then they probably don't get a whole lot of time
with someone helping them deal with these kinds
of issues."

Father Andrews suggested a variety of potential alternative
role models for boys without readily available fathers...

"...teachers are still primary in that role, and I think that
males in the church, the male staff members in this
program and other programs like it" ... such as the
"Police Athletic League and wherever there is an
opportunity for befriending, and teaching,"

...in which positive relationships can be developed that help to fill
emotional needs of young men living at risk.

Peers and Others

Other relationship issues which seem to have relevance include
male/female relationships and the supporting relationships of peers.
Mr. Ronnie, as well as Ms. Cheryl, expressed concern over different
aspects of teenage male/female relationships. Pertinent aspects of the
relationships involve sexuality, respect, responsibility and perceptions
of parenthood.

"...Well like I said they themselves, already know that
drugs ain't goin' to get it, (they) stay away from the drug
scene. But its the other scene, with girls man, and
its a common thing man, because I know how I was when
I was young. It's much too dangerous now. We try to do
a Christian thing also, so we plant those seeds and abstain
and just be cool about it, 'your too young'.. you know
what about the responsibility..."

With regard to perceptions of manhood the issue of sex also was an important factor. Manhood is also reflected in notions about sports and intelligence.

> *Question:* "What do you think are some of the perceptions of manhood that the boys in the center have? What do you think are some of the attitudes that they have, good or bad?"
> *Mr. Ronnie:* "To be a professional sports player and in college, seem to be the height of what they go to right now, finishing school, maybe too much sex.
> There's a couple of guys who are having sex and one guy in particular is really outrageous, and he thinks that's part of being a man. I try to tell him it isn't."

Ms. Cheryl conveys similar concerns about the young women and their attitudes about boys, sex and parenthood. When asked to describe some of the issues that girls talked about in her all female group sessions she stated...

> "We talked about responsibility to the female and her body and as far as taking care of her body and not letting other people touch her body, whether its a boyfriend or family member. We talked about the responsibility of a baby and how young girls look at babies as little innocent things that's going to give them love...not realizing that the baby is going to stay with them at least, the next fifteen years. Unwed teenage mothers seem to glorify part of it and that's why it doesn't really shake them, how it really is. Like I said, none of the girls in our program have been pregnant, to my knowledge, and they are not pregnant right now. None of them have babies. Some of them are sexually active, but what they consider (is) they are using a condom then its O.K. and, being that they are being taught about safe sex, they think that its O.K., but they're not being taught the responsibility that goes along with it."

The nature of male/female relationships is also revealed in a comment made by one thirteen year old girl about a boy and his relationship with his mother.

> "We have one boy here who just talks about his mother,
> for some reason he doesn't like her. And all the girls say,
> 'Well, how can he treat a female? He can't even treat his
> mother right!'... which makes sense."

In a group interview with the teenaged and pre-teenaged girls a picture of confusion emerged with regard to male/female relations. The image presented by the same young woman's comment, when juxtaposed with the more adult concerns of the staff previously mentioned, connotes an innocence typical of thirteen year olds poised on the brink of adulthood yet still mired in adolescent conflict. When asked "What things in life bother you the most?", she responded by saying "boys." When asked to elaborate she said "Yeah, they ugly."

A sort of juvenile bantering between boys and girls at the center was also the subject of discussion and a program activity developed by Mr. Ronnie during the boys Rites of Passage meeting one Wednesday afternoon.

> "These guys here used to play with these girls and hit
> them and run and fight and yell. For their session I asked
> them if they could just be good to the girls for two hours.
> If they fuss, don't fuss back. If they want to hit and play,
> don't hit and play. Be serious with them for just two hours
> and see a change."

The subject of respect and manners was also an issue which Mr. Ronnie defined as an important need in the realm of male/female relations. The following comment illustrates his concern over this issue as well as concern over the different rates of maturity and social development between the young men and their female peers...

"manners are out the window, they need to recoup that
respect for each other. I stressed just last week that the
young girls are skyrocketing over the guys man.
They're taking things more seriously and they're leaving
the guys behind. So pretty soon they're not going to even
need these guys. So if these guys step up their progress,
step up their manhood, not in a mean or a boastful
way but in a more sincere mannerable way, I think things
will work better in the future for all of us, because
they will have a better attitude about themselves and who
they have to relate to."

A final point on the subject of relationships can be made in
looking at the answers to research question of why do youth come to the
development center. Reasons given by youth reflected concern over the
negative influence of the streets; to get help with their school work; and
to learn things that they don't necessarily learn at home. Adult staff, on
the other hand tended to mention such things as a sense of community,
camaraderie and belonging that the center is designed to provide. One
young man said...

"I come to the center (because) most of the time there's
nothin' to do right after school. So its a place to, like,
come and be with your friends. Do your homework,
and then you can play around later."

Crime and Violence

The topic of crime and violence was not always a central point
of discussion, but concerns over these issues were revealed in
comments made by young people regarding what they would change in
their community if they could. Several of the young men identified
drugs, crime and violence as things that bother them the most.

Some suggested possible solutions such as "cutting the supply"
and "getting everybody that's selling or using drugs to stop." One
young man suggested "trying to get people to like each other." Others
seemed more fatalistic and resigned to the pervasiveness of drugs and

crime in the community. These feelings were reflected in such comments as "ain't no way," and general recognition of the center as a haven from the negative influences of the streets.

The young women at the center expressed concern over drug addiction and linked it to the subject of child neglect. This led to a lengthy, and somewhat angry discussion of what to do with addicted neglectful or abusive parents. One girl suggested that we "put them in prison" or that we "just kill them."

Values

The subject of values comprises a separate set of issues and includes statements relating to attitudes or beliefs pertaining to notions of right and wrong. The operational definition of values includes the system of priorities people adhere to as cherished ways of living, thinking or acting. Values range from specific personal interests to broad based global interests. They are often reflected in words or actions rather and are sometimes difficult for people to articulate as a general rule. Personal values reflected in the interviews center around individual goals, personal appearance, self esteem, pride and motivation. More general approaches can be seen in statements of need such as the need for discipline, religion, spiritual growth, leadership and commitment.

The subject of values is closely tied to the philosophies and guiding principles promoted by center activities and can perhaps be better understood in light of these factors. The basic components of the afternoon youth program include Homework Time, Rites of Passage, Girltalk, Conflict Resolution, Black History, Bible Study, and Friday Trips. By inference the assumption can be made that a high value is placed on education, adolescent development, nonviolence, cultural and ethnic pride, religious education and recreation. The dual nature of values is such that they provide both practical guidelines for behavior and help to establish philosophical priorities. Therefore values will be discussed in both contexts.

Race Relations

Race relations, or issues having to do with race and ethnic heritage, are another point of interest at the development center. This fact is reflected in program content as well as interview comments. Black History is an important part of the after school activities and guest speakers have, on several occasions, focused on African American cultural heritage as a topic of discussion. Mr. Carter asserts that having knowledge of one's history is an important part of establishing a sense of self worth and pride. He sees this as being an essential part of promoting hope and high aspirations and maintains that black youth need to know "who they are culturally."

Rites of Passage activities also incorporate discussions about race relations and addressing the problems of discrimination. One Rites of Passage activity involved a role play which focused entirely on the subject of racism.

> "Yesterday we talked about racism and we had a racist
> group and a non-racist group. And it was really
> weird, because you chose white people, or Caucasian
> or however you want to say it, and you chose Orientals
> and Jamaicans. I asked the racist group the good points
> and the non-racist group the bad points. It was really
> weird because, now everybody was reversed. You know?
> And it was a good session. They learned not to be prejudice.
> I asked them what they learned and they said...
> 'not to be racist,' 'not to take people for granted.'
> Then we started talkin' about stereotypes, to kill that,
> and it was a pretty interesting session."

Education and health concerns were also discussed during interviews but did not provide a central focus. The primacy of education as a program element, with daily tutoring and an emphasis on school achievement, will be discussed in greater detail as a part of the program activities.

Philosophies and Guiding Principles

The subject of spirituality and religious involvement was a common philosophical theme. Mr. Carter discussed the need for spiritual identity among youth at the center. Four guiding principles of character, vision, hope and spirituality were described by the director of the center as an accurate assessment of philosophical building blocks for programs at the center.

Guiding principles, according to Mr. Carter, include a holistic approach which connotes a balance in the meeting of educational, emotional and spiritual needs. Programs at the center are designed to help young people meet these needs through a variety of activities. Mr. Carter states...

> "...What we do is designed to come together at a point. When we do Rites of Passage, as I said earlier, it builds character. But I think if we only take Rites of Passage and feed them that, and we don't feed them the spiritual component...we don't feed or teach them the real importance of an education, that, within itself, will not work. It's my hope that, and it's my expectation as well, that the pieces come together because no individual component of our program will make an individual complete."

The relationship between hope, vision and spirituality is expressed by the director in a discussion of how children tend to lose their dreams as they grow older. Hope can be described as the process of encouraging young people to dream.

> "...but we designed a program to help them dream again so that the lawyer they wanted to be at five years old is not something that has faded away by the fifth grade. So that is the gist of what we're doing in the after school program, but then its all wrapped around a spirituality that exists within each of those components because I think spirituality is your hope and it is your

balance. It is the thing that carries you through
difficult situations and it is alsoyour hope of success."

Values often seem to be expressed in reference to need. These
include needs for such things as love, discipline, and leadership.
Different value systems also are adhered to by different factions within
the community as exemplified by previous discussions about work,
ownership and respect.

The conveyance of values that help young people fulfill their
goals and hold onto their dreams appears to be an essential objective of
the after school program. The young people interviewed for this study
seem to know and appreciate this goal as a fundamental philosophy and
guiding principle of center activities. This assertion is supported by
remarks relating to why they come and what they learn at the Diamond
Hill Development Center.

"The center helps me to stay outta trouble and stay
outta the streets"

"They help me learn what I suppose to learn."

"I come to the center to get help with my homework and
help with different things that I don't know and need to
learn about."

The programs that directly serve youth at the center are geared
towards providing an alternative community in which they are protected
from negative influences both at home and on the streets. This basic
principle is illustrated both in the reasons why kids say they attend the
center and in comments recorded during interviews with staff and board
members.

In addition to taking advantage of the help that is available for
them with school work, several of the older boys referred to staying or
getting "off the streets" as a primary reason why they come. This
reasoning seems to hold equally as well for girls and the young people
seem to be painfully aware of the negative influences of the larger
community.

The young people who come to the center regularly seem to have incorporated an understanding that the center is a vehicle through which they can "develop myself," "better myself" and "learn about things that they don't know and need to learn about." Two objectives mentioned by both Father Andrews and Mr. Carter seem to form the foundation upon which further program principles and strategies are built. The first objects is to provide an alternative community, a safe haven into which kids can come. Father Andrews talks about school and family as communities in which young people participate and offers the center as an additional positive alternative.

> "One of the highest, most important things that I think we can offer and that these kids desperately need is an alternative community...in which they have a home and friends and adults to relate to and support with standards and expectations for these youngsters."

As an example of how such a setting can positively influence peoples' lives, Father Andrews talks about violence and the conflict resolution workshops incorporated into the program activities at the center...

> "...Whatever these standards and expectations are and behaviors, what we really need to do is make them the norm for the community..."

> "I don't really think a youngster is going to accept and adopt those for the rest of their life in all those other communities. What really has to happen is that they really need to experience in this community, that there really are alternatives to violence and there are ways to resolve conflict without weapons. If we stay with that long enough, that becomes a part of their experience."

The alternative community principle can be understood as one of creating an environment that acts as a model. Youth at the center, through program activities and informal interactions, are exposed to new experiences, new ways of dealing with problems and new ways of living their lives. A second guiding principle of program development and implementation was expressed by Mr. Carter in the concept of serving.

> "...We need to understand that we are servants, and
> servants cater to the needs of the people they serve."

This approach, however, does not preclude the notion of leadership. Instead, the principle of serving emphasizes the point that serving and leading can be collaborative endeavors and that one can "lead as a servant." In terms of program evaluation, according to Mr. Carter, the first measure of success, the first indicator of whether a program is working, is whether the kids keep coming back. This, in itself, can be used as an indicator of whether their needs are being met.

> "..If you take that attitude into the programs that you
> are involved with, then I think you're going to see what is
> most important as opposed to what you think is important
> and what is most important is what the people whom you
> are serving gets out of the program."

Another measure of success is involved with the notion of "buying in." It is closely related to issues such as ownership, motivation and the adoption of standards or expectations mentioned earlier. "Buying in" is also a concept relating to program success that was echoed at other sites during the study.

> " And if they have some input in it, they buy into it,
> then the goal you are trying to accomplish will usually
> come to the forefront."

The weekly routine of youth activities was posted on a bulletin board located in the main room where most center activities take place. Another list entitled "Center Rules of Conduct" was also on display. It prescribed rules for acceptable behavior emphasizing values such as honesty, fair play and respecting others.

Program

Defining At Risk Youth

During formal interviews, informal discussions, and through observing how different young people at the center respond to adult leadership, it became apparent that not all youth could be served by programs such as the Diamond Hill Development Center. Resources are limited and not all young people wish to attend such a program. A most eloquent expression of how children critically in need of services can be identified, comes from the experiences of Ms. Molly during her daily duties of driving the center's sixteen passenger van. She tells the story of "a little gang of seven" preteen aged boys whom she encountered one day because they were throwing rocks at the van. While picking up the children who attend the center at the local middle school, Ms. Molly became so unnerved by these boys' actions that she said she was afraid to go back.

> "One night during the winter when I kneeled to pray,
> my head was flooded with all of these suggestions.
> First of all they are jealous because they want to be a part.
> So make friends, find a way to get them some Christmas
> presents....When I completed the plan to become friends
> with the seven and would go pick the group up for the
> center, they started seeing me on the van. They
> started pouring on the van and bringing their friends.
> So now we have a van full of boys and our kids do not
> want to get on because they can tease and holler and
> agitate and all of this. And so our kids stopped wanting
> to ride because they did not want to get tangled up with
> these guys. And so, I had to find a way to meet my
> responsibilities to our children and not run into
> these guys."

In an attempt to help address the needs of these boys, who were not members of the center and for whom there was no room in the program, Ms. Molly attempted to find services for them elsewhere.

"They loved to get on the van and turn the music up.
They wanted to belong. That's what they wanted when
they were throwing those rocks. That's what they need!
But we don't have the vans, we don't have the money,
we don't have the churches."

Another experience related by Ms. Molly illustrates what she describes as "emotional poverty", a condition which permeates the lives of these boys in this little gang of seven.

"He was with me on the van when I took somebody
home over at another housing project, and we were
riding along and he said 'There's my mother!'
She was walking along the street with some other
women, and she looked at him without recognizing
him at first, and he said 'Hi, Ma!'
And then she looked at him and said 'That's my son!'
But you see she's separated from him. She lives in her
own world.......and then one day he was getting on the
van and he said...
'Would you take me to Hollywood Court?'
He was going to find his mother. Well, you can see
the anger inside a kid like this."

In spite of the need, however, it was determined that there was not enough space to bring in additional youth to the after school program. There was also some concern over the ability of staff to control the group. The emotional need and the material deprivation experienced by these young men, at very early ages, compounds their ability to tap into available community services and seems to result in life style choices over which they are depicted as having little control.

Ms. Molly did, however organize some people and found some money to take this little gang of seven to the circus. While they were there, two of the boys got caught stealing. No charges were filed, but Ms. Molly was shocked and embarrassed by the experience. Her response, however, seemed to express a cold realization that larceny and deceit are already a fixed pattern of survival for many impoverished young people.

> "They must steal. If you can imagine that they were
> so desperate at Christmas for $30.00 worth of what some
> other child might call trash, just you know, any little
> something they were taking back. You know, there might
> not have been much else of anything that they were
> going to get. So, at the level that we're not really familiar
> with,...at poverty. Emotionally poverty stricken,
> materially poverty stricken."

> "I just think there is an insatiable desire for things.
> Oh, we may have one or two. That's why I say that group
> is another raw culture compared with the group of people
> we have here. But they just must steal."

> "I said, 'I am so embarrassed. Look what you have done.'
> One of these little boys used to go out stealing every night
> and the police would bring him home to his mother.
> He's now in a school, but...what I'm saying is that these
> guys are considered the worst little guys in the
> neighborhood. Our guys think they're bad.
> They're only in elementary school."

In attempting to identify the needs of the most needy, Ms. Molly exposes a problem referred to elsewhere in this research as "creaming." This is a condition which exists in social programs when those who need services the most are not served because they are so difficult to work with that program evaluation by most convention conventional standards would result in loss of funds. These are children who are so troubled that they are unreachable or deemed unsalvageable.

In order to insure a modicum of successful outcome, less difficult children are served. This recognition is not intended as a criticism of program developers or staff, but is an attempt to point out problems with evaluating the effectiveness of programs serving troubled populations. A more in depth discussion of the subject of creaming will be undertaken elsewhere in the study. The phenomenon is exemplified, however, in the following description which helps to provide a working definition for "at risk youth."

> "You've got this group that comes out of the projects,
> then you've got a group like those who will come with
> me, or somebody else. Then you've got another group
> on the periphery that just kind of stands back and watches
> and sees what you are doing....that's the group, around
> this group that's responsive. That's the group before you
> really get to the criminal group, and I don't know...
> beyond that, another circle...and I'm not talking
> professionally. I'm just talking about what I see out of
> the corner of my eye as I go by."

Activities

The most consistent and regular part of youth activities is homework time or tutoring. Young people typically start arriving at 3:00 PM, with the older kids arriving first. Ms. Molly and Ms. Cheryl pick up the younger ones at the local elementary or middle schools and they usually arrive a few minutes later. The older kids will talk and socialize with each other quietly either outside on the sidewalk, or inside, depending on the weather and other factors. The door to the parish hall locks automatically and usually must be opened from the inside or with a key.

When the younger children arrive things frequently become quite hectic for a few moments. They arrive in two groups of ten or fifteen according to how many were picked up on that particular day. Frequently the young children rough house or do things like throw their book bags down and take a running slide on their knees on the linoleum floor. Occasionally horse play will degenerate into fighting, but not usually. The initial scene could be described as energetic but not out of control. By about 3:35 P.M. Ms. Molly takes the youngest children next door to the Sunday School rooms. The older youth stay in the parish meeting hall and sit in groups of three or four around long, collapsible, fibre board tables. Often there will be a co-ed table where boys and girls sit together, usually couples with romantic interests. Then, there will also be a table with mostly boys and a third table with mostly girls. The oldest boys and girls (14-15 yrs.) tend to sit together, while the younger ones (11-13yrs) tend to divide themselves according to gender.

Mr. Ronnie and Ms. Cheryl provide help with homework as do any volunteers who might be working that day. During the course of the fieldwork there were rarely more than two volunteer tutors at any one time. One board member consistently arrived every Wednesday at 3:30 and left at 4:30. He worked exclusively with one young man. Other volunteers and staff offered general assistance to anyone who wanted it. The director did not actively participate in the tutoring but occasionally looked in to see how things were going. When he did participate he would frequently be called away to the telephone.

One day report cards had been given at school and all the kids were expected to bring them to the center. Ronnie, as he is frequently referred to by the kids, collected people's report cards and made xerox copies for his files. The incentive for bringing in your report card, or "grade sheets," was a trip to the circus. Several of the youngsters did not do as well as they had hoped. One young person expressed her anger about receiving an "F" in one subject when she walked hurriedly into the main meeting room and went directly to Ronnie. She said that she hated the teacher and said that she "had been doin' my work" and that she "wasn't goin' to do it no more." Mr. Ronnie responded by talking to her about her grade saying that she couldn't expect to get an "A" if she just started studying and doing her homework at the end of the semester.

Later that afternoon Mr. Carter talked to the entire group and expressed his disappointment in their overall performance at school. He announced that Friday's bowling trip was cancelled. He also said that if he could, he would take back the circus tickets because they hadn't "earned it."

> "You gotta want something for yourself, because if you
> don't want nothin' that's exactly what you'll get...nothing"

He talked to the group about academic scholarships and how much it costs to go to college. The kids were assembled in the large meeting room and Mr. Carter talked to them in a loud voice, with an agitated tone, bordering on anger and hinting at frustration. The group seemed to listen intently.

> "Stop settlin' for 'C's. You can do better than that...
> 'C's don't get you no scholarships."

> "When I holler at you the most, it's about doin' your
> school work!"

> "Say 'I am capable!'... say it like you mean it!...maybe
> that's what we need to work on. Y'all don't believe
> you're capable!"

During a subsequent informal interview Mr. Carter explained that it is the policy of the Diamond Hill Development Center that Friday afternoon trips are designed to serve as rewards for the youth after they have met the expectations set for them during the week. Fieldtrips are earned. For this reason, he expressed the desire to cancel the circus trip they had planned.

Rites of Passage

Although all of the youth programs at the Development Center address the needs of young black men in a variety of ways, the rites of passage program is the only one that specifically focuses on their needs as males. Whereas tutoring and homework time is allotted daily, Rites of Passage and the female counter part Girl Talk, take place every other

Wednesday from 4:30 until 5:30. Other activities scheduled for after the home work hour include black history, Bible study, conflict resolution, life skills, guest speakers and Friday trips. Specific days have been set aside for each of these activities. Guest speakers or life skills, a co-ed activity, alternate weekly with rites of passage and girl talk. Examples of guest speakers include a man who came to talk about careers in banking, a woman from Nigeria, and a man who recited some of Martin Luther King Jr.'s famous speeches.

The programs are intended to be educational in nature and each focuses on aspects of life not often covered in school. Black history is designed to help kids at the center "know themselves culturally." Ms. Cheryl expressed her own perspective about the value of educating African American youth about African heritage as well as helping them positively cope with the problems of race relations in American society. During one informal discussion she suggested changing the name of black history to black future, as an expression of empowerment and hope. On one occasion a woman from Nigeria talked with the entire group about contemporary African life. On another occasion a second woman came and talked about the historical contributions made by black people in America.

During Rites of Passage is the one time that teen age and pre teen boys are separated from the girls and expected to address issues relating to their expectations and obligations as young men. Mr. Ronnie oversees and operates the Rites of Passage activities whereas Ms. Cheryl works with the girls. The activities, themselves, vary each time and the curriculum Mr. Ronnie follows is one he develops on his own. He described his approach to developing daily activities for the Rites of Passage program was in the following manner...

> "I just get together with the fellas where we discuss
> various things. Some things I come up with,
> or Mr. Carter may insert some things and I deal with that.
> It depends on the situation."

> "On Wednesdays I have to be there at 3:00, and as I'm
> walking up the street to come here, I think of something
> to do. I usually come up with ideas that maybe my nephew

or my son might be going through or something I know
the fellas might be going through individually, and try to
bring that out and see as a group how they would deal with
it. Sometimes I come up with something about black
pride things. I think of a man pride thing. I think of
male/female relationships. It depends on how I'm
feeling really. It's not a set thing. You call it strategies.
It's not really any set strategies. It's whatever I come up
with that I think will be interesting to them, to help them
get their heads together."

In reference to the handouts and written material provided
during some of the sessions, Mr. Ronnie said that he usually writes his
own material. Often he will tell the kids that someone gave him a letter
or left something for them, without identifying himself as the author.

"I make things up in my head, come up with a situation
for the young person or a person of their age group in
a situation that I make up in my mind as I'm walkin',
as I said, or as soon as I get here. Something will hit me
and I'll jump on the typewriter and type up something
as if someone passed it to me. When I first did it, I put
it down and said that 'someone gave me this and asked
me to ask you all these questions.' But really, I had did
it myself, and typed it before they got here, and ran it
off. And, you know, lately, they've been catchin' me
typin' it up. They see me typing, especially on Wednesday
and they know somethings up and I was here early to
do something like that today."

On several occasions he provided the participants with
mimeographed sheets depicting an imaginary situation designed to
stimulate discussion. The handout usually presented the group with a
problem, which became the basis for a discussion.
One afternoon, the group of young men was called together for
Rites of Passage. The usual time for this activity is, 4:30 PM, right

after homework time. Seven boys, ranging in ages from 11 to 14, were in attendance. Each young man was given a copy of a letter, which Mr. Ronnie said had been left on his desk. It was written by hand and read as follows...

> *"Brothers,*
>
> *It is time that we stepped up the production of awareness on our parts. As young African American men we must be more aware of our place in society today.*
>
> *We should no longer have to live like our fathers and grandfathers, fearing what the other man won't let us do, and you know who the other man is, that I am speaking about.*
>
> *What must we do to become aware? How shall we meet the challenge that is before us? What goals are there for us to reach for? These questions I give to you my African American brothers. Please! We must be swift to get to the point of awareness that is needed.*
>
> *What is your opinion?*
>
> *Signed,*
>
> *Anonymous"*

Mr. Ronnie had the young men sitting in chairs, arranged in a semi circle, while he was standing before a portable blackboard. He asked one boy to read the letter saying that it was left on his desk by a "mystery writer". As the young volunteer read, he came to the phrase "young African American men" and he muttered slightly under his breadth, but loud enough for most to hear "That don't sound right." As he finished the letter Ronnie drew a diagram on the board which consisted of three vertical lines, representing columns, with the words "Challenge," "Action," and "Goals" written at the top.

As the boys laughed and joked Mr. Ronnie led a discussion about drugs, goals, life challenges and actions needed to achieve goals. He would ask the group what goals and challenges they had and then ask the people who responded to describe the action necessary to achieve that goal or meet that challenge. Every young man provided some input although some were more talkative than others. Table 2 presents a list of group and individual responses that the group leader recorded on the blackboard, at the Rites of Passage meeting.

Table 2
Responses recorded at the Rites of Passage meeting

Challenges	Action	Goals
"to get through school"	"study hard"	"make it through college"
"study hard"	"study hard"	"get a job"
"make it through college"		
"at least get through		
high school"	"stay in school"	
"get a job"		"better social standing"
"drug free life"	"say no"	"better life"
"stay out of trouble"	"stop hangin"	"be a policeman"
"life in order"	"get an education"	
"have a clean record"		

During the discussion it became apparent that some of the goals being talked about were also challenges. Actions were sometimes seen as challenges. There seemed to be more challenges mentioned than goals. Some additional comments from the young men, not recorded on the blackboard but overheard during the course of the discussion included...

"Make it *through* college, not halfway"
"I want a masters degree."
"I want a Ph.D."
"My daddy, he had to drop out of school 'cause his
    parents died, and now he has his own business."
"Life is too tough these days."

On another occasion the daily activity consisted of a Monopoly style board game entitled "Decisions." The game was played with dice and plastic figures that moved along a game board after each player rolled the dice. Card were then picked up game pieces landed on corresponding square. The player was presented with a scenario based upon which card he drew. Players were then required to make decisions appropriate to the scenario. This exercise provided opportunities for group discussion and reflection on why people made the decision that they did.

Sometimes, Mr. Carter came in during the meetings and participated, primarily by observing and being present. On one occasion he led the group in a discussion in which he talked about "giving back" to the community. The basic theme was that financial success is not the true measure of a man and that "giving of yourself" is a more important measure of character than having money. He said...

> "Money doesn't raise you up."
> "What do you call a tramp in a $500 suit?
> A tramp in a $500 suit."
> "Giving back is giving of yourself. Money is not the
> focus of who you are."

During one Rites of Passage activity the discussion centered on love, sex and values. Mr. Ronnie had given the young men several pieces of paper from which they read out loud in a group and answered questions. The responses were recorded on the blackboard this time as well. There was a great deal of laughing and joking among the boys, apparently because of embarrassment about the topics. The question "What is love?" yielded the following responses.

sharing	giving	having a relationship
trusting	caring	dedication
making love	attitude	emotion
honest	relationships	responsibility

Even though some of the young men were listening, the joking was plentiful to the point of becoming a distraction. In an attempt to settle the group down and have a serious discussion Ronnie said that the girls were talking about the same subject, but that they were apparently more mature than the boys because there was not a lot of laughing and joking coming from the room where they were meeting. A few minutes later we heard laughing and loud talk coming from the girls' meeting room. Several of the boys commented about this.

Mr. Ronnie discussed the idea of premarital sex as counterfeit love and said that sometimes people substitute sex for love. He began to show some signs of agitation because the joking and loud talk continued. He spoke to one boy harshly for wearing his headphones and asking when it was time to go home. The young man was told that he could go home now if he didn't want to participate. He decided to stay.

Some of the kids seem to have bought into the idea of Rites of Passage as exemplified by their interest in Mr. Ronnie's preparation for the day's activity. They also seem to have made a game around his deception regarding the mysterious author of the handouts and the source of the material.

> *Question:* "Do they feel like you were trying to fool
> them when you told them that someone had given
> you something and now they found you out?"
> *Mr. Ronnie:* "Yeah, they have. They found me out.
> So now when they see me typing on Wednesday, they
> expect that we are going to discuss something on this
> paper and everybody wants to read it or they want to
> get into it. But basically I just come up with things,
> nothin' in particular."

Regarding published material about rites of passage activities for youth, Mr. Ronnie expressed some hesitancy if not slight skepticism. He seemed to recognize the value of a more formalized curriculum but was somewhat critical about the relevancy and his own ability to use the material he had seen effectively.

"Mr. Carter gave me a booklet in September about
Rites of Passage, and I went through it, man. I'd never
heard of Rites of Passage until I came here, and really I
didn't understand what it was about. But when, you
know, I understand its about manhood and the rites
of your heritage, being a man or...I don't know.
I get confused so that's why I never really got into the
pamphlet and I kind of...from what he told me,
after I asked him what rites of passage was,
and Mr. Carter broke it down a little bit for me,
I formulated my own thing , you know. Something I
could break down and relate to them in my own way.
Because I think, what I read might be a little bit over
their head, to tell you the truth."

A similar concern over the relevancy of programs with a
strong African cultural emphasis was expressed by Ms. Cheryl. Though
she agreed with the idea of exploring issues relating to black awareness
and cultural heritage, she preferred to focus on relevancy and the ability
of youth to identify with messages conveyed during program activities.

"We were talking about so far as blacks relating to
Africa, and you asked me my opinion and as I see the
children, to them, Africa is something that is so far away
they really can't relate to that.I know sometimes in the
African studies we try to go back. We follow the
curriculum, and in the curriculum it tells us to and say
that they were kings and queens and, yeah, that's true,
and that's good, but the children can't relate to a king or
a queen. You know, they look at Prince Charles and
Princess Diana, and as far as royalty, they are not
really looking at that, unless they know alot more.
It's like...'so here I am, I'm in the projects.
I'm wearin' the same clothes, two or three days because I
don't have a coat.' If someone told me that black people
were once kings and queens, that doesn't click anything,
because I'm so far away from kingship, it doesn't move me."

As a compromise, both in Rites of Passage and in Girl Talk, the staff have chosen a flexible approach to developing program activities rather than a fixed curriculum. The greater emphasis from Black History seems to be to establish a sense of ethnic pride as black people or as African Americans, and developing methods to cope with the problems of racism, discrimination and material inequality in contemporary American culture.

A guiding principle in the Rites of Passage program is building character and respect. According to Mr. Carter, the purpose of the program is ...

> "to develop character and understanding of who you are
> as a male or as a female. Character as young men. Showing
> respect to each other. Showing respect to authority.
> Showing respect to the opposite sex."

In practice, Mr. Ronnie's central themes focus on male and female relations, perceptions of masculinity, responsible decision making and encouraging high aspirations for the future. Perhaps one of the most positive effects of these activities, from the researcher's point of view, is the simple provision of a forum within which young men can discuss issues relevant to their concerns without fear of unwarranted reproach or criticism. Independently of any preconceived goals regarding specific program outcomes, the mere act of getting together under responsible adult guidance, and confronting the struggles of adolescence in the Diamond Hill community may be Rites of Passage and Girl Talk's greatest contribution.

Follow Up Visits

Approximately four months after the initial data collection and interviews were completed at the development center, the researcher returned for follow up visits and to provide transcribed copies of the interviews to key people. Copies were provided to all center staff, and some informal discussions of recent developments were conducted.

Mr. Carter stated that recent financial problems at the center had resulted in the need to reduce personnel. In addition future funding from key contributors was in danger of being reduced. As a result Mr. Ronnie was no longer working at the center and some of the activities, such as Rites of Passage were being modified accordingly.

On three subsequent visits the researcher noticed that several of the older boys who had been regular participants during the spring were not present. A statement from Ms. Molly confirmed that several of these young men stopped attending after Ronnie left. Some other boys interviewed last fall were still attending regularly but the oldest members of the group seemed to be missing. Part of this attendance problem may also be due to fall sports activities at school.

Mr. Ronnie was contacted and he said that he left the center because he felt that some of the board members were not satisfied with his work. He is now working at a similar after school program at another nearby church. He was pleased by the fact that some of the young men he became friends with while at the Diamond Hill Development Center sought him out and continue to maintain contact with him. He said that a few even come to his house occasionally, to get help with their homework. Mr. Carter asserted that the board and he were very satisfied with the work Ronnie performed with the boys and girls at the center. His leaving was not a board influenced decision but was rather a question of managing limited financial resources.

Ms. Cheryl had also left the center, although the researcher did have the opportunity to speak with her during the summer and on one of the earlier fall visits. She stated that she had been accepted into a graduate program in education at a local university and was planning to start attending classes soon. She was hoping to get a masters degree in special education. On subsequent visits to the center in October the researcher was advised that Ms. Cheryl had left. Most of the girls who had been involved with the girl talk activities and who were regular participants at the center during the initial visits were still attending. Some of the older girls were not seen although no specific inquiry was made about their regular attendance.

During these follow up visits the center was populated primarily by younger, primary school age children. Many of them were the same children who attended in the Spring. The staff was reduced but several new volunteers were assisting with tutoring. Mr. Carter was also more actively involved in the tutoring and working directly with the children. It appeared that the center was going through a transition period wherein the program activities were being reshaped to meet the needs of the younger children who were the primary participants. Attendance averaged about twenty children per day, less than at previous times. According to Ms. Molly, they were no longer operating at full capacity. According to the director, there are thirty-five young people currently enrolled in the Development Center's youth program, with an average daily participation of seventy per cent.

Many of the teens have begun to return after fall sports. The center is currently in the process of creating a Saturday group for teenagers who can't attend on weekdays but still want to be involved in the center. Some of the older teens serve as role models for the younger youth in the program. Whether or not the Diamond Hill Development Center can retain an active teen and preteen population is probably not an easily answered question. It has been demonstrated in the comments and observations by the staff that there are many children in the neighborhood who need the services they offer. Whether these children will find their way to the Diamond Hill Development Center is another question.

Similarly, the question of ongoing financial support and the shrinking availability of funds is a concern. As is the case in many programs and agencies addressing human needs, people at the development center are being asked to do more with less. Whether or not they can sustain their efforts to provide an alternative community for children and youth is a question only time can tell. One gets the feeling that as long as they can find the money for a director, they will have a center for youth.

Support for programs like the Rites of Passage and Girl Talk at the Development Center is not easy to sustain. There is not a great deal of literature available to the general public that is designed to create an organized approach to coming of age ceremonies. There are few easy formulas that can be applied to every situation. Maintaining flexibility in programming is a central principle at the Development Center. This approach is coupled with an emphasis on school performance and spiritual growth. The effort is designed to produce a "holistic" effort to address the multiple concerns confronting young men and young women growing up in the urban community which is Diamond Hill.

Lessons and Reflections

The Diamond Hill Development Center's Rites of Passage program is a small part of the overall youth program. It uses an all male discussion group design to promote an exchange of ideas and concerns relevant to young men and their daily concerns. A parallel discussion group for girls takes place simultaneously.

Rites of passage, in the sense of exploring African based traditions have not been a central focus, as the available literature might indicate. Instead, both the boy's and the girl's group leaders have chosen activities and material that they feel are more relevant to the youth's daily experiences. These activities are derived from and focus on many of the issues that have been presented here. Such issues include discussions about black history, social justice and race relations, but also involve relationships, values and spiritual growth.

The informal nature of some activities allows for spontaneity and flexibility while occasionally succumbing to disorganization and discipline problems. Sometimes friendly horseplay deteriorates into more serious conflict. Frequently the young men buy into group activities, but on other occasions they do not. When an uncooperative mood prevails, the frustration and true difficulty of the task at hand becomes more apparent. It is then that group leaders are, sometimes, drawn into the conflict. Certain youth tend to be more difficult and less responsive than others. Disciplinary action usually involves lecturing, or being sent home and put out of the program for brief periods of time.

Education

Education, and making the most of educational opportunities is a central concern at the center. Homework time is the first order of daily activities and school performance is emphasized. This seems to be one area in which a more extensive use of volunteer help would benefit. Frequently the older boys and girls will get together at one table and talk or socialize without applying themselves. The girls, as a group, seem to be more task oriented than the boys. Some of the older boys rarely bring homework to do, while others, in the same grade and attending the same school, work steadily on their assignments.

During the field observations, the boys and girls group leaders were the primary source of academic help for most of the older youth. The director did little tutoring while Ronnie and Ms. Cheryl ran the after school activities. This arrangement has the potential for sending a mixed message about the importance of schoolwork. Since their departure Mr. Carter has taken a more active role in this regard. He also visits the youth's home, talks with his or her teachers and does individual counseling as needed.

Positive Role Models

A commonly expressed need during the interviews was the availability of positive role models for boys and girls at the center. Having more adults available to provide individualized tutoring was a suggestion made by one volunteer. Most of the volunteers encountered by the researcher during the field visits were women. One white male board member came regularly to help with homework related activities. Most of the black men, who were seen volunteering their time did so in the capacity as guest speakers.

One way of addressing the need for positive male role models might be to aggressively pursue a community service recruitment strategy at one or more of the local colleges. Potential black male, and female, role models are available at a local predominantly black college, and through black fraternities at a nearby state university. This resource might be explored. With two sixteen-passenger vans, the center has the means with which to provide transportation if needed. This strategy could fulfill the dual purpose of developing potential role models and providing more effective academic support.

Administration versus Program: The Tradeoff

A second important area of consideration for the Development Center has to do with the role of the director as it relates to running the programs. Administrative duties for any ongoing nonprofit organization require a constant effort to secure funds as well as human resources. This in itself is a full time job when you are talking about average attendance approaching thirty-five children every day coupled with an active senior citizens program in the mornings.

Securing financial support for the center's youth program is a constant problem, and one of the primary concerns of the center's director. It appears that he is continuously subject to conflicting interests over funding versus program involvement. If the director is expected to actively participate in programs, then fund raising may suffer. Conversely if a director spends all of his or her available time on fund raising, then program supervision, design and implementation may suffer. This concern is particularly relevant as it pertains to the need for an active presence of male role models. Resolution of this dilemma and clear expectations regarding fund raising versus program implementation are essential.

Support Networks and the Funding Dilemma

Whether the dilemma over funding or program can be resolved depends largely on the availability of an enthusiastic and hard working support network. Support of this nature must probably come from volunteers in the private sector. A paid assistant director in charge of program might solve the problem by allowing the director more time for fund raising, but it seems unlikely that such a staff position can be filled in the near future. Thus, a more vigorous effort to sustain and cultivate volunteer support is another viable alternative.

One logical source of volunteer participation is St. Augustine's Church. Whether the human resources present in the parish have the means or inclination to rejuvenate a commitment to youth programs at the center is beyond the scope of this research to determine. However, it appears that if these resources could be mobilized, they would allow for a more vigorous approach to fund raising while simultaneously providing a stronger focus on program quality.

A third possibility is to restructure the relationship between the Development Center and the church in order to create a combined position that serves both facilities. This goal might be accomplished by employing a Sunday school coordinator who is also an assistant program director at the center. This goal might be achieved by combining the financial resources of both the church and the center while seeking to bring in additional support from the diocese. If such a cooperative arrangement could be established, it might simultaneously free up the director for fund raising and enhance the life of the church.

Summary

The Diamond Hill Development Center is ongoing and surviving, but it appears to be struggling. Reductions in funding, shifts in personnel and reduced teenage attendance are ominous signs. The task of keeping a youth program alive and vibrant is a difficult one. It requires both money and enthusiasm for creative program design. Children are continually growing up and out of even the best programs. Adults do not always place youth programs high on their priority list for funding or volunteering. This is a luxury that we, as a nation, can ill afford.

The young people come to the center to get off the streets. They know the dangers of the community and they come "to learn what they need to know but aren't getting at school." They come to the center because it is fun. They come to the center, and sometimes they don't want to go home. Without well trained staff and enthusiastic volunteers centers like the Diamond Hill Development Center cannot survive. The crisis of young black men in our cities is only a part of the problem. It is a crisis that none of them created singly but in which they are all immersed. If American society fails to address the problems of underserved minority youth, and refuses to address this issue as a high priority for social reform, even "the good ones" might grow up to be the statistics about which scholars read.

Chapter 5: The Bunker Hill Young Marines

Setting

The Bunker Hill Young Marines are an outgrowth of the Bunker Hill Gardens Community Outreach Center, which is a nonprofit, community based organization located in a large apartment complex on the outskirts of a major mid-Atlantic city. In order to understand the origin, purpose and mission of the Young Marines it is necessary to first learn about the Outreach Center and the community it serves. Although the community is, technically, located outside the city limits, Bunker Hill Gardens was characterized by a local police officer as an urban community inhabited by a predominantly low income, minority population. This description is in contrast to the affluent, "mostly white," suburban neighborhoods farther from the city center.

The apartment complex is situated on a two lane highway bordered on both sides by sidewalks. There are two signs in the apartment complex parking lot which adjoins the road. Each sign has an arrow pointing in the direction of the appropriate facility. One sign reads "Rental Office" while the other reads "Bunker Hill Gardens Community Outreach Center."

There are no gardens in or around the apartment complex. In fact, there are very few trees except for a small patch of woods behind the building farthest from the road. The complex consists of a cluster of six large buildings, most of which are four stories high, made of brick, and linked together with walkways and adjoining parking lots. There are bars on the doors for the outside stairs leading to the upper level apartments. A swimming pool is located directly in front of the small rental office where the apartment management company is housed.

Bunker Hill Gardens is managed by a privately owned corporation rather than a public housing authority. "Most of the people in the complex are working," although some are "getting by on social security or welfare," according to the description of one resident. In addition to the pool, there are basketball courts and a small playground. The Outreach Center is located in a ground level apartment in the midst of the Bunker Hill Garden complex. The buildings and grounds appear to be in good repair on the outside. It is not readily distinguishable from the other apartments except perhaps by the flow of traffic to and from the center. The center is the creation of a Baptist minister who is also the presiding executive director. Reverend Ezra Knight is a physically large man who appears to be in his mid fifties. He has a deep, booming voice which was difficult to capture on tape because of its resonant quality. Reverend Knight appears to possess a vigorous physical stature which complements his extroverted personality and friendly demeanor.

The Bunker Hill Community Outreach Center occupies an apartment in a building adjacent to the parking lot, directly behind the management office. A visitor must drive around the first row of buildings and into this second parking lot in order to arrive at the center. Alternatively one could park in the first parking lot, adjoining the highway, and walk along a network of sidewalks, past the rental office, the pool, a small playground and across the second lot in order to arrive at the center. The distance is approximately one hundred yards.

Upon entering the Outreach Center one can observe that the living room of this apartment has been converted into a reception and waiting area. There is a receptionist's desk directly in front of the sliding glass door which looks out onto the parking lot. The desk itself faces into the room and as you enter the center there are two couches and a coffee table on your left. A small kitchen and eating area is located at the far end of the apartment which is open to the living room area. A clock on the kitchen wall said 9:17 when the researcher arrived at the center. It also said 9:17 when he left, eight hours later.

To the right, as one enters the center is a hallway where normally the bedrooms would be located. These bedrooms have been converted into offices for various activities that take place there. Rev. Knight's office is at the end of this hallway. Although he appears to be quite busy most of the time, Rev. Knight also seems to remain accessible to people. His office door is frequently open and you can hear his voice throughout the small apartment.

On one occasion a little girl of about 10 years old, dressed in pink, knocked on the center's door. She stuck her head through the open doorway and said "Is Reverend Knight here?"

As she spoke she stepped into the room closing the door behind her. The receptionist said "He's on the phone , Honey."

The girl sat down on the couch for less than thirty seconds and then walked down the hall to Reverend Knight's office. The receptionist followed her down the hall saying, "He's on the phone, baby." She came back to her desk a few seconds later without the little girl, saying, "You know, I'm going to lock that door someday."

Shortly thereafter the little girl came out of the Reverend's office and left through the front door, apparently of her own accord. Reverend Knight's voice could still be heard on the phone from the living room. On another occasion an older man dressed in a white sleeveless T-shirt and white shorts, with a red bandanna tied around his neck, came in. He nodded quietly to the people in the room as he came in and sat down on one of the couches. He sat quietly for about thirty minutes and finally went in to talk with Reverend Knight, then he left.

From the receptionist's room one could look out into one of the several parking lots which are a part of the Bunker Hill Gardens complex. A group of about twelve young men and boys were standing on the island in the center of the parking area. They seemed to vary in their ages from about 10 to 15 years old and they were clustered in a tightly knit group standing around several bicycles. One of the bikes had been turned upside down and one boy was spinning the wheels with the pedals while another was working on the chain mechanism. Others were watching and some were talking to each other. One boy was bouncing a basketball. They were all standing close together on the curb/island and had been occupied in this fashion for about twenty minutes. About forty-five minutes later the group on the parking lot island left. Two older young men, approximately 16 or 17 years of age, were standing on the sidewalk talking to three girls sitting on a split rail fence. A young boy of about 8 years old did a wheelie on his bike while riding across the parking lot. Three girls were playing double dutch jump rope. It seemed to be a festive atmosphere. The receptionist mentioned that school had just let out for the summer. The date was June 14th.

History of the Outreach Center

The Young Marines is a community-based program which coordinates and organizes activities for young men, and a few young women, in the Bunker Hill apartment complex. The complex itself has over 400 housing units which house approximately 3,000 people. The number of youth participants in the Young Marines is less than 30, only a fraction of the potentially eligible youth in the community. The program director and youth leader is a twenty-six-year-old man who volunteers his time on evenings and during weekends to conduct biweekly meetings, take the kids on trips and generally provide adult supervision for a host of activities. He is assisted by some parents and adult volunteers, but is largely responsible for the creation and operation of the group's activities.

Reverend Knight started the Bunker Hill Gardens Community Outreach Center five years ago when, after retiring from government employment, and after having successfully operated and sold his own business, he embarked on a third career as a Baptist minister. As a volunteer for a local Kiwanis club, he was tutoring children at a nearby secondary school and became familiar with the Bunker Hill Gardens community. In his capacity as a volunteer he was made aware of crime, violence and other social problems which were endemic to the community at that time. Reverend Knight asserted that when he heard about a murder in which an elderly woman was stabbed by her drug addicted son seventy-two times, he felt he was compelled to do something. It was at this time that he approached the management corporation for Bunker Hill Gardens with his idea for a community outreach center.

Before actually starting the center Reverend Knight said that he conducted three separate surveys in the apartment complex in order to "let them determine what they want." He described his work at the center "as working with the community in order to develop a church right there in the community." His strategy for community action includes "promoting leadership from within," while at the same time making use of the available community resources such as churches, schools, fire, police, health and social service departments. Reverend

Knight maintains that activities at the Bunker Hill Gardens Community Outreach Center are based upon a moral philosophy of "Loving, Caring and Sharing" and a practical strategy of "Loving, Living and Learning" together as a community. These mottos also serve as slogans or rallying cries found on much of the center's printed literature.

A wide range of community-based programs are conducted out of the Bunker Hill Community Outreach Center. The Young Marines represents only a small part of the center's activities, but it has been a very successful part, based upon the statements of youth, parents and community members. Tape-recorded interviews conducted at the Bunker Hill Gardens Community Outreach Center included some people involved in these other programs. These interviews provide a well-rounded picture of the full range of services provided at the Outreach Center. In many ways the responses are consistent with Young Marine experiences, but in some cases they are unique or specific to the person's individual interests. The focus of the interviews, however, was deliberately oriented to Young Marine activities, with other programs providing contextual richness.

Services at the center include a variety of programs designed to meet the social and spiritual needs of the community. All people who work at the center do so on a volunteer basis and operating expenses, according to Reverend Knight, are based upon the donation of space provided by the management company and what many churches refer to as a faith budget. Programs operated out of the center include Bridge to Life, a spiritual support group; an employment center, which operates out of space donated by a local shopping mall; a food bank, which provides food for people without money or resources; a substance abuse support group; tutoring for school children; counseling for housing needs; a dance group for girls; and the Young Marines, a young men's support group which also includes a small number of interested young ladies. Additional programs include Bible study and a playroom for smaller children. The Bunker Hill Community Outreach Center is also undertaking initiatives in community health care and expansion of the outreach center model into neighboring apartment complexes. Reverend K. has also devised a plan to provide transitional housing to homeless families by restoring vacant apartments in large complexes that suffer from low occupancy rates due to crime, poverty and related social problems.

Although many of the Outreach Center's activities seem worthy of study in their own right, it is beyond the scope of this research project to accomplish that task. The purpose of this discussion of Outreach Center programs is to serve as a background and a context for understanding how the Young Marines' activities fit into the overall picture of the Bunker Hill community.

Field observations and conversations with community residents led this researcher to believe that the Young Marines would not exist were it not for the Bunker Hill Community Outreach Center. On the other hand, it is also important to see the Young Marines as a vibrant and functioning organization independent of the outreach center to the extent that, once established, it seems to have taken on a life of its own.

One final observation is worthy of mention regarding the people and activities at the Bunker Hill Community Outreach Center. There is a sense of accomplishment to be found in the comments people made about their efforts at the outreach center. The consensus of opinion expressed during the interviews and informal discussions was that the existence of the outreach center has had a positive impact on the control of drugs, crime and violence in the community.

Bunker Hill Gardens was characterized by every respondent who claimed to have knowledge of its recent history as a dangerous and violent place prior to the establishment of the outreach center. While still recognizing the potential for additional and future social problems, interviewees consistently attributed improvements in the community to the establishment of the community outreach center. The following comments are typical of the things people had to say about life in this community and the effects of the outreach center after less than five years of operation.

"...this neighborhood used to be just shoot'em up, shoot 'em up."

"Years ago it used to be real bad. Selling drugs, shooting, stabbing. One kid stabbed his mother over here seventy-two times.

> In the building over here a girl was
> found dead in a car. Over here some guy's kid
> got shot in the leg. Some kids from other neighborhoods
> come in here, sit around with other kids and then just
> shoot their guns in the air. A lot of that has stopped,
> but the shootin' in the air.
> Sometimes, at night, a lot of the kids will say...
> 'Did you hear that shootin' last night?'
> I say ...'No, I didn't hear anything.'"

When the same respondent was asked why things seem to have improved in the community his comment was as follows...

> "What I see so far is, I believe since the outreach center
> come in, 'cause that has helped a lot of people that have
> been on drugs and bein' convicted. So they helped out a
> lot. Then the management is starting to come around
> and improve a lot of things like they're cuttin' the grass,
> puttin' fences back up, keepin' the neighborhood clean.."

In response to a question about the influence of the center on life in the community one person said...

> "Yes it has (had an influence), very much so, because
> when the center came to the Bunker Hill complex, there
> was a lot of violence, and now it's not so bad as it was
> at all. They have helped a lot of people here."

A mother discussed what she felt to be a sense of desperation and powerlessness that existed in the community , in years past, because of a pervasive fear people lived under due to oppression of the neighborhood by criminal elements one resident characterized as "the unwanteds."

> "..They would think there was nothing that could be done,
> it would always exist, you know. This way would always
> be no matter what. If someone tried, well, the first person

who come here, these guys are going to shoot you down,
and so you never get started. That was the fear.
If I went out and tried to make a difference, the fear
that someone wanted to kill you. So that was one of
the reasons that nothing really got started...fear."

The influence of such "unwanteds" elements on her son and
other young people growing up in the Bunker Hill complex can be seen
in the following description of activities on the neighborhood
playground .

"...hanging out on the playground... you had more or less
three groups of teens. You had your elementary age, you
had your junior high school age and your high schoolers,
and then you had older men. So you know, you had
like a conflict. You know, there were a lot of things that
really were sort of negative because, you know, the young
kids was watching the old kids. You had the drugs that
were going on and then to have the kids to have a
negative attitude. Not doing anything out of line, just
hangin' with friends. Watchin' what's goin' on. No one
doing anything. No leadership. No role models."

One mother depicts a level of intimidation that goes beyond
most popular notions of peer pressure. With regard to, adolescent drug
involvement she depicts what might be better described as peer fear.

Ms. Sheri: "Yeah, shooting crack in the hallways. I mean
that just doesn't make sense. These older guys, like 20's,
20's and up... 23... 24. Like the older guys had already
gone through school or half gone through school.
I won't say they completed it. And to have a younger
age group, or preteenage group see that, you know,
that's a bad... you know... influence on them, because,
eventually, if they continue to be in that, they're going
to end up where those other guys are."

Researcher: "Well, do you think that the younger men, or younger boys, let's say 16-18 years old were looking up ..."

Ms.Sheri: "They weren't looking up..."

Researcher: "...to the older men who were doing these things or..."

Ms. Sheri: "From what my son told me it's like fear when someone approaches you and asks you to do drugs and here, you have this guy that looks like he's doing weights and he's sitting out and...you know... he's older and there's that fear.You're young, and so they try to press you to do that. You know... you hear on T.V. 'Say No to drugs.' You know it's easy to say that, but then when you are approached with that...and you're young and... that fear is there, then what do you do?"

In contrast to this rather grim depiction of life in the neighborhood before the Outreach Center was established, a sense of accomplishment and community pride can be found in the comments made by people who have been working at the center for some length of time and seen its effects on people's lives. The recently established tenant's association appears to be an example of empowerment within the community, resulting from the outreach center's activities. Similarly one board member of the outreach center takes pride in the progress he feels they have made towards taking back the community by removing the drug dealers and reducing the violence.

"When we first started working in this area you couldn't drive your car on the parking lot because of young drug dealers and fear of your life....they were shootin' all kinds of things out here, out of control and totally unsafe."

This same gentleman recognizes that, since the development of the outreach center, there is "...still a little shootin' goin' on, but not to the extent that it was." With respect to the drug dealers he maintains...

"...they have left. When they find that the environment
has changed then they will leave. They don't want to
be around an area where they will be scrutinized."

These ends are accomplished through the cooperation of
various factions in the community, young and old, professional and
volunteer.

"The young people tell us what's going on because they
consider us as being a friend because they figure they
might need us sooner or later, which they will because,
if they happen to get in trouble we will follow (them)
all the way to jail and to court."

Depicting a brief overview of all of the center's services Mr.
George Brown, an elderly gentleman who serves on the board, describes
a "holistic approach" to the needs of the neighborhood. "We provide
whatever services are required" for a particular family, by finding
resources, making referrals and interceding for them, while also
"providing a religious outlook".

Issues

The issues that affect the community and the Bunker Hill
Community Outreach Center are largely the same issues that guide the
development of programs and philosophy of the Young Marines.
Because of the neighborhood's past history, crime, drugs and violence
are major concerns.   Jobs, opportunity, housing and community
leadership are also important community issues.   The central issues
identified by Young Marines, parents and related stakeholders at Bunker
Hill Gardens Community Outreach Center are represented in Figure 5,
while Appendix 3 provides a complete list of codes.

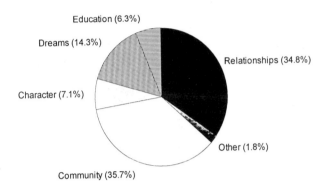

Figure 5. Bunker Hill Young Marines-Issues

The outreach center has enlisted the cooperation of not only the management corporation but also a local mall developer who has provided space to set up an employment agency run by community volunteers. People at the center can tap into employment services through this operation. Other community concerns relate to perceived needs and community organization.

Regaining control of the community through developing leadership and resisting the drug dealers was a major concern and source of pride for people at the Outreach Center. There was a clear sense of accomplishment in the progress that has been made over the past five years, coupled with a recognition of the need for continued vigilance. Community organization and the development of community leadership seemed to be the primary strategy for accomplishing this goal. Other important issues were addressed in a similar manner.

Relationship issues for Bunker Hill Young Marines were seen as important considerations. Comments about relationships emphasized the importance of family members, especially the supportive roles of mothers, fathers and grandparents. The need for role models was also a central interest, along with the positive and negative impact of peers. One typical example of the positive effects of role models and the influence of peers can be seen in the quote from one young man regarding his membership in the Young Marines.

> "I just feel good about myself knowing that there's
> people like Bobby and the Young Marines to look after
> me and make sure I'm doing what I'm supposed to do."

Three more important considerations for youth were dreams, education and character. Throughout the interviews with youth the question of future hopes and dreams was asked. Each young man expressed his aspirations and life goals. Some talked about being professional sport stars. Others talked about having their own business or becoming computer engineers. It was apparent during the interviews that these young men had plans. They were aspiring for a better future, some realistically, and other perhaps not so realistically. It was plain that hope was abundant and most of the young men felt they had a future. Part of this hope might have been related to the frequent references made to improving themselves through education. As an issue, education is an important part of the Young Marines program. Several youths reported improved school work and a sense of pride over becoming Young Marines. Parents consistently reported better attitudes about school work among their sons.

A final issue relating to the young men at Bunker Hill Gardens was the notion of character building. Many of the principles and values discussed in interviews and those reflected in Young Marines activities stressed the concept of character. Values like respect, pride and honesty were stressed along with an emphasis on religious commitment and spirituality. These issues will be discussed in greater detail as we examine the Young Marines program more closely.

Philosophy

Philosophical approaches used in the Young Marines program are depicted in Figure 6, and have been divided into three primary components, philosophies, principles and values. Philosophies include religious, spiritual and broadly based belief systems. Principles imply basic tenets of behavior which guide program activities and emphasis. Values comprise the fundamental ideas and ethical orientations defining what is good and bad. The philosophical bedrock upon which the Young Marines is built can be found in the group motto which is recited at each meeting.

> "DRC. Discipline, Respect and Caring. Discipline is to try. Respect is to have high regards for, and caring is to have a heavy load of responsibility."

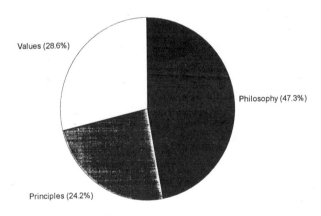

Figure 6.Bunker Hill Young Marines - Philosophy Code Groups

Principles and Values

There is more, however, to the Young Marines, than slogans and mottos. With the discipline, self respect, and the knowledge that someone cares evolves what appears to be a sense of power and ability in these young men. This phenomena is not unlike the sense of empowerment that is conveyed when the adults talk about the Outreach Center and it is not an entirely tangible thing. It is a positive force in the community albeit not always measurable. It is observable however in the comments and enthusiasm brought to the descriptions people convey about their activities and plans.

The concept of ownership, as defined previously in this study, seems to be relevant to the Young Marines as well. At the Diamond Hill Development Center, ownership is presented as a principle which not only affects people's sense of responsibility in their community but it is also a basic principle for involving the kids in the program. A similar idea exists in the Young Marines in that much of the emphasis at the meetings is on youth leadership.

Once the program was started, Bobby came to grips with the fact that providing positive activities for young men in the community was a demanding and difficult task. In response to this, he came up with the idea that the youth should have more of a say and more responsibility in making the program work. The following quote expresses that sentiment.

> "Everything I used to do was by myself, with just a little
> help with Mr. G. who used to be here. He used to
> do the typing for me, but I used to do the filing,
> and the...everything that needs to be written down and
> so on. And so, now I say 'Well hey! This program is
> not for me. It's for them.' So, we decided to make
> officers for the program. So we have a President,
> Vice President, two Secretaries, the Treasurer and
> we're supposed to have a Sargent-at-Arms. So as
> to the organization, when we started coming as one,
> that's when the meetings really started to get up tempo."

This statement exemplifies several key concepts and the emergence of a strategy for program activities that is operating today. At first, Bobby was trying to do most of the organizational work by himself. In recognition of the somewhat disproportionate demands of this task, he seems to have adjusted his style of leadership to include additional help from adults and sharing the responsibility of program success with the kids. During site visits, another adult volunteer was helping with record keeping, and the youth had taken on some of the responsibilities of group leadership.

The officers and the committee system is one way that leadership skills are taught and shared. Promoting leadership from within is a key strategy for community organization used by Rev. Knight. He describes this approach as being fundamental to the success or effectiveness of any program. Bobby's work with the Young Marines exemplifies this guiding principle by making the youth responsible for each other. He establishes strict guidelines for behavior and high expectations for achievement, but attempts to create an environment in which the youth look to each other for support and mutual discipline.

This emphasis on discipline and structure can be seen at the Tuesday and Thursday night group meetings. Attendance is mandatory and tardiness is not ignored. People are expected to arrive on time (with a five minute grace period) and take the meetings seriously. Specific rules about attendance and membership are enforced and adherence to parliamentary rule of procedure is generally expected. One person speaks at a time and others are expected to listen, without cross talk, whispering, or laughing at other people.

On one occasion an older youth was sent out to find out where the President was when, after fifteen minutes, he had not arrived at the scheduled group meeting. He was found by the messenger and brought to the meeting. When the President arrived he was asked in front of the group where he had been. He said he was talking to a girl and had lost track of time. Bobby, who was presiding over the meeting, scolded him for setting a bad example and then insisted that he resume his position as an officer in the front of the room when the young man tried to sit surreptitiously in one of the back row seats.

There seems to be a fine line between adult guidance and adult control which is inherent in the facilitation of youth leadership as it relates to maintaining an organized and structured program. Another example of the youth leadership principle can be seen in the use of older Young Marine members as examples or role models for younger members.

" I work with my officers very close, because I see
them out there and tell them. 'Look, you can't do this
because, remember, you have all these other marines
running around here and they'll come to me, and say...
'Well, he did it! So, why can't I?' ..."

Another way this principle of youth leadership manifests itself
is in the homework help projects and in the creation of a Concern
Committee, wherein club officers visit members' homes to talk with
parents about homework and behavior. Young Marines are available to
help each other with their homework. They do it in the meetings and at
specially arranged times if somebody needs individual tutoring.
Several of the young men have experienced marked improvements in
their school work, their behavior and their grades, since joining the
Young Marines program. Two mothers expressed similar assessments
about the effects of the peer support for homework and the positive
effects of the program on schoolwork.

"Schoolwise, at one time it seems to me his report cards,
his grades were so bad, I was afraid to look at it.
I'm bein' honest, and during the summer I'd be gettin'
him little books, like in the 10th grade you have little
books that you go into. Maybe thirty minutes, I'd try
to make him sit down and do math or whatever, right?
And at the time, before he really got involved with
Bobby, he would have still, you know.... he could do a
little, but he wouldn't do it. You know? I wouldn't
stay over him. But I had to have, within a week,
so many things that he had to do, and he wasn't doin'
it and then he was gettin' pressure from the
outside...and you know the guys. An he approached
me with it and I appreciated it and I thanked God
for that because he didn't...I look at it in a way...
what if he didn't tell me, whatever...and anyway...
the positive effect about it is, his grades have come up.

> He went from an 'E' to a 'B', "E" to 'B' and we're
> really very proud of him."

Interviewer : "When you say pressure, (do) you mean
from the guys, to not do well? Pressure him not to
do well or pressure him to do well? Pressure of what
kind?"

Ms. Sheila: "OK, in other words as far as the Young
Marines and the effect that it has had on my son,
is that it has made him...took him out of being a
follower into a leader."

Another mother made the following statement.

> "..he wants to be the best that he can be in the program.
> And his homework, everything that I used to have hard
> times getting him to do as far as study, period...
> and things like that. He has to do it at a certain time...
> 'Mom, I want to get it over with. I want to make sure I
> can be at my meetings, and when Bobby asks some
> things I want to be able to give him a positive answer."

Researcher: "Does it surprise you to hear him say that?"

Ms. Gwen: "At that point I had gotten so disgusted
'cause he had received an 'E' in English. He had
a 'B' in Spanish and an 'E' in English. I couldn't
understand that. 'E' is failing. He brought it up to a 'B'
......after being with them in the study periods."

The positive effect has also extended to reducing the level of
stigma associated at school with the youth who come from the Bunker
Hill apartment complex. Ms. Sheila related that prior to the formation
of the Young Marines teachers and administrators would frequently
label students from the apartment complex as delinquent or suspect.

Subsequent to the Young Marines becoming known to school officials, she expressed the feeling that this tendency has diminished.

Spiritual Growth and Positive Attitude

Like all of the activities affiliated with the Outreach Center, the Young Marines incorporate a spiritual emphasis into its program philosophy. This religious orientation is manifested in a variety of ways, but is perhaps applied most effectively to the Young Marines in a program activity referred to as Real Men. This particular activity attempts to foster an understanding of manhood that looks beyond the physical and includes spiritual development through a Christian/Biblical focus. A quote from one of the lessons handed out to the Young Marines during Real Men exercises is as follows...

Before the fall man, man was a companion of God.
The perfect will of God is for man to be His companion.
For a man to be all that God wanted him to be, he must
walk with God. One of the most vital areas of
developing yourself to be all God wants you
to be, is learning to walk and to fellowship with Him
day by day. Be God's companion.

Real Men activities incorporates program values and principles relating to discipline, respect and hard work. This point is illustrated in comments from young men during several interviews.

Researcher: "What's this real men thing about? Tell me about that. I've seen some papers about that."

Jason: "It's like spiritual as well as, you know, physical. We study like how to be a real man, like, a real man should be able to endure eight hours of work on his feet. A real man should be able to take care of his family. Stuff like that."

Researcher: "So it emphasizes hard work , responsibility..."

Jason: "Discipline and respect."

A second young man discussed how Real Men lessons teach values, such as responsibility, and apply to young women as well.

> "We have a lesson we is learning that we just started,
> called Real Men. We just learning how to be real
> men and women. To take on responsibility and stuff.
> It's teaching us the responsibility of life. Like if your
> older and you have a child, you have learn that,
> you know, you can't do everything for yourself.
> You have to help other people or you have to
> like pay the bills. You can't just spend all your money
> on clothes and stuff. You have to pay bills so you will
> have money to live."

An older gentleman, who is active in Outreach Center program development, and who expressed support for the Young Marines, emphasized the need to teach and instill values in the younger generation. He saw, as one of the main goals of the Young Marines, the instruction of values for boys and girls. Referring to the Boy Scout oath model for teaching values Mr. George said...

> " Yes, it will work for these kids, but it needs to be started and
> you've got to have somebody who knows how to instruct these
> young people in those doctrines. You have something that
> you've got to instill in their minds in order to compete with
> the drug dealers. You've got to have something that will wash
> them up. In other words, clean their minds to the extent where
> these youngsters will say...'I don't want no part of this here.
> I want to live different. I want to do something different.
> I have another way I want to live.'...But you've got to bring
> them to this. You've got to instill this stuff in them, because
> at their age, they're not able to deal with all the other forces."

Maintaining a positive mind, focusing on the positive, and having a positive attitude are also pervasive themes incorporated into program philosophy and activities. Mr. George talks about exposing young people to the "positive side" of things. Rev. Knight talks about refusing to dwell on the negative. Meanwhile, Young Marines refer to keeping a positive mind or a positive focus. Additional values and a sense of priorities are conveyed in the Young Marines program through the organization's mission statement which accompanies a pledge that every member must sign. The mission statement emphasizes self help, recreation, community service, schoolwork, and self respect.

The Young Marines also have a rigid code of rules and regulations regarding attendance, dress, behavior at meetings and behavior in public. Club officers have additional rules and a list of duties which they are expected to perform by virtue of their title as officers. Disciplinary action relating to noncompliance with any of these rules is spelled out and described in writing. Similar to the Boy Scout oath the Young Marine pledge is signed and recited at the meetings. It emphasizes commitment to the goals of the Outreach Center and highlights values pertaining to service to God, country, family life, mutual interdependence loving, caring and sharing.

The Bunker Hill Young Marines appears to utilize a highly structured approach to organizing the activities of the youngsters it serves by providing clear guidelines and applying consequences for noncompliance. These consequences tend to emphasize peer pressure, reprimands, or, in extreme cases, exclusion. This strategy can be observed in the previously mentioned case of reprimanding an officer for being late, and in the way consequences for inappropriate behavior are delineated in the program rules. Exclusion, however, is never final, and a process by which members can be voted back into the organization has been implemented so that, in practice, the kids have the final say over whether a person's behavior warrants sanctions. Based on their own comments and the comments of their parents, participation in the Young Marines seems to have positive effects on the self esteem of the young people involved. These positive effects seem also to spill over into their reputation at school and in the community.

Membership in the Young Marines is not automatic and for someone to be fully accepted into the organization he or she must attend five consecutive meetings. One young man talked about how he quit the organization and then returned. Procedures for allowing ex-members back into the group had been discussed at the previous meeting. This particular person had very recently been accepted back in by a vote from the membership. He made these comments.

> *J.R.* :"I quit it like a couple of weeks ago, but I'm gettin'
> back in...I had things to do. I wasn't able to make
> all the meetings. See...I wasn't into it at all...I just
> couldn't handle it at all. Now I could.
> So that's why I'm back."

> *Researcher*: "So there are lots of rules the Young Marines
> have about coming to the meetings and being late.
> Can you tell me what some of the rules are?"

> *J.R.* : "Yeah, you know not coming late. If you come
> late it gets put on a little sheet they got. You know,
> if you be smart, you get something I forgot what it is,
> on the other sheet there, you know. It all adds up."

> *Researcher*: "..and apparently you left, you weren't
> kicked out?'

> *J.R.* : "Kicked out? No, I left for awhile."

> *Researcher*: "Then you just got back in last night?"

> *J.R.* : "They voted me back in...I had come to the meeting
> and you know, all the members had to vote me back in,
> and everybodydid, so now I'm back."

Philosophically the Young Marines is oriented towards the spiritual and personal development of young people. This is accomplished by encouraging growth through the teaching of values, self help and building leadership. The guiding principles for achieving these ends are creating a safe and positive environment that models

Christian religious commitment tempered with discipline, respect and caring. Strategies for implementing these principles include peer support, hard work, mutual interdependence and trust.

Program

The Young Marine Activities

The Bunker Hill Young Marines is largely the effort of a few dedicated adults and about two dozen responsive pre-teen and teenage young men. Although the program accepts young ladies, during the field visits meetings and activities were mostly attended by males. One young lady, Christine, takes great pride in her membership and has been with the organization since its beginning. There was a general consensus among several adult volunteers and supporters that something more must be done in the community to provide activities for girls. Efforts to provide some activities geared to be attractive to females have been initiated but are still in their developmental stages. During the time of the fieldwork for this study the Young Marines at Bunker Hill Gardens was a mostly male organization.

Bobby Petrie, an African American man of twenty-six and a longtime resident of the neighborhood, is the person most frequently mentioned as the adult responsible for the formation and success of the Young Marines. His involvement with the Bunker Hill Gardens youth started when he became the coach for a boy's basketball team in a police-sponsored athletic league. Having grown up and subsequently left the neighborhood, Bobby was familiar with the experiences of the youth in the community. He subsequently returned to the community, and although he was already committed to working with youth at the time, he began the Young Marines as an outgrowth of his basketball team. He was encouraged to do so and supported by Reverend Knight who was already operating the Outreach Center at the time.

It should be stressed that the Young Marines was described as a successful program, by virtually all people who participated in the study. Different people had different reasons why they thought it was worthwhile, but the opinions expressed by participants, parents, adult volunteers, and independent community agents were overwhelming in their praise of the Young Marines and their activities. The program design and leadership is primarily through Bobby's efforts, with the support of Reverend Knight, several concerned parents, and Ms. Sandy who acts as the club recording secretary. Many of Bobby's ideas for group work and program activities have come from the personnel manual at his place of work. His employer, a major grocery store chain, has been very generous in providing support for Young Marine activities in a variety of ways. Recently, the group was also highlighted in a local television broadcast, a fact which has boosted morale and had a positive effect on membership.

The activities, both formal and informal, comprise the basic motivation for participation in the Young Marines. Over seventeen different activities were identified as things that Young Marines do in addition to attending the bi-weekly meetings. These activities include basketball, black history, community service, cleanup, the concern committee, cookouts and dinners, homework, recycling, real men, tutoring, trips and the word of the day. Additional plans include female cheerleaders, recycling , building an obstacle course, and having a boot camp.

Some examples of community service programs that were mentioned during interviews include planting shrubs at school, recycling, acting as pall bearers at a funeral, and community clean-up. Along similar lines, Bobby has worked out an arrangement with the management company for the apartment complex where the Young Marines will be responsible for maintaining order on the basketball courts. This will be accomplished by giving the actual breakaway baskets to the Young Marines and they in turn will share the responsibility of putting them up at 9:00 AM and taking them down at 9:00 PM. during the summer. At the time of the fieldwork the baskets had been removed by the management company because of problems with crowd control and undesirable activities on the basketball courts.

The young people who attend the Young Marines do so for a variety of reasons. When asked why they come, answers typically conveyed three distinct themes. The first has to do with avoiding the negative influences of the streets. The second is a desire to do something positive. The third is because they have fun. In spite of the

rigor, the high expectations and the compulsory homework, the kids
have fun and they feel good about doing something positive. These
basic themes was conveyed in a variety of ways. Responses to the
question of why they come included the following:

> "Because it gets me off the streets and doin' bad stuff
> that I'm not supposed to do."

> "Because it's an all right thing to do. I mean its better
> than to just be standin' out there on the corner.
> You go in there and you learn a couple of things.
> That's why I come. I have fun."

> "It's fun! We have trips, we have picnics, all kinds
> of good stuff."

A slightly more ominous reason for participation was
expressed by one youth who echoed the sentiments of others when he
said...

> "Ain't nothin' to do around Bunker Hill. Things be
> happenin' around here. And you can't be outside unless
> you have a gun."

The Young Marines provides a safe environment where there is
mutual support and positive fellowship. This observation is exemplified
by comments such as...

> "..we sit down and talk and stuff, you know...just friends.
> Everybody's just friends and they talk. And people they
> started drugs and they be shootin' at each other.
> So, you know, he (Bobby) tries to keep us off the streets,
> and he's doing a good job."

In addition to providing a safe environment, participation in the
Young Marines seems to positively affect self esteem as well as a
person's reputation in school and the community. These effects were

seen earlier in the comments of a mother who felt that Young Marines' participation helped to offset negative labeling of Bunker Hill students at school. The heightened self esteem factor can be observed in the comments of organization members.

> "I feel more mature and confident in myself. At first I was,
> like if I had to do something in front of a whole group
> of people, I be kind of shy and they taught us to feel
> good about ourselves and that made me stronger.
> To know that there is nothin' to be afraid of .
> To do what you have to do."

> "Adults look at you differently, in a good way"

The organization of Young Marine activities seems well suited to incorporate philosophy and guiding principles with program strategies. The committee process, a loose but disciplined parliamentary process at the meetings, and the expectation that meetings be taken seriously all work together to provide a program structure that seems to have a positive effect. The need for structured youth activities was stressed by people at the Outreach Center and is also an essential program element at other sites.

Youth leadership is fostered by having higher expectations for older members and by making members responsible for each other's behavior. The officers check on the younger boys with their concern committee activities, and Bobby checks on the officers. This process sets up a system of mutual accountability that does not short cut individual responsibility.

Education is also a highly valued commodity and major source of pride among many of the Young Marines. Educational achievements have been mentioned by parents and Young Marines alike as a means of substantiating the positive effects of participation. Education extends not only to school work, but also to the teaching of values. This reality can be seen in the real men activities, the slogans and mottos used at the group meetings and the expectation that members attend church at least once a month.

In conclusion, it is apparent that the Young Marines has had a positive effect on the lives of its members to date. Although only a small portion of the eligible youth at the Bunker Hill Gardens apartment complex participate in the program, Rev. Knight's response to that reality was uniquely indicative of the philosophy of positive thinking that he instills into his work with the community. Rev. Knight's remark is reminiscent of the recent popular movie about the Iowa farmer who built a baseball diamond in his corn field because he heard a voice that said "Build it and they will come." For Rev. Knight and Bobby Petrie, the voice seems to be saying "work with the ones you have."

> "What you do is you keep workin' with what you have...
> build a drawing card...anytime change starts takin' place
> there's a fight or a hassle...in order to play the game you'll
> have to join...I just came back from a local health spa,
> they're gonna go marchin' into the health spa...
> so I'm talkin' about the best physical athlete you want
> to see. When you see these young marines you're
> talkin about somethin'. You ain't talkin' about nobody
> walkin' around with his pants hangin' down....
> You gotta produce something."

Lessons and Reflections

There is something taking place at the Bunker Hill Community Outreach Center that is extremely positive and uplifting for the people there. This is apparent not only in the Outreach Center, and the Young Marines, but also in the comments made by people who are slightly removed from the situation. A local police man, the apartment complex manager, and a state employment counselor all spoke highly of the center's activities and their effect on the community. Reverend Knight sees it as the work of "God through Christ and the Holy Spirit." Others would probably talk about community organization, political empowerment and a sense of common purpose.

Regardless of the energy source or where the impetus comes from, persistent observation reveals that Reverend Knight's style of leadership and his ability to empower others to lead, is a profoundly effective vehicle for social change. People in the community have responded to his enthusiasm, encouraged by his message of self help and motivated by his positive outlook. Bobby Petrie is one of those people who has responded, and Bobby has had an impact in his own right.

Role Models

The Young Marines is a working example of role models in action. It also represents a tool for community organization and an illustration of how larger efforts at the Outreach center are being conducted. Bobby is someone the kids in his program look up to, admire, and appreciate. He has been given, and deserves, a great deal of credit for the success of the Young Marines. He does not, however, do it by himself. He has the support of some dedicated mothers, friends and community leaders. The Young Marines could benefit by the added support of fathers and other responsible young men in the community. This has not happened yet.

One promising, and potentially valuable, observation from the Young Marines program is the example of intergenerational role modeling. Reverend Knight and those mentioned earlier are the people behind the scenes creating the venue in which Bobby Petrie realizes his own leadership abilities. There is a symbiotic relationship that benefits four generations. Older community leaders and young potential leaders grow out of a positive interaction between retirees, parents, young adults and children. This chain of interaction has the potential to bring the community together through the building of intergenerational relationships and mutually shared resources. It is unlikely that Reverend Knight could do what Bobby does, but it is just as unlikely that Bobby could do what he does without Reverend Knight.

Community Support and Recognition

Another ingredient that seems to have had an especially positive effect on the Young Marine members is the recognition they are receiving both individually and as a group. Both the reputations of the individual members and of the overall community have been enhanced by the presence of this Young Marines program. This phenomenon has taken place in the neighborhood, in the schools and in the mass media. Published newspaper articles, television news coverage, interviews with community police all attest to this enhanced reputation.

Young men expressed pride over this recognition during the interviews. The outcome seems to be a growing confidence that they are individually and as a group, doing the right thing. The influence of media and positive recognition seems to have provided fertilizer for positive growth. This lesson should not be lost in the shuffle.

One of the center's board members stresses the importance of remembering that previous attempts to establish a similar program in the community have not been as effective. He, therefore, emphasizes learning from the mistakes of the past in order to avoid similar shortfalls in the future. During a follow-up interview, Reverend Knight referred to a natural tendency for programs to grow and then taper off. The challenge facing Young Marines in the future may be to sustain their growth through new membership and community support.

In spite of the fact that things seem to be going well for the Young Marines, the question of what would happen if Bobby left needs to be addressed. Would they "peter out" in the same way efforts have done in the past? This is a concern that probably should be addressed. Working with youth is hard. It requires time, energy, financial resources and enthusiasm. These are commodities which one person has limited amounts of, even under the best of circumstances. For this reason additional group leadership, especially from males, should be recruited.

If Young Marine activities are to be expanded and membership increased the possibility of volunteer burnout could have a devastating effect without the development of active volunteer participation. New leadership should be based on high ethical and moral standards that offset some of the chaotic pressures encountered on the streets and in the larger world. The code of ethics established by the Outreach Center as well as specific screening policies for volunteers working with youth is one way to protect the interests while serving the needs of young people in this community. At the risk of becoming overly bureaucratic, these issues should be considered if aggressive recruitment efforts are undertaken.

Summary

Beyond the immediate example of an emerging program for young men, the Young Marines demonstrates the reverberating effect that one caring, interested adult male can have on the lives of teenage boys. The program demonstrates the capability of caring adults to lead and encourage young men from high risk communities to develop in positive and productive ways. The key to Bobby's and Reverend Knights success comes from a variety of sources. Community support and positive responses are vitally important. Collaboration between corporate, public agencies and private charities is another part of Reverend Knight's recipe for success, both at the Outreach Center and with the Young Marine's .

It is apparent from comments recorded by youth and parents alike, that membership in the Young Marines has positively influenced young men, individually, and the community, as a whole. Improved school performance and attitudes towards personal responsibilities at home are two examples. Commitments to community service, to self discipline and to respect for others have also been made. Like the community as a whole, many of the Young Marines have embarked in new directions by turning around a negative situation and "focusing on the positive."

Chapter 6: The Comprehensive Youth Services Center

History and Setting

The Comprehensive Youth Services Center was established in the early 1980's by two concerned professional women whose vision was to create an agency that provides a wide range of services to high risk adolescents. The center is comprehensive, because its mission is to provide a complete array of services under one roof. The logic for this approach is based on the observation that high risk young adults often have multiple needs and services targeting them tended to be fragmented. It was observed that human service agencies are frequently located in different parts of the city and for this reason, there is a lack of follow through among young people in need. Ten years ago, the Comprehensive Youth Services Center was founded and designed to fill these service delivery gaps.

The C.Y.S., as the organization is often referred to by its staff, is situated in an abandoned army hospital located in a downtown residential area. There is a subway station and a city transit bus stop within walking distance. This easy access to public transportation allows young people from any of the city's several wards to participate in the various programs. The 100-year-old building in which the center is housed is leased from the city and is in fair condition, considering its historical status. It is a four-story structure, including the basement and is made of brick in the fashion of many old school buildings. There is no central air conditioning and the building has high ceilings, so that it is difficult to cool in the summer. At the time of the site visits, some of the rooms had window unit air conditioners while others did not. During the course of the fieldwork temperatures ranged in the mid nineties, frequently approaching 100 degrees Fahrenheit. On several occasions the center's activities were adjusted or modified in order to locate an air conditioned room.

The C.Y.S. building is a large facility which houses a wide variety of activities conducted by the center's staff. Located on the first floor are the main offices, a conference room with an adjoining waiting area, a children's nursery, a main hallway. Pictures of African American leaders and historical figures line the walls ascending a central stairway connecting the top three floors. The second floor has offices for the educational director, the administrative coordinator and four classrooms. One classroom is filled with computers, while the others have arm chair style desks for students in a traditional lecture arrangement. Each classroom has a blackboard and some were equipped with tables and chairs.

On the third floor there is a self defense training room that is a large open area with a gigantic central radiator heater in the middle of the floor. The heater looks like something designed during the turn of the century and reflects the technological sophistication of the building's heating system, early 20th Century steam radiator heat. Around the walls of the training room are pictures of martial arts figures, black religious leaders, and martial arts training equipment. Hanging on the walls were pictures of Malcolm X, Muhummad Ali, Joe Louis and other famous black men along with poems and famous sayings. Over approximately one-third of the lacquered plywood floor is a mosaic of rugs and matts which comprise the sparring arena. This is where the students practice their role, throws and other techniques during the training session.

A full basement is finished with linoleum floors and plaster walls. Located there is a medical clinic, the furnace room, and several more offices, linked by a central hallway. The basement houses offices for mental health and substance abuse counselors, the accountant, and the weatherization program. While the interior of the building is in fairly good condition, in some spots, the walls are flaking and in need of paint. Several youth were working on the conference room during the course of the field work. They were scraping and filling plaster holes, preparing to put up drywall. The project appeared to be about 90% finished by the time site visits were completed three weeks later.

The neighborhood in which the center is located is highly urbanized. It is located on a busy city street with bus stops and subway stations within walking distance. The area is mixed in terms of residential and commercial dwellings. There are gas stations and restaurants nearby as well as apartment buildings and single family row houses. The center is surrounded by a wrought iron fence and situated on approximately a one-half acre plot.

The community was described as diverse in terms of economic and social character. There are affluent and upper middle class professional people living nearby, as well as several public housing projects. Housing projects "surround the area" but are "kind of intermingled" and located "on the edges" of the more affluent neighborhood.

Up the street about two blocks away there are several boarded up storefronts and signs of economic distress. Down the street, in the opposite direction are commercial establishments that seem to be thriving, or at least their buildings appear well maintained. Since the center's mission is to serve youth in all parts of the city, the characteristics of the immediate neighborhood are not as relevant to the programs and activities when compared to the two sites previously examined in this study. Young people come to C.Y.S. from all wards of the city and each of which has its own unique physical and social characteristics.

The Comprehensive Youth Services Center is a privately operated, nonprofit agency which incorporates a blend of full time professional and part time volunteer staff. According to the center's accountant, the agency has experienced a "shrinking budget" in recent years, but funds have been characterized as "stable." Last year the center operated with an annual budget of $800,000. This figure represents a $50,000 reduction in funding from the previous year. The number of full and/or part time staff employed at any given time varies from year to year depending on funds and the nature of programs in progress. Currently, there are approximately ten full time staff on the payroll. Over ten years time the center has, reportedly, served over 6,000 students. Funding sources include the United Way, federal grants, private contributions and corporate donations. Volunteers also provide support services in a variety of ways including tutoring, medical care, and professional counseling.

Although C.Y.S. does not provide services exclusively to males, it was selected as a site for several reasons. In 1994 a coalition of five city agencies was selected for a nationwide study designed to identify the needs and create services for minority males. C.Y.S. was selected as one of these five agencies and is currently involved in a three-year needs assessment and service development pilot project to that effect. The population served by the center is over 90% African American, 60% of whom are males. Some of the programs include an all male discussion groups and a male-oriented health clinic. C.Y.S. has a policy of nondiscrimination and serves all youth in the community between the ages of 14 and 21, male or female, regardless of race or religion.

Issues

Defining At Risk Youth

Although the young adults who attend the Comprehensive Youth Services Center are older than youth at the previous sites, the practical definition for being at risk status is similar. Most of the concerns referred to when defining what it means to be a young person in a high risk situation relate in some way to crime and violence. In the words of C.Y.S. executive director, Mr. C. J. Robertson, the phrase high risk applies to young men and women who are involved with drugs, come from dysfunctional family backgrounds and/or are in trouble with the criminal justice system.

A second working definition for being at risk relates to being a school drop out, having unresolved family issues or having been incarcerated. Mr. Goodwin, commonly referred to by students as Sam, is one of the substance abuse counselors. He provides a definition for being at risk that relates to drug dependence but can also be applied to other situations. In doing so he tends to challenge preconceptions about what the term "at risk" means, and how it applies.

"At risk youth don't necessarily come from low income situations. At risk youth, in the definition that I understand, have problems or issues that deal with self esteem, deal with feelings or feeling inadequate, which would make them vulnerable to situations that center around the drug problem."

One final reflection on what it means to be at risk can be found in the comments of a summer intern. Lloyd is a college junior, age 20, who worked at the center for eight weeks during the summer. He is a young black man who, like most of the interns there, was recruited through the Minority Leaders Fellowship Program. He falls well within the age bracket of young people served at the center. This young volunteer, along with the other summer interns, provided concrete examples of positive role models for young adults. He has also been fortunate enough not to need the center's core services. Lloyd's observation was a simple and succinct.

"Just by living here, in this city, they are at risk. Even the good kids are at risk."

On another level, Lloyd, and the other summer interns, do benefit directly from the services that C.Y.S. provides. By being afforded opportunities to participate in program activities and lead, within the context of their internships, these young people are gaining invaluable experience that should serve them well in the future.

The population served at C.Y.S. is significantly older than those found at the previous sites. The average age of young men interviewed was 18 to 19 years. It is logical to assume that their perceived needs and ideas about how to confront problems will be different, but the range of issues discovered at the Comprehensive Youth Services Center includes many of the concerns voiced at the previous sites. In many ways, the structure of the center programs provides some guidelines for understanding which issues are deemed most relevant to the needs of young black men in high risk situations. Ten years of operation seem to have resulted in an organizational structure which is consistent with several areas of need.

The basic services available at the center encompass a broad range of activities designed to address a variety of social issues. These services include   education, employment, counseling, recreation and health care. Figure 7 depicts the broad range of issues discussed at the Youth Services Center during interviews with participants and staff.

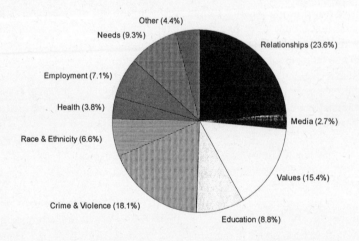

Figure 7. C.Y.S. - Issues Code Groups

Issues, as depicted during these interviews appear to be interrelated. Concerns over employment tend to complement issues relating to education. Education was very clearly a vehicle for employment and not an end in itself. These differences may serve to demonstrate what the executive director of C.Y.S. found to be a high level of diversity within the population of at risk minority males between the ages of 13 and 21 years of age.

Frequently mentioned issues included relationships, crime and violence and values. Education and employment were also important considerations. Additional prevailing themes included race relations, and a general discussion of needs.

Crime and Violence

References to court ordered attendance, drug use, and emotional trauma resulting from exposure to violence all point to a social environment where crime and related violence have a profound negative impact on peoples' lives. One comment by a C.Y.S. staff member echoes those made by others during the interviewees at other research sites, but provides an even darker tone regarding the emotional effects of violence on young people.

> "They've seen so much of this that's the thing, that after a point, you almost become numb. I have a young man, he was not my counselee, and he happened to be talking with me on this occasion and he had this little notebook, loose leaf, that he was carrying around. And what he had was like pictures of all his friends who had been killed, newspaper articles showing the bodies. It was...and he was just going through it telling me 'Well, this is my friend so and so, and this is ...' And it's the kind of thing that I would do if I would just pull out one of my photo albums an I was showing you... 'Look , this is my mother, and this is....' and he just goes on like this, and I'm sitting there thinking. And I was upset by the extent of loss that he had experienced in less than a year or just about a year's time. It's almost an average of one a month, and what do you do with that kind of pain?"

Violence is news worthy. Violence is dramatic. Even the good guys resort to violence in the end. This is a major theme which "bombards" our society. Public officials who haven't had combat experience are questioned about their ability to lead. The glorification of violence, state sanctioned or otherwise, is seen as impacting values and behavior. It allows for the justification of assault and even homicide as a praiseworthy means to achieve fame, recognition or notoriety. For some people there is not much distinction between these various "claims to fame", and even negative prestige is better than no prestige at all. Although the high level of violence in many urban neighborhoods seems to defy logical explanation, for many it is an ongoing reality. In a classic understatement one young man said...

> "If I could stop the violence I would but, no one person
> can do that. Everybody has to join together to do that.
> There's no need for violence and all the killin'.
> I don't think that's necessary."

Relationships

The subject of relationships is a broad topic which includes references to parents, family, peers and a variety of other subtopics. Within this context the issue of role models emerges as a prevailing need and primary interest. Despite the researcher's deliberate avoidance of the specific term, the subject of role models has been mentioned in depth at each of the three research sites. Once initiated by the interviewee as an issue, however, the subject was explored thoroughly. Closely related to this issue, and a potential driving force behind the perceived need for positive role models is family relationships.

Many of the young men who attend programs at the C.Y.S. come from single parent homes where the biological father is absent. When asked about the typical profile of young men and the basic assumptions that he uses when working with a new member one counselor maintained that he assumes the family has dysfunctional characteristics, until proven otherwise. Two additional assumptions relate to poor academic achievement and at risk status for drug involvement, crime and other self destructive behaviors.

The roles of fathers, absent or present, is an important part of the family relationship issue. One young man said that he never really knew his father and that his grandmother would hide his father because she thought his mother would take him to court for child support. With respect to the subject of fatherhood he provided the following quote.

"Hopefully, when I have a child, I will always be there
for him. I'm gonna do for my child what my father
didn't do for me."

When asked whom they admire the most, several of the young men enrolled in the center's employment program said they admired their mothers, while others referred to some member of the center's staff. One young man described his relationship with center staff as being "like parents to us" asserting that they "motivate us," "keep us doing the right thing" and "look out after us."

The family was also seen as an important support network. This point is exemplified in programs emphasizing family skills, child care and family planning. There were references made to the importance of family in educational development, and the perceived breakdown of the family as a positive socializing agent. In response to the need to address the problem of family disruption, it is suggested that structured programs must provide assistance for meeting the basic needs of high risk young people.

Since a majority of youth entering into C.Y.S. programs were described as coming from single parent homes with absent fathers, discussions of role models are often associated with family issues. In reference to a question about violence in the streets and the perception of society becoming increasingly more dangerous, one of the senior staff members explains violence in society as resulting, in part, from the deterioration of the nuclear family.

"Yes, I am definitely inclined to agree with that. I think
that you have to look at things like the breakdown
of the nuclear family. Certainly in terms of a lot of
people that are part of this program may be in single
parent households. In households where there are
two parents, both of them need to be working in
order to maintain certainly,... some time ago
it was feasible for a parent to be at home with children
for part of the time. While mothers in many cases
and the father was out working, and caring for the
family, providing. Now many of the fathers of these

young people are absent. They are missing positive
role models. The role models that they see in terms
of people in the community, when you look at the
movies, there are a number of movies that have come
out that are supposed to have positive messages but
the bulk of what you see is violence, and the
negative stereotypes of black people and then the
message is tacked on at the end. So if you get to that
part and you're busy focusing on the killings, and
the drive bys, who is bad, and the gun is powerful,
all these things....then, when the message comes...
I would imagine that many of the young people miss it."

The same person also makes reference to overall values in our
society which depict and glorify violence as something positive and
respected by men. The subject of celebrity role modeling and negative
messages enountered in the media, which place a high value on
expressions of violence, was also seen as a contributing factor.

Mr. Robertson, the executive director at C.Y.S., describes the
role of the center as providing a structured response to the needs of
young people caught in the breakdown of family relationships. He also
emphasizes the responsibility of society as a whole to address the
alienation of many urban youth.

"There is a breakdown simply because there is generally
no father there. The woman is there. The father may
be incarcerated or dead, but he has left the home. The
child is not adequately trained by the household, by
the parent.

So we are not good parents in this society. Therefore,
those are the three basic needs, and if you start with
parenting, then those other needs will probably be met.
But its going to take us a long time to get to parenting
so we as a society have to provide some structured
programs that will assist in giving structure to
young people."

One aspect of that assistance seems to be the development of programs with built in opportunities for young people to enter into relationships with caring adults who lead by example. Evidence from comments during the interviews suggest that the development of a caring, trusting and committed relationship seems to be the operating definition for positive role models. The effects of meaningful relationships on a young person's life can be profound. One staff member relates how, during his own youth, he was at a stage where he had come into serious conflict with the law. He describes his life and his character as having been filled with negative influences. One person whom he describes as having had a profound influence was a group home director who took a special interest in him. The relationship allowed this man to develop a belief in himself that carried him through these troubled times.

"For the first time in my life someone had more confidence in me than I had in myself. Someone who went to the court system with me, paid my fines, put himself and his job on the line for an opportunity for me to live, brought me back to the program. I had never seen that demonstrated. First of all, he was a male. Second of all, he was white. Thirdly, he was on a professional level much higher than the rest of the counselors I was working with. He was the director of the program, and I was greatly overwhelmed by his kindness. He took me to his home, had lunch, showed me his home. He trusted me more than I trust myself. My thought was, 'If this guy takes me out to his house he has got to be crazy.' I was in the midst of the most negative point in my life, where anybody was easy takings, easy pickings."

The same person went on to discuss how two other people, one a black male and the other a gay woman, also demonstrated levels of caring and kindness that had a profound impact on his own life. These experiences were juxtaposed with a discussion of his own prejudices and early conditioning about the nature of human relationships. The same counselor is the staff person most frequently referred to in the interviews with youth as someone who helps them or whom they admire the most.

The notion of celebrities and black politicians as role models was refuted as an ideal during several interviews, and was referred to in the negative light, on more than one occasion. A telling criticism of famous people as role models can be found in relation to the belief that black celebrities often lose contact with their communities.   One philosophical position is that people are obliged to give back to their community so that less fortunate others may benefit from their achievements as well.   This notion of community service and responsibility is a strong theme found at each of the sites visited during this study. Exploitation of poor people, and the black community in general, through celebrity endorsements or catering to white majority interests for selfish gain is seen by one person as an example of misplaced priorities. In contrast, personal commitment and hands on involvement was seen as a praiseworthy sense of social responsibility.

> "I'm not talking about dollars and sense. Anybody can
> contribute to the black educational fund or the black
> college fund. Fine. That's real nice. You wrote a check.
> I'm talkin' about coming back to the community.
>
> I think the President had a great idea of educating people
> and then having them come back to the community to
> serve two years as a kind of payment for their tuition.
> I think that's great. Its a good idea. Where is it?
> You understand?
>
> I think that black people in show business,
> they got billions of bucks...money they'll never spend.
> I think its cool, but I think they ought to give block parties.
> I think they ought to come back to the communities
> that are in trouble and I think they ought to make a
> contribution on a personal basis. You got to give back
> what you have or God will take it away, is my feeling.

Take someone like Michael Jordon, sure he makes a
contribution. He makes a contribution, but he spends
more money in Vegas...you understand...than the
contribution he makes...and I'm not talking about just
dollars and cents. I'm talking about coming out and
seeing people.

These kids rob, steal, kill, sell drugs, so they can make
enough money to buy Michael Jordan tennis shoes,
which cost about $160-$200. For a kid that doesn't
have the money in the first place. The parents don't
have the money. The shoe doesn't cost that much
to make. It's a set up, and this cat's on television and
acts out all these little things and gives the impression
that if you do what...?....you can make what...?
...understand...?
You got to go to a different level with that."

In spite of the recognized need for positive role models and the
effects of negative messages contained in the media there is also a
recognition that role models, alone, are not enough to solve the
problems of inner city young men. One volunteer staff person related
his own experiences growing up in a troubled neighborhood.

"I don't think there could ever be enough good role
models out there. Particularly now. We have a lot of
bad role models. I look at my situation and how I grew up.
I grew up in the mean streets of Brooklyn, New York
...in Bedford Stuyvesant. If you look at the conditions
in which I grew up, I wasn't supposed to make it.
A lot of times it depends on the particular baggage
that a youth may bring with him."

This particular individual completed four years in the U.S.
Marines, is currently finishing college, works full time, teaches martial

arts in the evenings, and is planning to enroll in law school. In his own words, he wasn't supposed to make it.

Communication

Closely related to the subject of relationships, communication is frequently mentioned as a factor influencing the lives of young black men. Communication has been mentioned in reference to several facets of social development including education, mental health and service planning. Two aspects of this issue stand out in the interviews.

The first aspect is the idea of communication as a form of expressing oneself, communication as it relates to speaking well. This issue centers around practical skills such as the use of language, vernacular and pronunciation. The lack of these skills are described as a hindrance to young people's ability to function outside of their own immediate communities, thereby interfering with education, employment and other critical areas of social development. The use of educated speech versus that of slang or dialect was described as an object of derision among young people at the center. Those who speak well or correctly were subjected to criticism from their peers as acting white.

The second aspect of the communication issue has to do more with the concept of expressing feelings and talking to people about problems. This type of communication can be perceived as therapeutic communication, and is more of an emotional need rather than a practical skill. This type of communication is recognized in programs designed to create a forum where young people can talk about their problems in community meetings thereby venting some of the frustrations of home, community and other critical needs.

"We also have community meetings which are held everyday during our school year. We have a community meeting and that's sort of like a big group session where the young people can talk about whatever. Current events, issues that are going on at home.

Some of the people came from homes where they didn't sleep all night. Where parents were fighting all night. Where ladies had to stay up all night so some man won't fall in their bed. Where crack heads were in their house all night doing drugs, where they were abused for some reason or another. So they had to come off of those, come from those homes.

Or they had to fight their way out of their neighborhood or what have you. Come from all these dysfunctional arenas to our center. This was a place where all that acting out would happen. We found that if we did something first, before class, the transition of going into class would be a little better, and they would be able to stay in the classroom. Pay attention a little more."

The lack of communication was described as a major barrier to recognizing and dealing with the needs of young men and youth in general. The "warehousing" of young people in schools, and other institutions was seen as a symptom of society's basic refusal to recognize the potential contributions of its young.

"My thought is that you have to stop warehousing young people and start to move in a direction where they can feel that there is a purpose or a reason, a rational reason for not selling narcotics and having hope. You're going to have to present that case to them sometimes on their level...No one communicates. It's not just tell you what to do and you go do it. It's not just that kind of situation. No one communicates. No one sits down and can exchange ideas and thoughts and no one perceives that these young people have the ability to have an exchange in an appropriate setting. And so you build this wall between these black youth and the society that they live in."

A philosophy of inclusion was seen as necessary for correcting these problems of communication and serving the needs of high risk youth. One staff member suggested that churches and community recreation centers could play a viable role in meeting the needs of troubled youth and that currently too few such institutions are meeting the challenge.

> "They're not playing a strong enough role in terms of letting these young people in and really working with them. Locks on the doors, locks on the gates to the churches, locks on the recreation centers, locks in places where activities could be present. At 6:00 or 7:00 o'clock in the evening there is no alternative for a young person after 7:00 o'clock but the library, and that closes at 9:00, so you force people into situations with that kind of environment. You must create an environment that is inclusive, that includes young people. And you must bring people in who have community with young people, have the desire, or have the ability to communicate with young people. And that's at any age. You'd be very surprised at people forty and fifty years old who can communicate with young people."

Education

Many of the center's programs and activities focus on education of one sort or another. As a major concern relating the perceived needs of young black men, education is not only a political issue, but also a primary area of program development at the youth center. Education also has some philosophical aspects that need to be explored. The educational program itself will be discussed in more detail later in this case study. Educational needs however were articulated by several staff and in a variety of ways. When asked to identify the most glaring areas of need for young black men in our society, Mr. Robertson, a tall professionally dressed man and executive director of the agency, specified education first, then employment, and then, family concerns....

> "There are three glaring needs that have been around for
> years that everybody should now know about.
> That is academic skills. That's a need they all have
> male or female. They don't have it. The school system
> is not doing it Employability skills. They are not
> prepared for the work force. The year is 1993, by the
> year 2000, blacks, African Americans, Hispanics
> will be the work force. They are not prepared for that.
> Then, basically, the family."

Another staff member was somewhat more direct in his account of the public school system.

> "The other piece is that the educational system is
> ridiculous. Here we are in the greatest country on
> earth and the educational system stinks. A public
> school system even the President won't send his
> daughter to."

An essential need in the area of education is the fine tuning of basic skills such as reading, writing, and communicating effectively. Most of the programs operating out of the center emphasize basic and fundamental life skills as a platform for achieving excellence. This broadly based approach to education is consistent with the comprehensive philosophy at C.Y.S. but is not typical of the public school setting. Instead, the center's educational approach combines practical instruction in basic subjects with the learning of survival and social development strategies. As in observations from the two previous sites the issue of education goes beyond basic reading, writing and math competencies. Education at C.Y.S. also involves learning how to be a parent, learning how to advance in your job, and learning how to control the anger that many young men inherit from their surroundings.

Educational deficit is a fundamental concern and it is coupled with self esteem factors sometimes associated with ethnic and racial identity. One of the educational instructors expressed his support for a multicultural focus in education, associating it with self confidence and the emotional well being of black students.

> "Those students that come to the Center come with
> great educational deficits. It's something that doesn't
> happen over night. It's something that happened to
> them in school as early as third grade. Being passed
> through the system and ultimately falling through
> the cracks, they've been allowed to move from grade to
> grade, sometimes graduating, without having the skill
> that was necessary.
>
> One of our strategies, dealing with that is to try and raise
> their educational levels by instructing them with resources
> and materials that depict blacks and the contributions
> they made."

When asked how this approach differs from the mainstream education and other efforts to develop cultural awareness that these young men and women may have already been exposed to, the response was...

> "It's a self esteem issue that we're dealing with over the
> years of working in the traditional educational system
> it is my belief that they could find no positive contributions
> by black people, other than the fact that they had been
> brought to this country by being slaves and working
> in that capacity in the cotton fields on over to
> industrial society."

There is a perceived notion that one way the educational system has failed is in legitimizing and recognizing the value of ethnic traditions and the contributions of non-European peoples to American culture. Recognition of American society as a pluralistic mosaic rather than a monolithic entity is a source of major concern especially as it applies to educational needs of black children. As a follow up comment to the above statement an inquiry about multicultural education efforts in public schools, the same educational instructor said...

> "Within the education system there has been a lot of
> work that has gone on, to try to change the curriculum
> to give more emphasis on multicultural kinds of resources.
> but up until now this has been done on a very small
> level, if at all."

One of the self defense instructors at the center's upstairs dojo, a martial arts training hall, clarified this point and simultaneously placed the issue of education in a historical/cultural perspective. While talking about the value of martial arts as a confidence builder which provides lessons for life, Sensei Turner expressed concerns about public schools and a philosophy of education which typifies the spirit of achievement stressed in the martial arts program and elsewhere at C.Y.S.

> "It doesn't necessarily have to be martial arts, as long as
> it's a place that's going to teach black youth who they
> are and what they need to do to educate themselves.
> Carter G. Woodson wrote a book in 1939 called
> *The Miseducation of the Negro*, and in that book he
> said that this education that we give here today is
> really the imitation of all things European. So we need
> our churches, our parents, we need these martial arts
> schools and any other organizations that are out there
> that are dedicated to helping these black youth out
> here, we need them all to teach from a black
> perspective, as to who we are.
>
> We have to become the center of that and take it from
> there. We need to get right down to education. I was
> reading something the other day. Words are truly
> so deep,...and I was reading up on the word 'education'

...and what I've learned is that 'education' has its root
in 'educere'. In Latin, 'educere' means to draw out,
or to lead out, to draw out from.

So that means that a proper education must start with
the assumption that there is something of value placed
within the individual at birth and the role of the parent,
the role of the teacher, the role of society is to nurture,
to develop, to coax out of that child that which is already
there. And it shouldn't be a process of cramming down
their throat some type of ... somebody else's course
just so they can regurgitate it on an examination."

Employment

Employment and the closely related issues of economics,
poverty and work are also important concerns. The fact that one of the
center's main programs relate to employment and job training is
indicative of the relative importance of employment as an issue.
Employment is associated with economics because it impacts other
concerns such as poverty, opportunity, career and hard work. One of
the most frequently mentioned reasons why young men come to the
center has to do with employment and jobs. One young man said that
he dropped out of the Jobs Corps because he "wasn't doing anything up
there."

The same person said he came to the Comprehensive Youth
Services Center to learn a variety of things including carpentry, drywall
plastering and how to do job estimates. The attraction of learning
management skills in addition to specific trade skills has an appeal to
young men at C.Y.S.C., some of whom are looking for opportunities
and have dreams of owning their own businesses. This observation is
also consistent with the entrepreneurial spirit promoted by the
employment training staff at the center.

Also the Summer Youth Employment Program, a federally
sponsored jobs project, was in full swing during the time of the

researcher's field visits. Approximately one hundred fifteen-year-old young men and women, from low income homes, were participating in summer youth employment training and related enrichment classes coordinated by a group of college interns supervised by C.Y.S. staff. The relative importance of employment can be best represented by the programs that the center offers. The philosophical and practical application of skills relating to and influencing employment is a common theme and will be explored in more detail when examining the weatherization program and other employment related projects.

Race and Ethnicity

The final group of issues that will be highlighted here are those which relate to race, ethnic heritage and race relations. Since the vast majority of people who attend the center are African American a great deal of discussion about race relations was not encountered unless the subject was intentionally brought up by the researcher. Whether this experience represents an outgrowth of the researcher's status as an outsider is not known.

The impression inferred by the researcher was that, within the relatively homogenous community, discussions about race relations emphasized affirming black people and black heritage rather than worrying about what white people do. Nevertheless, the subject of power relationships between black and white males was addressed by one staff member which might provide insights for people working across ethnic, racial and gender differences...

"I think the other side of the coin is that young black
males sense fear a mile away. Smell it, just like a lion
smells its prey. Females present that and white males
a lot of the times present that whole thing. And not
that you have to stand up to a young black male, but
certainly if they smell that kind of fear they will
manipulate that situation as much as they possibly can.
That is the difference in terms of the contrast between a
white young male and a young black male in almost the
same environment."

Whereas this generalization may not be applicable to all young black males, it represents an observation made by a man who has had considerable experience with troubled or high risk adolescents. The researcher interprets this comment as an observation that fear or discomfort, when working with people across ethnic, racial or gender differences, may contribute to barriers that inhibit positive communication and meaningful relationships. Additionally, the statement reflects an ongoing racial tension in our society that can be observed in more than just a few social situations.

The nature of frequent contacts between black and white men, when white men are involved in some sort of institutional role or other position of authority, was presented by the researcher as a potential barrier to communication. This suggestion elicited the following response.

> "It makes a good excuse for the kinds of problems that
> pre-exist and exist continually between blacks and
> whites, especially men. We're not seen as leaders,
> although we come from a generation of leaders and kings
> and governors and people who have learned languages
> and written books and have done great things in this
> world. We are not seen on that level. We are still seen
> as people who are very limited in our own abilities
> to do anything. Even though we have launched
> astronauts, and been mathematicians. We have seen
> political persons come from nothing to something.
> We are still not seen as leaders. We are still not seen
> as men who have great ability."

Mr. Smith, the educational supervisor, expressed his discontent with the way black people are represented in school curriculum and history books. He also professed belief in a white majority conspiracy to continue the oppression of black males through substandard education.

A third person expressed her exasperation with ongoing injustices experienced by young black men who, by expressing their frustration and rage, become victims of violence as frequently as they become victimizers. The general impression points to a consensus that race relations in our nation have deteriorated in the past twenty years rather than improved, and that aggressive action is needed to improve living conditions for urban minorities. Concentrating these efforts and organizing the resources of the African American community is one of the underlying principles for mobilizing on behalf of positive social change.

There is also a great deal of emphasis on ethnic pride, cultural heritage and black awareness. Black history and maintaining an awareness of African cultural influences has been expressed as a concern by several interviewees. References to maintaining an Afrocentric perspective and focusing on the cultural origins of black people in the United States demonstrate the perceived importance of racial and ethnic pride. Enthusiasm for African cultural heritage and racial pride is balanced by agency policies promoting nondiscrimination. There is an awareness of ongoing discrimination and racism in our society, and a desire to avoid the rekindling of new hatreds.

Philosophy

Philosophy codes at the Comprehensive Youth Services Center have been divided into three main groups, philosophies, values and principles. As previously defined, philosophies refer to broad ideological concerns. Values refer to notions of right and wrong, perceptions of good or bad, and statements regarding priorities. Principles refer to basic guidelines or parameters for program development. A more complete understanding of practice principles is probably best achieved in the context of the programs and related activities to which they apply. Entrepreneurship, for example, is more meaningful when considered in relation to job training and other employment activities. For this reason philosophical issues and values themes will be emphasized here. An expanded discourse on principles will be included in the examination of specific programs and activities.

Figure 8 depicts the different philosophical orientations that tend to guide program activities and perceptions of issues among the center's staff.

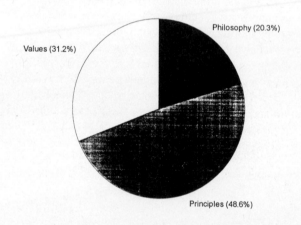

Figure 8. C.Y.S. - Philosophy Code Groups

Proactive Philosophy

Being proactive is an underlying philosophy professed by Mr. Robertson and is an idea that corresponds with what others might call a "can do" philosophy, or a positive focus. To be proactive is more than just agreeing to a principle. It is a philosophy that emphasizes action rather than reaction. It is an approach to viewing the world that is akin to the old saying that, "Actions speak louder than words." It is typified by the notion that if you see something you don't like, change it. A proactive philosophy emphasizes action over funding and human centered problem solving over programmatic constraints and bureaucratic limits. This is not to imply a sense of reckless activism, but rather a spirit of determination, persistence and dedication.

> *Mr. Robertson*: "We need to be proactive, to find out what do young people need, develop program around that and then find funds for that. What we do as nonprofits is, we find funding and try to develop a program that will match the funding. So we are reactionary instead of being proactive."

> *Researcher*: "So you would define proactive as seeing the need, going in, starting the work and then getting financial support once you've already entered the field?"

> *Mr. Robertson*: " Absolutely. That's what C.Y.S.tries to do."

A similar sentiment is reflected in a statement made by Ms. Debra Host, the program director, who talked about creating new programs at the center. When asked about the steps that she takes, Ms. Host related the following procedures.

> "We basically would talk about it. We'd talk about an idea somebody may have, talk about how it would fit with the staff. Generally, they will bring it to my attention. We'll talk about it a little further. Expand upon it. Come up with an idea. Present it to the executive director, who is very open, and if we think it will work we try it and see. Give it a try."

Being proactive is consistent with an attitude of empowerment and moving forward on behalf of positive change. These basic principles are embodied in the concept of ownership. Members at the youth services center are described by staff as owning the program. Rather than being merely a place where young people come (e.g. a helping agency), C.Y.S. strives to provide a vehicle by which troubled youth can help themselves. The distinction is subtle but the connotation can be made clear. Ownership implies having a voice. Presenting one's involvement in terms of membership, encourages a collegial quality to the relationships that exist between youth and staff. Young adults are there to be advised, to be listened to, to be guided. They are not perceived as clients who just come in for treatment. They are enjoined. They become members. They become people who belong.

> "When young people come to the center asking for
> services, one of the unique things about the center is
> that they don't just become a client but they
> become a member. So that they take ownership
> into the services and they take ownership into the
> building so that they are a member. They belong
> to something. They're not just somebody who comes
> on a regular basis. They take ownership in it."

The degree to which people buy in to the philosophy of ownership varies. It has a different effect on different people. Ownership bears a dual responsibility. If a member succeeds he is responsible for his own success. If he fails, he must own up to that failure. Rick, age 19, has apparently bought in to what they are doing at C.Y.S... He is employed in the weatherization program and his statement exemplifies what is meant by a proactive philosophy and the ideal of ownership.

> *Rick*: "I want to start my own business. They help you
> learn how to start your own business. Get a little pick
> up truck."
> *Researcher*: "If you could do or be anything what would
> that be?"
> *Rick*: "Be successful. Don't let anybody hold me back.
> Go forward."

In addition to owning his business, Rick's dream is to buy a house, get married and have children. Ownership, as a philosophy, seems to encourage self respect and competency. These qualities promote values and attitudes which are deliberately intended to instill emotional growth, motivate youth towards positive change, and inspire a renewed sense of an ability to achieve.

Serving

Another strong ideological position is the philosophy of serving. This orientation is demonstrated in a variety of ways. Giving back and serving are terms used at one of the previous research sites and they are both applicable to the ideologies expressed at C.Y.S. The idea of giving back is frequently associated with celebrities and famous people but also applies to a more sweeping notion of remembering your roots and helping those less fortunate than you. Giving back is closely related to the idea of returning and actively participating in the life of the community from whence a person has come.

One staff member at the center stated that "you've got to give back what you have or God will take it away, is my feeling." Giving back is not intended to imply simply providing charitable donation, instead it entails a hands on commitment and personal involvement. This observation is based in the assertion that black celebrities should go to the urban neighborhoods and engage people personally.

Service is also a basic approach to working with people. This concept is closely aligned with the ethical orientation of caring, an ethical notion that was frequently mentioned during the interviews. The philosophy of serving is at the core of the whole issue of providing services and is embedded in the very essence of the Comprehensive Youth Services Center's program identity. Serving is the guiding light which allows the agency to exist. It is reflected in the notion of child care, and each of the other services provided by center staff. At the heart of the serving philosophy is a commitment to non profit status and the basic policy that all services at the center are free to members. No fees are charged.

Services provided by the center are intentionally designed to be comprehensive in nature reflecting a holistic approach to serving the needs of youth. The wide array of programs serve a variety of needs, some of which are educational, while others relate to health, emotional needs, and employment. This holistic approach provides a rationale for encouraging young men and women to achieve excellence in their lives through acquisition of skills, recognition of their own abilities and the passing of important values. The intent is to assist them in achieving excellence whenever and wherever possible. At C.Y.S., service is simultaneously a philosophy, a duty, and a strategy.

Values

The exploration and clarification of values is a deliberate part of the C.Y.S. program, and is ingrained in the approach to service. The first thing a new member does after initial orientation is to participate in a values clarification workshop. One underlying theme in the exploration and articulation of values is clearly that values are reflected in the way people treat each other. Another way of saying this is that people communicate their values through their actions. The implication for having values clarification as an assessment strategy is to drive home the point that a person's values control his actions and his actions control his world.

Values comprise the second largest piece of the philosophical pie after principles. Many of the values conveyed during interviews apply to ways of relating to other people. Other values have to do with what might be referred to as character building traits. A third set of values might be labeled counter productive or negative values. Examples of each of these values-related code groups are provided and discussed based upon the comments and opinions of study participants. A full range of values-related codes can be found in Appendix 5.

Relating to People

Basic orientations about how people should behave towards one another provide the framework with which to define relationship values. Helping, trusting, caring, are three examples that imply a sense of cooperation and commitment to others. These values can be seen in the way the staff members characterize their individual strategies for working with youth. Trust and trust building is a counseling strategy which is described as a good starting place when establishing relationships with troubled youth, according to Sam, a popular substance abuse counselor.

> "Personally I myself want to feel a rapport with that individual, which is solely based on trust...that's one of the basic fundamental issues with most of the young people. There is a great deal of mistrust for one reason or another."

Ms. Pendleton, the mental health coordinator, reiterates this point by adding the following observation about a young man who was having some difficulty buying in to the idea of expressing himself during a values clarification workshop. When she was asked about his resistance she said...

> "I don't know if it's a macho thing. I don't know if I've got to prove myself. On the street, that's how they have to be. Or is it just because 'She's new' and, 'I don't know her' and, 'I don't really trust her yet so I'm not going to say anything.' That's kind of the way it is. I get some of that from the females, but mostly from the males. And I guess I say that because the majority are males that come here, and sometimes they haven't decided about me yet....which is fine with me, because I know where I'm coming from and, eventually, they do too."

Respect is also a highly valued commodity and is expressed in a variety of ways. Rules at the center are designed to encourage people to show respect towards one another in their daily interactions. One example of this is in the rules about using profanity. In the martial arts program respect is associated with discipline. In this context showing respect entails bowing and greeting people as you enter the training hall. Respect is also associated with self confidence, and discipline is associated with self control.

"You're learning how to vent out those angers and
how to replace them with something more positive.
So, I think of martial arts as not only doing the physical
thing, but it also teaches you discipline, confidence,
self-respect, respect for others, control and all those
different aspects that you would learn on a physical
level, you also learn on a mental level."

Kindness, patience and nonviolence are also terms that reflect
an ideal way of dealing with people or resolving conflict. Sensei
Akeem, the senior martial arts instructor, made an important comment
about nonviolence and the value of having enough self confidence to
"take low" by not having one's self esteem be easily threatened..

"Well, our philosophy in terms of violence... we teach
self defense, not just physical self defense. We teach
mental and psychological self defense...being able to deal
with situations before it escalates to the physical.
Although we train ourselves to be able to handle
physical situations, what we hope and pray is that
through learning the martial arts, people will be able to
better communicate with each other, to be able to
avoid situations that seem to want to escalate into
something that will become violent. So we teach people
how to use their heads, not their bodies, not physical
... mental skills.

Aikido is an art where you don't resist any force coming
at you. Use the other person's energy, strength, speed,
against him. And so that's what we try to do. If you talk
about my momma, I'm not going to get mad because I
know who my momma is. I'm going to laugh and smile
and turn away because I don't have to deal with that.
I don't have to fight you. I'm not going to fight you
because, again, I know who my mother is.
If you step on my shoe, I'm not going to make you

apologize to me. I might apologize myself, say
'Excuse me.' Because, again, I have self pride. I know
who I am. I can take low and be okay with that.
Whereas, with somebody else, they will probably
want to fight or be mad."

Character Building Values

Another values-related phenomenon emerging from the interviews is the emphasis on character building traits. These traits can be defined as personality characteristics that foster personal growth and enhance a person's opportunities for success. Personal growth values include concerns about morals, spiritual development, pride and self esteem. References to perceptions of manhood, black pride, and style relate to character building and personal development, as well.

Success oriented values include references to hard work, achievement, motivation and commitment. In a printed leaflet, provided for new members during orientation meetings, seven valued qualities were recommended as guidelines for success. These characteristics were stated and defined as...

Attendance:	The act of being present at school or work.
Punctuality:	The act of being on time at school or work.
Conduct:	To follow rules and demonstrate appropriate attitude and behavior.
Adaptability:	The ability to adjust or fit in to a different situation.
Preparedness:	The act of being ready to do something.
Reliability:	The act of giving the same result over and over again.
Follow-up:	To carry a task or assignment to its completion.
Thank you:	The act of acknowledging one's approval for support given.

Negative Values

The third set of values is especially important because these are values that serve to construct the barriers and obstacles preventing many young men and women from fulfilling the potentials C.Y.S. staff are trying to evoke. These beliefs and values are those that lead to counter productive or self destructive behaviors. Some of them may be unique to the urban social environment in which many of the program's participants find themselves, but others are best described as reflections of adverse value orientations in the larger society.

Examples of counterproductive values of the former type include a sense of hopelessness, anger, frustration and rage. An emphasis on survival, as opposed to success or achievement, provides another example. The notion of negative prestige, defined as developing notoriety through violence or intimidation, provides yet another example, and was discussed in reference to drug dealers as an explanation for violence in the community.

Counter productive values in the larger society are demonstrated in reference to tokenism and race relations. Materialism and commercialism are also referred to as negative values and philosophical perspectives interfering with the quality of life of black people. One person expressed the belief that black against black violence and male/female relations were adversely affected by a materialistic worldview.

> "As I look at black people, the black youth, they're
> killing each other out here on the streets and I'm
> saying to myself, 'Why is this happening?'
> A lot of this is over materialistic things. I remember in
> the 50's and the 60's we didn't have a lot of black
> on black crime. In fact black people had very little.
> But when we had very little we had an agenda that
> brought us a lot. Now we're living in a time when
> we have a lot, I'm talkin' materialistic wise. And now
> our agendas are bringing us nothing. So I think
> we have traded our spiritualism for materialism."

Regarding male/female relations, the same person goes on to say....

"And then they've got these new songs ...'Ain't nothin' goin' on but the rent.'...'You've got to have a 'J'...'O'...'B' ...if you want to be with me.' So yeah, we live in a materialistic society. You got the president going over and dropping bombs on people for materialistic things, for oil, or what have you.

Whether a black youth kills somebody for some tennis shoes on the street or the president kills somebody for oil in an Arab country, I think a life is a life and materialism is materialism. We can go from the top to the bottom, we live in a society that is very materialistic."

This respondent's observations mirror the nihilism described by West (1993) and the maladaptive behaviors described by Wilson (1991) in his causal explanations for adolescent black male violence. Recognizing their negative effects provides opportunities for diffusing the barriers they create. Defense mechanisms which encourage values that promote negative adaptations like machismo, bravado and egoistic self absorption might be confronted with strategic attempts to encourage positive counter balances such as effective communication, a sense of male responsibility and self respect.

One example of where this type of reframing takes place can be seen in the martial arts program. The basic philosophy of martial arts, as presented by one of the center's instructors is to promote self control so that violence can be avoided. He maintains that most of the young men coming to his classes know how to fight. What they often don't know is how to control their tempers. His emphasis in martial arts therefore is to teach people to cultivate self control through developing self confidence. This overall strategy can be described as the act of taking something negative and reshaping it into something positive.

Program

Programs at C.Y.S. are varied and deliberately comprehensive. Although relatively few activities specifically target males, the nature of the agency's mission and the social circumstances of the larger community work together in such a way that the majority of people who come to the center are young black men. Even programs that do not intentionally limit themselves to male oriented problems, tend to benefit young men as a group.

Strategies for program implementation reflect an emphasis on service with frequent references to practice principles such as listening , inspiring, assisting and mentoring. A brief overview of the basic programs offered at C.Y.S. includes educational services; employment services; mental health; day care; counseling; a medical clinic; and recreational activities. Additional services include family intervention, crisis intervention, group counseling and referral services.

An example of how less specialized, more inclusive, strategies still benefit young men can be found in the weatherization project. As a job training and employment opportunity the weatherization program hires and trains young men and women in energy conservation and construction trades. The weatherization programs include a long term for profit, subcontracting business in which center graduates can apply to become full time employees. There is also a short term training project in cooperation with the local office of employment services in which referred candidates are taught basic skills. A third aspect of the weatherization program is a low cost lighting installation service run in cooperation with the local power company. All of these activities are referred to by center staff generically as the Weatherization Program.

Neither of the three programs restrict participation due to gender, and one of the three job site supervisors is female. The nature of the work, however, tends to appeal to the traditional interests of males. More males seem to take advantage of this opportunity than do females. Other programs, more by circumstance than by intent, disproportionately benefit women. Child care services are available to all center members. Some fathers have made use of this service in the past, but it is more often used by mothers. The extent to which males or females benefit from certain services, tends to reflect the demographics of the community and the interests of the people being served rather than a policy or intent to favor one group over another.

The chart in Figure 9 represents the way various program codes have been grouped in order to better understand various aspects of program structure, development and implementation.

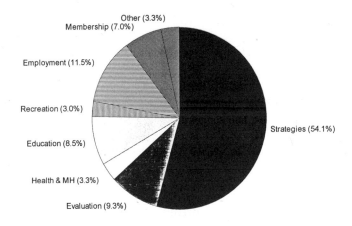

Figure 9.   C.Y.S. - Program Code Groups

Program Strategies

Without question, the most frequently identified aspect of program behavior has to do with the strategies that people use in order to be effective in the things they do at C.Y.S. This question was approached during the interviews in a variety of ways. People were asked directly about strategies, but were not always consciously aware of a deliberate process. When asked about what works for them or what advice they might have for others who are working with at risk youth, a different picture begins to emerge.

On the one hand the different program activities represent a mosaic of agency strategies designed to serve the needs of at risk youth. These include the way programs are structured, the organizational make up of the staff, their professional credentials and their various job duties. On the other hand different individuals have their own personal strategies as well. A brief list of the responses made by staff members, when asked about how they do their jobs, provides an interesting look at strategic approaches adopted by staff members independent of their individual job duties. (See Figure 10)

The code group labeled "what I do" is relatively small, but it is particularly revealing because the comments represent people's perceptions of how they conduct themselves during their daily interactions with youth. It includes comments made by staff members about how they build relationships with young people at the center. The codes seem to embody the sense of mutual respect and interpersonal communication that is central to many of the approaches thus far discussed. The list includes the following strategies: listen, inspire, manipulate, assist, hug, install, do paperwork, build confidence, direct, dialogue, and defuse.

Another important aspect of program structure is the collegial approach to professional relationships that seems to apply. Many if not all of the staff have multiple responsibilities. As a result, the authority structure at C.Y.S. seems to encourage a sense of equality and mutual respect. This observation is supported by several references to interdisciplinary case management practices at staff meetings. Ms. Host, the program director, also describes a family atmosphere among staff as one feature that makes the center attractive to youth.

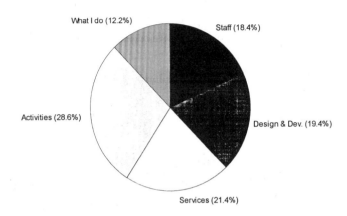

Figure 10. C.Y.S. - Strategies Code Groups

Orientation and Future Plan

Once a person enrolls as a member, he or she must participate in a five-day orientation process. Any Monday a potential member can come to the center and participate in a two-hour orientation meeting. Orientation includes testing for educational placement as well as an overview of services offered. If the prospective member decides to participate in the program he then returns the following Monday to begin developing a future plan.

During future plan the new member comes to five one-hour sessions, one each day beginning on Monday and ending on Friday. If the new member misses two sessions he or she must begin again. Future plan meetings are group oriented lectures and discussions that cover five basic areas. The first meeting is a values clarification workshop. The second meeting looks at environmental influences and the idea of achieving success. Day three covers the subject of communication. Career development is explored on day four and the final day involves a discussion of drugs and substance abuse.

After completing the future plan workshops the new member is scheduled for the first meeting with his or her primary counselor. During this interview they begin to examine the essential obstacles to the members achieving those goals he or she would like to accomplish. Together they develop a plan or strategy for diffusing those barriers and achieving those goals. This process having been completed, the new member and the primary counselor work together to accomplish the agreed upon goals. An Individualized Treatment Plan is created for each member and revised periodically, in an effort to inspire progress and to encourage growth.

Employment Services

Two employment related activities were in full swing during the three weeks that field observations and interviews were taking place. The weatherization program, is an ongoing energy conservation project described earlier. John Deer, the program coordinator, is one of two white males currently employed at C.Y.S. He is a soft spoken man in his mid thirties who says he has two undergraduate degrees, one in social work and another in theology. Mr. Deer said he grew up in the building trades since the age of 14 and worked in construction during the summers while attending college. He describes his trade skills as a meaningful supplementary source of income for his social work career.

Employment training has been a part of the center's services for almost nine years but recent funding from the Department of Employment Services has allowed for an expansion of these activities. Mr. Deer has been operating the Weatherization Program in its present form for the past two years. During that time, the center has trained approximately thirty young men and women. Ten of these ex-students are currently employed at the center in different capacities. The center has a very limited supply of construction related equipment. It is primarily the student's and staff's responsibility to acquire and take care of their own tools. These expectations are consistent with a philosophy of ownership and the principle of self help. Students and staff are expected to take responsibility for themselves.

One important goal of the Weatherization Program is to cultivate a sense of entrepreneurship. These work related activities are intended to cultivate employment experience as well as leadership potential. The concept of entrepreneurship is based on the principles of free enterprise, market values, and performance driven outcomes. The following quote from Mr. Deer reveals the nature of how these practical principles are applied to employment training at the center.

> "An entrepreneurial spirit is one of being able to instill
> in the young people the concept that they could run their
> own business. That they could become part of an
> organization or entity that they could put ownership into.
> A private, for profit type of enterprise they could become
> a part of, not only in a labor aspect but also in a
> management aspect. So, we tried this. At its inception it
> didn't really work too well and then, two years ago, we
> started the weatherization activity which provided more
> of an opportunity for young people to buy in to it, to
> learn a skill, to learn management of it, to be able to deal
> with vendors, subcontractors, and other organizations
> that were in the business."

Presently, they have three crews operating in the community simultaneously. They seal drafty windows and doors, install insulation, install energy efficient lighting and perform minor household repairs. Crew members also perform some building maintenance tasks at the center, under contractual arrangement. Employment related activities at C.Y.S. are intended to lead to career enhancement, not just hard skills training. In addition to installation tasks, participants are taught managerial skills such as inventory reconciliation, invoicing, and site inspection.

A second project sponsored by the Weatherization Program is also run in cooperation with the local power company. The power company project involves selling and installing compact florescent lighting as a means of promoting energy efficient lighting. Support from the power company comes from the receiving a reduced cost supply of low energy light fixtures which center members then market and install for a fixed rate per unit. Based solely on a free enterprise, performance driven model, this project provides opportunities for the development of meta-employment skills such as marketing strategies, personnel management and financial management.

The weatherization projects have become so successful that they have had to separate themselves out from the center's financial operations and maintain their own financial records. Interest in the weatherization and lighting projects among center youth has become so strong that there are not enough spaces available for permanent jobs, and Mr. Deer has had to find placement for people with contractors outside of the center. The fact that center graduates are competitive in the job market and that the program is doing so well as to be filled is described as a positive situation and a measure of program success. Another measure of success can be found in the story related by Mr. Deer during his interview. This is Joe's story.

> "A young man came through here about four years
> ago and sat down across the table from me.
> I said, 'Joe, why are you here at the center?'
> He said, 'Well, I couldn't make it in the Job Corps?'
> 'Why couldn't you make it in the Job Corps, Joe?'
> 'Well I complained.'
> 'Then what happened?'
> 'Well, I got kicked out of three Job Corps.'
> 'Well, we don't play here. If I accept you into this
> program, I expect you to be serious and get
> something done because, you know, you're already
> down for the count.'
> So he looked at me very seriously and said
> he understood.
>
> So he came in. At that time. Joe was selling crack,
> he was also using it. We were able to provide him a
> host of services here; drug counseling, some
> medical counseling and treatment.
> We were able to provide him vocational skills.
> He was the most serious young man I think I ever had.

He didn't have any foolishness about him. He didn't
mingle with the other kids and laugh and horseplay
and he finished the program.

We placed him with an employer. He stayed with
that employer for about a year and then he went on
to work with a health organization somewhere else.
He's been there ever since.
Got married, has a family. He has his life on track.
When he first came here he was on a downward spiral.
In the last six years that I have been here there
have probably been about ten of those cases."

Another employment related project that was in operation
during the site visits was fully separate from weatherization and
coordinated by Ms. Pendleton and the crew of summer interns she
supervised. The Summer Youth Employment Program (S.Y.E.P.),
sponsored by the federal government and administered by the city, sent
one hundred of the city's low income high school students to C.Y.S.
enrichment classes and to job work sites each day. Each summer the
center contracts with the city to oversee the placement of high school
students into jobs in the community. Although they had originally
expected seventy-five summer employment participants, at the last
minute they were asked by the city to provide spaces for twenty-five
more.

During the field visits, Ms. Pendleton, the mental health
coordinator, and her summer staff of college interns were working
furiously to accommodate the overflow. During the summer, when
regular membership enrollment is usually low, C.Y.S. contracts with
the city to help coordinate the Summer Youth Employment Program
(S.Y.E.P.).

College students are hired as summer interns to provide
support and help supervise placement of high school students in
summer jobs. They canvas the community for potential employers,
help train the youth for part of the day and check back with employers
to make sure things are running smoothly. Enrichment services,

supplemental education, drug awareness and other services available to C.Y.S. members are also provided.

Summer Youth Employment Program participants attend the regular Orientation and Future Plan classes just like regular members. They are provided with educational services and participate in the same basic assessment processes as do the regular members. Future Plan and Orientation for regular members was continued throughout the summer. Usually the groups were conducted separately, depending on the numbers in attendance.

All Male Discussion Group

All participants at the center are required to attend the traditional orientation and future plan curriculum before developing individual goals related to their enrichment activities. The all-male counseling groups in which the researcher took part were attended, primarily, by S.Y.E.P. youth. Two summer interns, Clarence and Jerry, led the workshop. Both wore clean white shirts and ties. They were both eager, intelligent, concerned young black men with high goals and aspirations.

Ten high school students, all of whom were young African American men, participated in the group session. The meeting was held in one of the second floor classrooms. The ten 15-year-old males sat in armchair desks, arranged in a semi circle. Clarence and Jerry talked to the group from in front of a blackboard.

Although a variety of topics were covered, the general focus of the discussion was centered around the value of education, hard work and achieving success. Both group leaders tried to emphasize the need for college athletes, or people whose dreams were to become professional athletes, to get an education. The emphasis was on taking advantage of opportunities to learn rather than allowing yourself to be taken advantage of by an athletic system.

One young man asked about running for President. This led to a discussion about voting, networking, and black politicians in general, including Jesse Jackson, Douglas Wilder, then governor of Virginia, and other black political figures. The discussion was lively and people seemed engaged. Both Clarence and Jerry seemed pleased with the level of participation that day. Their goal for the day seemed to focus on motivating the young men to take on leadership roles and not to fall prey to exploitation or false dreams.

One week later, the same two interns led another all male group wherein they tried to focus on the subject of race relations. They handed out a document entitled *Integration and Desegregation* and tried to engage a group of fifteen to twenty young men in a discussion about this subject. It was a very hot summer day and the group was on the floor of the third floor martial arts training hall. The air conditioning was not working. The young men took turns reading the handout aloud while others stretched out on the mats and closed their eyes. Several of them had difficulties reading some of the multisyllable words, such as "institution" and "rehabilitation." Others read in slow cadence and appeared to be struggling with the material. Finally, Jerry read the last paragraph and attempted to facilitate a discussion.

Clarence and Jerry seemed to be having trouble leading this group, and getting them to focus on the subject at hand. There was frequent whispering and lots of jokes being cracked. Later Clarence confirmed that he had felt some frustration with trying to lead the group that day due to their apparent lack of interest. Whether this was due to the heat or the topic is not known. Clarence attributed it in part to his style of communication but it seemed more likely to the researcher that the other circumstance were significant barriers to producing the desired results. Misjudging the group's overall reading and emotional maturity levels, might have also contributed to the difficulties.

When asked what was the perceived value of having an all male group Jerry, a college intern, said he felt that the young men could better express themselves without having women present. This was attributed to the fact that there was "no need to impress someone." He expressed disappointment over the fact that they had difficulty getting the young men to talk about the handout on integration versus desegregation and said that he thought that "many black youth don't feel that black history is important."

When asked about how well he thought the all male groups were going with the S.Y.E.P. youth in general, Jerry said he felt that the meetings needed to be more structured and controlled. He said that, because they did not consider themselves to be in school, it was "something they did not want to deal with." Clarence, the other group leader and also a summer intern, said he felt they were being tested. On two other occasions, during group meetings, the researcher observed more experienced, staff members in situations where it appeared they were being tested by young men who were reluctant or unwilling to participate. One event was discussed earlier and another occurred during a drug awareness session when one young man became quite vocal and agitated to the point where the group leader told him to calm down.

The All Male Medical Clinic

On Wednesday evening at five o'clock a community based free medical clinic operates out of a basement office set up for this purpose. Young adults within the specified age requirements for the center, can attend the clinic free of charge and receive primary medical services. The effort is made possible with the volunteer help of local physicians and medical professionals. Services include AIDS and other sexually transmitted disease testing, family planning, nutrition services, drug testing and basic health care.

Within the context of this ongoing service the observation was made that many of the young men were lacking basic medical and physiological knowledge. In spite of the streetwise stereotype and worldly image, many young men attending center programs were found to be ignorant about important medical issues.

"We have in the past couple of years, targeted an all
male clinic, when we have a male doctor. We see all
males and the doctor not only gives examinations, but
talks to the young men about safe sexual practice,
about growth and body changes, and those kinds of
things. It comes directly from a male physician and we
follow these young men for a period of time."

"A lot of these people are inner city youth and because
they seem to be so streetwise, some of them, it's just
assumed that they know everything that there is to know

about development and how to take care of themselves,
and the proper use of a condom and that sort of thing.
But it's not necessarily true. The assumption is very
false, and they need to know a lot of things they have
not been taught."

Education

Educational programs at C.Y.S. emphasize assisting people in preparation for taking the high school graduate equivalency diploma (G.E.D.), helping to correct basic deficiencies and remotivating young adults to pursue educational accomplishment. These strategies can include improving self confidence about educational achievement in a variety of ways. Instruction is based primarily on a small group model that allows for individualized attention. Individual volunteers are used as tutors when available. There are also opportunities for computer related skills development and the cultivation of computer literacy.

Each entering member is tested for educational proficiency during the orientation process. Standardized tests are used to determine reading levels and math skills. Following a determination of academic proficiency the member's Individualized Treatment Plan includes an educational component as a part of his or her program goals. Identifying and overcoming obstacles to educational achievement are an integral part of the holistic approach to serving young people's needs Efforts to provide guidance or resolution to those obstacles are part and parcel of the center's educational approach.

One male teacher stressed the importance of building self esteem and combining that with a caring approach to teaching discipline. He identified the perception that being highly educated is unmanly, as a major obstacle to academic achievement for black males. This same educator attributes this misconception to a scarcity of black men involved in primary education.

"..because there is no male, black male role models,
at all, in the educational and home environment,
...so in the absence of these role models, they tend

to think education, for instance, is for women only,
or its a sissy thing. So they shut off at an early age."

Changes in public education to combine African American
cultural education with positive male role modeling were seen as
potential solutions to this problem, by this male staff member.

Substance Abuse Counseling

Substance abuse counseling and treatment are services
provided at the center both through the medical clinic and as a part of
the future plan process. An outpatient drug counseling program was
created but was discontinued after one year. Sam, one of the substance
abuse counselors hired for that project, is still employed as a counselor
at the center but is planning to move to a more highly specialized
program in the near future. He led a group discussion on substance
abuse which focused on the hazards and temptations associated with
drug and alcohol addiction. The discussion group included one new
member but was comprised mostly of S.Y.E.P. youth. It was robust and
humorous presentation which Sam said he had toned down for the
younger youth. In the fall, when they tend to have older youth, the level
of awareness and actual drug involvement tend to be more serious. He
began the discussion by saying...

"Last week we identified substances. This week we're
gonna talk about cocaine. You're gonna tell me what
you know about it. I'm gonna tell you what I know
about it."

Sam handed out a booklet to the class of 18 males and 11
females. He talked to the group about the different ways people use
cocaine; snorting, free basing, and mainlining. He would ask someone
to read a page or paragraph from the pamphlet entitled *The Dangers of
Cocaine Use* by W.R. Spence. He led the discussion by using humor
and soliciting responses from different students as he spoke. Using a
dictionary, Sam asked someone to look up the word alkaloid, and then
had him read the definition aloud. All the while he encouraged

discussion and communication. He talked about male sexuality and addiction to sexual feelings. He talked about the differences between young men and young women with regard to their sexual feelings. The class concluded at 2:00 P.M. after an hour's worth of discussion.

During a previous discussion about drug education Ms. Host said that the substance abuse workshops sometimes need to be tailored to the group being served. Whereas many of the younger members of the S.Y.E.P. program may benefit from basic educational information, she expressed the feeling that older groups, with more experiences in the "drug scene" might be dealing with different issues and need a different approach.

In spite of the lost funding, Sam said that he still counsels with youth regarding drug addiction and drug use. Two publications were found on a table outside his office. The first pamphlet was entitled *Tips for Quitting Cocaine*, and although there was no indication of authorship for either of these works, the suggestions they offer are worth repeating. The first book lists ten important suggestions for escaping the shackles of the cocaine habit. The second pamphlet provides useful advise for staying clean and sober. This information provides young people with practical tools for fighting drug addiction and the knowledge that others fought these same battles in the past, and emerged victorious.

"Tips for Quitting Cocaine"
(author unknown)

Tip # 1. Stop using cocaine all at once, not gradually.
Tip # 2. Discard all cocaine supplies and paraphernalia
Tip # 3. Break off contact with dealers and users.
Tip # 4. Limit your access to cash.
Tip # 5. Structure your time to support abstinence.
Tip # 6. Identify your cocaine triggers.
Tip # 7. Stop drinking and taking other drugs.
Tip # 8. Identify your support network.
Tip # 9. Set reasonable goals.
Tip # 10. Stay clean. No matter what.

"Six Facts About Cocaine Cravings"
(authorship unknown)

1. Cravings are impulses or spontaneous desires to use cocaine.
2. Cravings are usually triggered by something people, place, things, feelings associated with your cocaine use.
3. Cravings tend to be strongest and occur most frequently in the first weeks after you have stopped using cocaine.
4. The intensity of craving does not fade merely with the passage of time, but as a result of not reinforcing the cravings with cocaine use.
5. Cravings are always temporary and tend to disappear quickly, especially when immediate action is taken to short circuit them.
6. Ignoring cravings is a poor defense against them.

Although he referred to a continuing need for drug counseling services at the center, Sam said that he felt the program they were doing was based on the wrong model. He said that an inpatient approach was not appropriate for an out patient program like C.Y.S. was trying to run. Because of this, he said that he felt the program was not as effective as it could have been. The researcher was unable to determine from subsequent interviews with staff, exactly what direction drug counseling at the center would take in the future. Drug awareness and drug education are still a part of the future plan and needs assessment process.

Recreation

Activities centering on recreational outlets are a voluntary but valued part of the centers program. There are recreational sports teams such as basketball and other less strenuous activities which promote informal relationships between students and staff. One counselor sees coaching basketball as a way to strengthen interpersonal relationships between himself and his counselees.

Ms. Host characterizes recreational activities at the center as being both structured and unstructured. Highly structured activities include different sports teams and the martial arts classes. Less highly structured activities include cultural outings such as trips to the movies and museums. These events serve an educational as well as an entertainment function. Exposure to culture and the broadening of horizons is a principal rationale for these activities.

In addition to the sports teams which are clearly attractive recreational activities for males, the martial arts program is perhaps the best vehicle encountered during this research for understanding the principle of providing strong African American male role models. Every Tuesday and Thursday evening self defense classes are held in the third floor training hall. Sensei Akeem, one of two martial arts masters who share the program leadership responsibilities oversee the Thursday night classes. Young men and women from throughout the community attend. Some are as young as six or seven years old. Others are preteens and some are merely young at heart. Adult men, women and children all practice together.

The style of martial arts taught at C.Y.S. includes aspects of karate, jujitsu and aikido. The latter is a unique form of self defense which emphasizes a philosophical approach requiring the practitioner to become in touch with a spiritual force referred to as "ki." This force can be conceived of as an inner power requiring total calm and mental relaxation to evoke. Practically speaking the aim of aikido is to teach students how to disarm their opponents by meeting aggression in the least violent manner possible. This discipline requires that the practitioner become mentally, physically and spiritually in tune with his or her inner strength. Self defense becomes dependent upon a passive response to violence which results in the aggressor's actions providing the source of energy for his or her own demise. Aikido could easily be described as passive resistance with an exclamation point or turning the other cheek with emphasis.

Both jujitsu and karate are martial art forms which tend to be more aggressive in nature but which also emphasize mental, physical and spiritual development (Hyams 1979). The sensei, a Japanese term for teacher used in martial arts, stands at the corner of the mat and tells his students to switch from jujitsu to karate to aikido during a sparring exercise. It can be likened to having a conductor change the symphony piece from classical to blues to jazz without missing a beat.

When asked about the rationale for teaching children who live in violence ridden communities a martial art and whether this might be construed as promoting violence, Sensei Akeem gave the following response...

> "Most of the time these young males are so angry
> because their lives have been screwed up, not just by
> society, but by family situations, that they don't have
> many communication skills.
>
> They have learned how to fight from the womb to the
> grave. So the martial arts system gives them a chance to
> take a look at another way. How to resolve situations
> without physical force.
>
> But yet again I say we do train to learn how to protect
> ourselves because everybody does not walk around
> in this society with the skills and knowledge we have.
> So again we are prepared to defend ourselves when
> it's necessary. But hopefully we will be able to do it
> without physical force."

During the course of one of the martial arts classes three little boys, ranging in ages from four to six, were playing and talking while the sensei, or teacher, was instructing another student. He stopped what he was doing and made them go to one corner of the room. They were told to remain in push up position with their full weight resting on their knuckled fists as is customary in many martial arts programs. One of the boys started looking over to his mother sitting near the entrance of the dojo, or training hall. Sensei Akeem said...

> "I told you once and Sensei Turner told you once and
> you didn't listen. I won't have that in my class.

Don't be lookin' over there at your momma.
Momma can't help you. You're mine now."

After one or two minutes, some of the boys began to falter. Sensei Turner, a black belt and Marine veteran, went over and assumed a similar position on his fisted knuckles, facing the small cadre of would-be warriors. As they struggled to resist the temptation of propping themselves up with their knees, their backs arching and their bellies sagging towards the floor, he exhorted and encouraged them saying...

"Hang in there! Be tough little brother. You can do it!"

After about five minutes Sensei Akeem let them get up and return to the mat to join in the practice session. One little boy was pouting with his lower lip stuck out and his head hung down. He was not the youngest of the three and was probably about six years old. Sensei Akeem said...

"Hey! You see that expression you got on your face there. That don't mean nothin'. Hold your head up! Change that expression! Change that expression!"

After class everybody exchanged bows and hugs. On the way out the researcher overheard the same little boy saying to Sensei Akeem,

"Practice makes perfect, don't it sensei? You have to strive for excellence. That's what I do."

The boy was six years old. He stood about four feet tall. He was learning basic principles and important lessons about self discipline, perseverance, striving for excellence and personal development. If he learns these lessons well, one day he will stand ten feet tall. When asked about this incident, which was far from an unusual event during the martial arts classes the researcher attended, Sensei Akeem said...

> On one hand I have to do that because I know his
> potential. I know what he can do. If I allow him for
> one moment to just cave in, then I've failed him and
> I can't do that. So I got to do whatever I'm supposed
> to do to raise him up to that level of excellence.
> 'Go over there on you knuckles. This ain't because
> I'm mad at you. I am not mad. I need you to refocus,
> so that you see what's goin' on. I ain't mad. I love you.'
> I'm going to give him a big bear hug. 'I love you.'
> So when he leaves, he knows that sensei loves him,
> that sensei cares about him. 'No matter what he made
> me do, sensei gave me a big hug.' So he can say
> when he leaves, no matter what he is thinking, he'll say
> ...'Well, sensei gave me a hug.' "

Program Evaluation

Whether a particular program is as good or bad as it should be is a subjective evaluation. Criteria for measuring outcome are not always as objective as might first appear. Program evaluation was found to be an important consideration at C.Y.S. because many of the program activities are evaluated by funding sources with continued funding being contingent upon an acceptable evaluation. The process includes detailed reporting and measurement of specific indicators that are designed to calculate program outcome and effectiveness. According to the center's executive director, evaluation criteria do not always adequately represent program effectiveness, especially as it relates to high risk youth.

Ms. Host suggested that a more appropriate way of measuring program effectiveness is by looking at improvement, such as academic growth. Attendance is also seen as an indicator of whether people are getting something out of the programs. Some programs are easier to document in terms of contractual success. One example of this is the employment programs. Securing outside employment is a clear and tangible indicator of success. The educational program is more difficult to evaluate unless people achieve their G.E.D. This year eleven people passed their G.E.D. tests, receiving general equivalency diplomas. It is more difficult to measure academic progress for among those learning more rudimentary skills.

Mr. Robertson refers to the concept of creaming wherein evaluation criteria are such that many agencies screen out youth who are thought to have low potential for success, in order to meet the pre-ordained objectives for program evaluation. The Job Training Partnership Act and the regulations governing continued funding was mentioned as a prime example of a program that, due to its evaluation criteria, automatically excludes high risk youth.

> "I think we're somewhat effective, but society does not
> allow us to be effective at serving those that have the
> most critical needs, simply because funders today want
> to see some tangible evidence of a positive impact
> of their funds. In order to show positive impact,
> they're looking at 'Did they achieve their G.E.D.?',
> 'Did they increase their academic skills by one grade or
> two grades?', 'Did they get that job they were looking for?'
> Something very tangible. For high risk youth, who are
> selling drugs, on drugs, coming out of dysfunctional
> families, one parent families, no parent there at all,
> being in the criminal justice system, ...as long as they
> feel good about themselves after they go through C.Y.S.,
> that's something very positive.
> How do you measure the impact of that?
> If they come to class everyday and even though they
> haven't attained any higher education level,
> they're coming, whereas before they weren't coming.
> That's something positive. So for us to be able to
> measure the smallest successes and for that to be
> satisfactory to the funders is most difficult.

J.T.P.A. is an example of one side of that.
The Job Training Partnership Act was funded by the
federal government to help young people gain
employability skills so they can get jobs.
Well, you take a young person who has dropped out
of school for the last five years, off the streets and
try to put him in a training program, for him to come
everyday, learn everything and within six months to
graduate and get a job. That's a very difficult thing to do.
If you don't do that and you've said you're going to,
under the contract you've failed."

Lessons and Reflections

The importance of relationships, in terms of building trust,
positive examples and a general support network is solidly supported by
the findings at C.Y.S. Many of the strategies for counseling and the
values conveyed by staff during program activities have to do with
relationship building. Developing supportive interpersonal relationships
with significant adults and family members is a highly valued priority.

A general belief and faith in the ability of young people to
know what is good for them when provided with reasonable alternatives
from which to choose, is another operating principle. This fundamental
assumption is supported by a proactive philosophy which empowers and
encourages people to take control of their lives. This empowerment
model can be seen in the concept of ownership exemplified by the
membership approach to providing services. It can be observed in the
concept of performance driven outcomes found in the employment
training program as well.

Needs assessment and program evaluation strategies at the
center are also conducted by involving young people in planning and
goal setting. Evaluating program success and overall effectiveness
involves the recognition of individual growth based on relative progress
for individuals as well as using more traditional evaluation criteria. An
inclusive approach to program planning was exemplified by the
minority male consortium retreat, where young black men participated

in needs assessment and program planning. The importance of program evaluation which is grounded in realistic individualized strategies can be observed in the previous discussion about evaluation and in the policy of developing individualized treatment plans for all center members.

Principles guiding different program structure and design are consistent with a philosophy of caring and community service. They promote self help and individual achievement. These goals are accomplished through a highly professionalized cooperative effort which utilizes community volunteers, sophisticated fund raising strategies, and a philosophy of ownership which permeates the program design. Youth at the center are encouraged to take control of their own future and to plan the outcome. They are discouraged from perpetuating negative adaptations to what is frequently viewed as a hostile but not impossible social environment.

The Comprehensive Youth Services Center is structured to provide a comprehensive array of organized services to high risk youth. The agency's goal is to make programs available in a single location and thereby facilitate positive growth towards personal success for its members. These services include mental health, education, recreation, employment, child care, medical care, and a network of support that provides personal relationships with adults who serve as mentors, advisors, counselors and examples. An inclusive and nondiscriminatory philosophy at C.Y.S. precludes too heavy an emphasis on programs that are not available to all members. Nevertheless, there is a general recognition of needs that are gender specific. Services for young black men are available but they are usually not reserved only for men. Exceptions to this rule are found in the all male clinic, the male discussion groups and the development of a community wide consortium to assess needs and develop services in the future.

The lesson to be learned from this site is that there is a need and there is the will to change. Youth would not come if they did not have the desire for something better. Certainly many people are coerced to attend by courts and probation officers, but others attend voluntarily and some thrive. Young black men make up the majority of people who attend the center's programs.

Many young adults have responded to the offerings provided at C.Y.S.. Some have done so more vigorously than others, but still even extremely troubled youth have been changed. Many of the quotes and references in this case study attest to that fact.

The members of the Comprehensive Youth Services Center recognize the dangers they face. They have witnessed the violence and the drugs. They have felt the frustration and difficulties associated with finding meaningful work. Those that buy into the center's activities have discovered a meaningful alternative to the temptations of the street. They enjoy the company of their peers and the leadership of older adults who listen and who care. Some of them even seem to enjoy the idea of somebody "gettin' on" them when they don't "do right."

They have witnessed the examples of men and women who have resolved to make a difference in their community. These relationships and the experiences that emerge from membership at C.Y.S. promotes self-determination and planning for the future. These young men and women are planning for a future that many of them felt had little promise but which is now rich with possibilities.

Chapter 7: Conclusions

The framework established for this research examined three domains of program planning. The first question was one of issues. In remaining consistent with the constructivist methodology, the research sought to explore the relevant issues as understood by people intimately involved with the problem. This can be described as a needs assessment from an idiographic point of view.

The second domain was that of philosophy. This aspect of the inquiry focused on how people construct their perceptions of the problem. It asked what point of view has been applied to understanding the problem. Understanding the philosophies that govern the perceptions and behaviors of people who are directly involved with a problem is seen by the researcher as an important first step in creating solutions that fit.

The third domain of research interest was program design. Program was operationally defined as the practical applications and strategies people use to confront the issues. They consist of individual practice techniques as well as general guidelines for broader activities. By applying this threefold approach to understanding program rationale, it was possible to create a framework which may inform policy development.

The important questions to be answered are what is the problem; how is it understood; and what should be done in light of that understanding? Program evaluation and policy review, then, becomes a matter of answering the question: how well do proposed solutions meet the needs, as they have been defined? The answer to this question depends to a large extent on what criteria are used and what expectations have been established.

The literature review for this study described how socialization takes place within the context of community. It looked at different agents of socialization such as schools, family and peer groups and described some of the psycho-social processes that occur in order for people to assume productive roles in their communities.

One observation across all three sites has been the theme that, for many young black men, traditional social institutions are not serving them well. Families are handicapped by absent fathers, drugs and financial difficulties. Schools are not always effective in teaching children, especially black children, the things they need to know. Peers and informal community networks frequently provide negative models for adjusting to the pressures of growing up amidst urban poverty, crime and violence.

One traditional institution which has served African American people well has been the church. The literature describes how African oral, mythological and religious traditions were passed on by holy men and women (Herskovitz 1958; Mintz and Price 1976). The history of the civil rights movement also attests to the historical role of religious leadership in the black community in the form of Martin Luther King Jr., Ralph Abernathy , Malcolm X and others. For this reason it should not be surprising that efforts to address the crisis of positive social adjustment for young black men in the 1990's are being carried out within the context of black churches. Only two examples of church related programs were discussed in this report. A host of others could have been provided. The sampling challenge was one of finding non-church affiliated programs, in order to provide some philosophical variety, as secular perspective.

The findings were presented in a framework that is designed to provide key areas of focus in order to heighten the readers' understanding. The distinction between issues, philosophies and program is not always a rigid or solid line. These categories are artificial constructs designed to guide the discussion and intended as tools to aid understanding. The essential themes guiding the research were a description of important issues; indications of the philosophical understandings brought to bear on those issues; and illustration of program efforts to provide guidance and structured leadership for young black men attempting to deal with these issues. Each case study has attempted to demonstrate how this relationship between issues, philosophy and program unfolds within the context of the communities in which they take place. Each program must be understood as a product of the community from which it is derived.

Transferability of the findings depends largely on whether the receiver of the message, the reader, can find observations in the case studies that apply to his or her own situation. Whether he or she chooses to replicate program activities in a different setting is a judgment the reader will have to make. The author has attempted to make this decision easier by providing the thickest possible description of three unique situations.

Prevention: The Tie that Binds

The findings in the case studies, both support and refute certain aspects of the literature. Field observations indicate that the broad based issues found in the literature review are clearly reflected in the perceptions and sentiments conveyed by study participants. The commonalities at each site are strong with variations that seem to reflect local conditions rather than fundamental differences of opinion.

A common thread running throughout is the unstated ideal of prevention. Prevention is necessary because of the dangers of coming of age in a hostile environment. The problem then becomes one of socializing young black men to be able to resist the negative temptations confronting them in high risk urban communities and the larger social environment. These temptations stem from a host of environmental influences, some of which they have control over, and many of which they do not.

Each program is designed to prevent these negative influences in young people's lives from usurping their future opportunities. Prevention applies to school failure. It applies to drug involvement. It applies to premature parenthood, and it applies to the dangers of becoming disconnected from the vision of future possibilities. Figure 11 illustrates the author's perception of how the relationship between issues, philosophy and programs have been combined in these cases to create preventive approaches to serving the needs of adolescent black males in high risk settings.

Concerns, interests and needs interact within the context of the social setting to help people shape and identify important social issues.

These factors comprise the total environment within which policy decisions and program planning takes place. They lay outside of the realm of program structure and design but constitute the milieu within which decisions take place. Perceptions and priorities are, then, defined regarding the relative importance of issues as determined by existing philosophies and worldviews. Once people have applied their own unique understanding to the problems at hand, attempts to find solutions are brought into play.

Observations from the different sites also support the idea that the boundaries separating issues can best be described as fluid. They change shape depending on the social climate and critical needs of the day. Though a basic structure is maintained variations occur over time and space. Issues may differ from person to person or from site to site yet basic similarities are sustained   With these fluid and dynamic processes in mind a theoretical model for program design and program fit has been created.

Programs suggested in the center circle of diagram are examples of the types of approaches used at the sites and correspond with the larger issues as defined in the outer circle. They are not intended to represent all of the possibilities The straight lines in the center circle demonstrate how rigidity in program design may conflict with community needs, thereby creating a lack of fit between structured services and the nature of important issues. The challenge of program design emerging from this study is to create enough flexibility to match the fluid nature of the social world without losing the structure or integrity of the program's original vision.

Wavy lines separating issues represent changing events, circumstances, and issues endemic to any social environment. This fluid nature is evident in numerous common themes identified during the research. For the sake of simplicity, only a few of these common themes have been selected. The model's intent is to provide examples for stimulating reflection and planning.   Interested readers are encouraged to apply their own issues, programs and philosophies to the design, identify the boundaries and employ their own notions of flexible program structure.   The purpose of this is to assist in that effort, not to dictate it.

Figure 11. Theoretical Model for Program Design and Program Fit

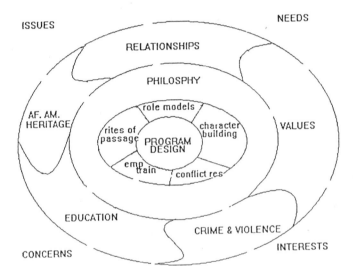

Boundaries separating basic issues are perceived as being semi-permeable (Falck 1988), firm in places but not impenetrable. Breaks in the lines separating the various segments of the diagram represent this open-ended quality in to the nature of the issues found in the study. They are discreet concepts but they are subject to constant influences from several directions. Values, for example, are influenced by education, which in turn may impact, or be impacted by relationships. Constructivist inquiry supports the concept of a dynamic and changing social world. For this reason the model should be envisioned as a spinning, moving representation rather than a static picture, transfixed in time, space or place.

Observations from the field indicate that inflexibility in program structure, such as funding limits, eligibility concerns, and evaluation criteria, can result in a failure to meet the needs of the most critically needy constituents. Conversations and interviews with study participants suggest the need for flexibility in program structure sufficient to match the fluid nature of changing issues in a dynamic social world.

Cross Site Findings

Common themes found across the various sites should also be examined in terms of the three foreshadowed research questions. They include an emphasis on positive relationships, education, and personal achievement combined with a holistic or comprehensive approach. Efforts to provide structured services occur in the context of creating a sense of belonging and membership, coupled with the passing on of key values such as respect, responsibility and community service.

Issues

Relationship Building

The importance of relationships, and how they play into the positive adjustment of young males is a critical concern. For many of the young men, the most influential and admirable person in their lives is their mother. The opposite side of this coin is the issue of absent fathers. Numerous references were made regarding the negative consequences of fathers being absent from the homes and the lives of young men at the centers. Staff and youth, alike, referred to problematic concerns regarding the absence of fathers. As strong and positive as the relationships with mothers seems to be, paternal relationships are equally compelling. Those young men whose fathers live at home seem to appreciate the value of that arrangement.

The importance of family relationships is reflected in frequent comments about parenthood. The responsibility of parents towards children is graphically portrayed in the group interviews with the Diamond Hill girls and their perceptions about what to do with child abusers. Similarly, the needs of teenagers who are already parents is an implied rationale for development of the child care program at C.Y.S. Each program attempts to systematically convey messages about parental responsibility, parenting and family values.

Family members, other than parents, such as aunts, uncles, grandparents and older siblings also provide an important means of social support. Center staff, teachers and coaches are frequently in positions to positively influence the lives of these young men as well. At each site, specific examples can be observed where key personnel are serving as important role models for young men of different ages.

A statement by one C.Y.S. staff member that "no matter what you do, you will have an effect," is a particularly ominous message. This comment recognizes the fact that young people have the final say in whom they choose to emulate. The implication is that helping professionals can have negative influences on personal growth by being overly judgmental, inaccessible or just poor examples. This assertion underscores the importance of human relationships and the value of productive, positive and caring role models.

Role modeling is an important aspect of relationship building. Role models can come from diverse backgrounds, and the process does not necessarily stop with adolescence. The observable consensus is that more black men are needed as mentors and or professional counselors, but there are also references to valued relationships developing across multiple social boundaries such as age, gender, race and sexual preference.

The subject of relationships also extends to male/female relationships and they affect family, attitudes about love, caring, mutual support and responsibility. Problems regarding marriage, sexuality, pregnancy and AIDS are additional concerns affecting male/female relations.

Education and Employment

An issue common to each of the three research sites is the primacy of education as it relates to both school and career aspirations. Addressing perceived deficiencies in the educational system and providing support for school achievement is a basic program element. At C.Y.S. these same educational goals carry over into the realm of employment training and complement efforts to develop marketable skills.

Broadly based enrichment activities where young adults are exposed to cultural experiences and learning opportunities are seen as an important part of the educational curriculum. Activities, such as museum trips, guest speakers and field trips to cultural events, are designed to promote educational experiences and make learning fun. The goal for these activities is one of expanding horizons in order to make young people aware of their future possibilities.

Young men who are attending school are persistently encouraged to strive towards academic achievement. They are encouraged to either help each other or get tutoring help from available adults. Those who have left school, as is the case for most C.Y.S. members, are assisted in furthering their basic education while also learning new career skills.

The findings indicate that, in some cases, the young men are rising to the challenge, especially when an atmosphere of mutual peer support is promoted. The Concern Committees of the Bunker Hill Young Marines are an example of how peer support can stimulate academic achievement. Older youth encouraging and helping younger youth at the Diamond Hill Development Center is another model which promises mutual benefits. At all three sites, academic assistance is an ongoing program concern and continuing need.

Coping with Drugs and Violence

A third common theme found at each of the research sites is the pervasiveness of drugs as a social problem and the violent crime with which it is associated. Although people did not frequently dwell on the subject of drugs and violence during the interviews, there is a constant awareness of their dual presence in the community. Frequent casual references to drug related experiences, shootings, drug dealers and other related societal evils are documented in the field notes. Two of the three sites have active drug counseling programs. The prior history of the Bunker Hill Gardens apartment complex and the interview with one Young Marine's mother about peer pressures to take drugs, confirms this observation.

Frequent references have been made to young people witnessing or experiencing tragic acts of violence. Efforts to teach and promote alternatives to violence can be found in program activities promoting conflict resolution skills, counseling as a means of venting pent up anger, and martial arts a means of learning discipline and self control. Related to the subject of violence is the problem of constant negative stereotypes associated with young black men both in the media and in the community. Media violence and the depiction of aggression as synonymous with masculinity is described as shaping adolescent opinion and behavior by placing a high value on expressions of violence as an alternative to frustration and rage.

Philosophy

The Holistic Approach

A holistic or comprehensive approach to program design was found at all three centers. Each program offers a broad range of services designed to fulfill a variety of social concerns. Although the centers are fundamentally different in many respects, they all emphasize a balanced approach to serving the needs of black youth. Where they tend to differ is in the specific ways they attempt to serve and in the ways they develop resources.

The holistic approach also includes the idea that a person's needs are interconnected. Educational needs cannot be addressed independently of emotional or physical needs. Financial needs, such as getting a job, are dependent upon interpersonal skills, such as communication, as well as vocational skills. Health needs can get in the way of economic needs, and spiritual needs can interfere with emotional needs. This perception of interconnectedness is central to the rationale for creating broadly based, comprehensive, or holistic programs rather than highly specialized approaches.

The Diamond Hill Development Center includes Rites of Passage activities as an integral part of an overall youth program which emphasizes intellectual, spiritual and social development. The center provides an environment which represents an alternative community designed to encourage school performance, enhance social development and promote spiritual growth. This end is achieved by providing a variety of opportunities and activities which are designed to stimulate, challenge, entertain and reward young people for positive growth.

By including Rites of Passage in the overall youth program at the Diamond Hill Development Center the program embraces an aspect of teen age development that centers on gender sensitive concerns. It emerged as an essentially spontaneous approach which provides a forum for young men to discuss and explore issues that they may have difficulty bringing up in a co-ed setting. These concerns include topics such as male/female relations, sexuality, fatherhood, masculinity, and other potentially sensitive subjects. Recognition of the need to provide such a forum is, in itself, an example of holistic emphasis.

The Bunker Hill Community Outreach Center also incorporates a holistic or approach by emphasizing mind, body, spirit and community. The highly structured program includes a formal creed, homework help, a sports team, spiritual development, and community service. The Young Marines emphasize character building by teaching values, such as respect, discipline and caring. They provide a solid base of social support in an effort to encourage young men to resist the negative temptations of drugs, crime and other self destructive behaviors.

The Young Marines represent one aspect of an extensive community organization plan developed by Reverend Knight and provide an example of how a small group of adults can make a big difference in the lives of youth in a community. The experiences of the Bunker Hill Young Marines demonstrate the willingness of many young black men to respond to positive male leadership, given the dedication and commitment of someone like Bobby Petrie, and the moral support of the community.

At the Comprehensive Youth Services Center the emphasis on holistic development includes a commitment to comprehensive services provided under one roof. Whereas strategies at the previous two sites are on primary prevention, C.Y.S. specializes in secondary prevention by working with young adults who have already been in trouble, either in school or in the community. The center's services focus on educational deficits, counseling needs, health needs, family concerns, and career development. To a lesser extent, spiritual and recreational concerns are also addressed. These efforts are accomplished by means of a highly professional staff with an interdisciplinary, cooperative approach. All services are free of charge and provided under one roof, but expectations are high. They demand positive growth and individual achievement.

Inclusion versus Exclusion

Another similarity found at the three research sites is their attempt to assess needs as they pertain to young men, and provide services targeting young men without excluding or ignoring the needs of women. None of the centers serve only young men. All have made efforts to include females in some way without ignoring the differences in needs and interests traditionally expressed by men and women. A dynamic tension emerges between recognizing certain problems as being gender specific without creating programs that are exclusive or discriminatory. Diamond Hill has a girls' group counterpart to Rites of Passage led by Ms. Cheryl entitled Girl Talk. This same approach is used at C.Y.S. where they have all male and all female group counseling sessions as well as gender specific health care.

The Young Marines has incorporated young ladies into its program, but has not quite determined how to achieve a balance. This observation is exemplified by the fact of disproportionate male membership and recognition of the need to develop more program activities for girls. Since many of the people who provide community support for the Young Marines are women, this should not be a difficult obstacle to overcome. The potential for cultivating female leadership is great and the need to develop more community support has been recognized.

Spiritual Development

Spirituality was an issue expressed as part of the holistic approach. Two out of the three sites are directly affiliated with churches. This fact arises more out of circumstance than by sampling design . During the course of networking to find appropriate research sites, several other potential sites were church affiliated. Spirituality was also expressed in reference to Afrocentric philosophy and martial arts training.

At C.Y.S., which is not church affiliated, two of the interviewees called for higher levels of involvement by churches to help alleviate urban problems such as providing constructive recreational opportunities for youth. Religious commitment was given as a rationale for developing programs and performing community service. Clearly the church is seen as a potential resource and important institution for mobilizing communities on behalf of positive social change. It is assumed that religion is important not only because of the additional resources churches can bring to bear but also because of a perceived value in having a spiritual component in one's life.

Membership and Ownership

Membership is a fundamental principle at each of the three research sites. Linked to this notion is the idea of belonging, mutual responsibility and ultimately, ownership. When someone takes ownership over something there is a sense of empowerment. As represented by center directors and staff, this sense of empowerment leads to taking responsibility for one's own future.

The success or failure of each center depends largely on its membership. Conversely, the success or failure of any member depends on his or her performance in the program, in school, at work or in life. The concept of ownership is exemplified by the term "performance driven" used by the employment coordinator at C.Y.S. This phrase assumes that people must take charge of their destiny by taking dynamic action, and performing at a high level of achievement.

The fact that the challenges, obstacles and barriers are great is recognized by all. Performance driven connotes an emphasis on achievement rather than training. Job training implies getting ready to do something. Performance implies achievement beyond mere preparation. The "entrepreneurial spirit" implies that people go out and bid for jobs, even create jobs where they previously did not exist. Ownership, in this context, is the difference between trying and doing. Membership promotes ownership.

The Challenge of Values

A philosophical and practical challenge for each of the programs in this study is that of balancing out negative realities with positive values. This concern corresponds to the idea of teaching cherished values in an effort to ward off the negative influences of the streets. A fundamental struggle over basic values is reflected in concerns over the breakup of families, negative messages from the media, commercial exploitation and the agony of urban violence. This struggle to sustain a positive focus on principles like community pride, cooperation, love, and legitimate aspirations, are at the heart of the conflict. These are binary opposites to the forces of nihilism (West 1993) and anomie (Merton 1968).

Each of the centers has devised strategies to promote cherished values in response to social conditions that foster frustration, anger and despair among young black men. Problems of racial injustice are confronted by applying educational strategies which promote awareness of valued traditions, cultural heritage and a sense of ethnic pride. Each of the programs attempts to instill character building qualities such as discipline, personal responsibility, and appreciation for the benefits of hard work.

Program

Common program themes include a recognition of of the need to address problems of education, values clarification and relationship building. All three sites have established multiple activities designed to provide positive recreation, and community support from responsible adults. There is an emphasis on experiential education, as it relates to employment, as it relates to expanding young peoples' knowledge about career opportunities, and as it relates to their understanding of the larger world outside their own communities. Program efforts include field trips that enrich basic education and expand global knowledge.

Improving employment potentiality by developing meta-employment skills is also valuable. A solid commitment to developing practical job skills and market competitive abilities is clearly observable at each center.

Crime and violence in each setting impacts people's lives significantly. Strategies to avoid the temptations of becoming involved in criminal activity are employed. Efforts are made to address this issue by providing an alternative community which provides practical opportunities and emotional support. In that setting, group and individul counseling efforts are employed, adult participation and guidance is available, and recreational activities are provided. At two sites youth are expected to participate in community services and in all cases they are expected to assume group values and norms exemplified by structured rules of behavior.

At the Development Center, youth participants go on field trips, discuss concerns in group meeting and are afforded opportunities they might not otherwise enjoy. The Bunker Hill Young Marines have similar opportunities and provide meaningful peer support through their Concern Committees and their recreational basketball team. At C.Y.S. young adults are provided with a professional agency that offers a variety of services designed to address many of the same issues relevant to slightly younger participants of the other centers.

The clientele at each of the three sites is overwhelmingly African American. This fact is not by design so much as it is a reflection of the population of the communities the programs serve. In each setting the programs designed to meet the needs of young men also provide opportunities for young women. Efforts to meet the unique needs of young black men are tempered with a commitment to inclusion and nondiscrimination. Each of the three sites have developed programs that function under the umbrella of a community based center. The concept of a center entails the notion of an organization providing a wide range of services in a central location.

Finally, there is a pervasive recognition of the need to provide positive male role models for adolescent black males whose fathers are absent from the home. Whether this need results from the breakdown of the nuclear family, drugs in the community, racial oppression or some other cause, is not readily agreed upon. What is agreed upon, however, is that there is a need to provide positive, caring, dependable male guidance for many young black men living in the communities that these programs serve. How to accomplish this task is yet another problem. It is generally agreed that role models need not be fabulously successful entrepeneurs, sports stars or media personalities. In fact, just the opposite seems to be the case. Role models are seen as people that must be intimately involved in people's lives on a daily basis, through times of triumph as well as times of trouble. Sometimes they don't have to be black and some times they don't have to be male. Nevertheless, the scarcity of willing and interested adult males and the acquisition of resources to hire experienced social work professionals creates ongoing challenges. One program director expressed a fervent interest in the recruitment of black men as social workers, teachers and counselors and lamented over what she saw as the inability of such professions to attract large numbers of black men. The use of volunteers, summer interns and professional staff are three strategies that have been employed to achieve this end.

In spite of this apparent shortage this research bears witness to a number of dedicated black men working both as professionals and volunteers to serve the needs of youth in their communities. These few good men include the parents that send their kids, the volunteers that recite speeches, tutor school children and coach teams. It includes the the college students who could easily spend their summers elsewhere, the grocery teller who gives up weekends and two nights a week, the minister with a mission and the professional with a vision. These are real role models in action. They may be forgotten heroes, but they refuse to be victims.

Policy Implications

Community Based Organization

Bunker Hill Gardens is owned by a single corporation. To a certain extent community organization is made easy as long as the cooperation of the management company can be secured. It is a credit to the management company that it is convinced of the merits of assisting in the creation of a community based advocacy project like Reverend Knight's. This is a fundamental difference between Bunker Hill Community Outreach Center and the Diamond Hill Development Center. Corporate support is centralized and accessible. It also means that there is a higher potential for establishing some control over community affairs because every tenant is answerable to the management corporation in some capacity. This fact provides considerable leverage for community organization, and is not unlike the public housing developments at Diamond Hill where a central authority oversees community.

Reverend Knight has developed a model for community organization which incorporates public agencies along with private interests. He has branched out using Bunker Hill as a central hub in a strategy designed to take over a whole zip code region by setting up community centers in apartment complexes. He has secured free rental space from a local shopping center in order to set up an employment counseling office. His basic strategy is to bring every conceivable public service into play, while simultaneously securing the voluntary support of private corporations and people in the community.

He has also made deliberate attempts to facilitate leadership from within the community by working with potential community leaders, like Bobby Petrie, and facilitating their growth in that role. He has enlisted volunteer participation from retired citizens which brings them into contact with younger people, both children and adults, in an advisory capacity. Out of these efforts emerges a sense of community and a sense of empowerment. Out of these efforts emerges a sense of membership and a sense of ownership.

One cannot help but wonder if this same approach to community organization could be applied to public housing projects.

By organizing police, social service agencies, and charitable efforts in a central accessible, location the potential for positive social change appears to be enhanced. A key element of the Bunker Hill model is commitment to religious values. This might be problematic for a publicly owned facility, but the use of church related organizations to contract public services is a model that has been used in the past. Even without a religious affiliation, the organizational model warrants further interest.

Bunker Hill Community Outreach Center is effective because it is present right there in people's lives. They do not have to get a ride or make an appointment. It is nearby and accessible. It is next door or downstairs. It is designed to help young people help themselves. It doesn't give away money, so much as connect people up with resources. It provides a friendly place where the local police officer can come in and sit, come in and be present in the community. It provides a place where kids can come. They can do homework after school or take dance classes. They have meetings and go on trips with the Young Marines. It is truly at the center of the community.

Practical Policies for Working with High Risk Youth

It may be impossible to say exactly what program or what counseling strategies are most effective when working with young black men, especially when confronting class, cultural or racial differences. What works with one person, or group may not work with another. Diversity seems to be the rule in every population. People have different needs, different opinions, different points of view. Keeping this fact in mind, several of the people encountered during the research provided their own ideas of what approaches are most effective at facilitating positive communication and encouraging cooperation.

The following suggestions are aimed at the program, or agency policy level. They represent pearls of wisdom from people with experience in the field. The guidelines are derived from direct quotes or paraphrases of common themes articulated by staff from each of the centers. Commentary was added by the author for clarification.

1. Be yourself. The notion of realness and the importance of developing a relationship that promotes trust is critical. A trusting, caring relationship is something that takes time to develop and which requires a high level of consistency to sustain. Trying to adjust or shape oneself to the perceived expectations of others can result in suspicion and distrust thereby negating one's effectiveness as a professional consultant.

2. Focus on people. People are the essential components of the human service professions. To set priorities that devalue the concerns or interests of people would be to place oneself in contradiction to the reasons for providing services. Treating a person as an object rather than as an end in and of him/herself represents a fundamental lapse in ethical standards.

3. Be sure that you will have an effect. No matter what your intent or what the outcome you will influence the person you are working with one way or the other. The goal is to maximize the possibilities that the outcome will be a positive one.

4. Be dedicated. The job is too difficult to be anything else.

5. Diffuse barriers, don't erect them. Enough boundaries, walls, keep out signs and defense mechanisms have been constructed between people to stifle meaningful communication for generations to come. It is the job of the professional counselor, youth worker or community organizer to build coalitions. This might mean that occasionally you will have to, in the words of Sensei Akeem "take low, and be okay with that."

In terms of helping people build self esteem, Ms. Host at C.Y.S.. recommended that youth counselors *1) emphasize the positive 2) stress ownership and 3) affirm success.*

Evaluating Effectiveness

Relevancy is said to be important because of the practical needs many inner city youth face and the desire to see immediate results from their efforts. Global knowledge requires expanding ones' horizons and gaining exposure to the magnitude of possibilities that exist beyond the limiting confines local communities. Making people aware of opportunities and helping them to realize their own natural talents was likened to harvesting a crop. If it is not harvested at the right time it loses its sweetness or rots uselessly on the ground.

The program director at C.Y.S. provided three indicators that a young person is "buying in" to the vision and becoming motivated for positive change. If they come, you know you've got them. If they talk, you know they're interested. If they call, you know they need you. Mr. Carter, from Diamond Hill, said he felt that buying into a program was connected to the idea of service. Indicators of whether or not youth have bought into a program can be found in how frequently they attend and how much time they spend at the center. Stability in attendance, whether the same people keep coming back, is a second sign of effectiveness. Another criterion for program evaluation can be found in signs of incremental growth, both on the individual and the program level.

The problem of equity, regarding females, illustrates the ethical conflict over providing specialized services and opportunities for one social group over another. This same conflict arises in other programs or policies wherein eligibility is defined by gender, race, or class. It demonstrates both conflict and confusion about how to confront specialized needs without violating principles of fairness and nondiscrimination. The policy implications are clear. Programs that are not universally accessible run the risk of being challenged for violating principles of nondiscrimination. This problem is especially relevant to programs using public funds. For these reasons, program proposals for alleviating inequities suffered by specialized groups need to be carefully constructed and well thought out on all levels of policy formation.

Another important observation relating to program effectiveness addresses the concept of fit. In order to be effective a program must be designed to meet the needs of the specific population it serves. This principle can be applied in different ways. It can refer to how well people work together, it can relate to differing perceptions of need, and it can refer to a good idea with improper or faulty implementation. Several examples come to mind.

The first definition of fit has to do with how well people get along and whether they can depend on or trust each other. Barriers to trust can arise out of ethnic, educational or class differences. They can arise out of personality differences or miscommunication. They can also arise out of trying to be something you are not, trying too hard to fit in and thereby losing touch of who you are, realness.

It is possible for programs to be created by people based upon a perception of need that is not shared by the population to be served. Efforts to change people can be thwarted or stultified if they do not themselves see the need for change. For this reason Reverend Knight performed three separate surveys at Bunker Hill Gardens before attempting to establish a community outreach center. He canvassed the community in order to find out what were the problems people wanted to address and then devised a strategy to confront those problems. This is the second example of fit. Programs, in order to be effective, must be received.

An example of how this complicated issue can play itself out can be found in the needs assessment process conducted by the Comprehensive Youth Services Center in conjunction with the minority male consortium. A weekend retreat was set up for young black men to voice their concerns. The intent was to assess what services or programs might be useful and how identifiable needs might be met. During the retreat it was discovered that the target population of minority males was exceptionally diverse. Concerns and interests relevant to thirteen-year-olds were not applicable to twenty-year-olds. Programs targeting one set of needs did not fit the needs of others. In response to unanticipated circumstances the consortium agencies decided to regroup and plan separate retreats. By maintaining flexibility, they reconceptualized the issues and planned a new strategy to enhance program fit.

Programs that are effective in one place might not be effective somewhere else. This may be due to the idiosyncrasies of the population being served or due to the talents and abilities of the person providing services. In a moment of enthusiasm Sensei Turner expressed the desire to have martial arts programs opened up in every church or community center. Sensei Akeem balanced this suggestion with cautious restraint. His point was that the quality of a martial arts program is dependent on the character of the instructor. Programs in and of themselves are not good or bad. What makes a program good is the people who run it, their dedication to the people they serve, and the quality of the lessons they teach.

Criteria for evaluating programs could be interactive as well. Members and participants could be asked what they get out of a program. This strategy was attempted during the interviews with questions about why people come, what they learn and how are they helped by the different programs? By comparing predetermined program goals with participant interviews and comments an alternative strategy for program evaluation might be provided. This approach would allow greater flexibility in program assessment while simultaneously opening up new possibilities in accounting for unanticipated positive or negative outcomes.

Possibilities for Future Research

Future research might examine more closely the question of whether issues of philosophy and program structure vary according to secular versus sectarian affiliations. Although a strong emphasis on spiritual growth was observed at the two church related sites, this spiritual emphasis was not conveyed as strongly at the non-church affiliated program. Differences between groups with different church or religious affiliations may also be discovered.

Additional interesting possibilities for future research have emerged from this work. One concern relates to the emotional effects of persistent exposure to violence. The experiences of one young man, chronicled in a photo album, attest to the need for research in the area of post traumatic stress for victims of urban crime. This research should not only be limited to family or direct victims but it should also explore the effects of violence among peers for adolescent males. Some whose friends have all been blown away can hardly help but suffer emotional trauma.

More research needs to be conducted to supplement and add to what has been done here. This particular research model could be expanded upon by examining additional stakeholding groups whose voices were not heard, such as program drop outs,   more parents, funders and the like. The choice, in this research, was one of breadth over depth, in an effort to several sites within the constraints of time and financial resources. Another design might choose to develop a more in depth analysis of a single site.

Further research could also be conducted in the area of specialized programs for minority youth that emphasize an ethnocentric socialization model, not only for African American males but also for other ethnic populations at risk. These might include Native American or Hispanic communities. Since the problem of access to culturally specific programs, such as Afrocentric or Native American rites of passage, for non group members might be problematic, and minority researchers could take the lead in such endeavors. Such research might assist in the development of new programs as well, by providing working models to interested people.

Although the research design chosen for this study was constructivist, this choice is not intended to imply that a more quantitative approach to the same issue would be inappropriate. On the contrary, theories and hypothetical possibilities might easily be extracted from the vicarious experience of this research. Many of the comments made by people in the field imply a theoretical statement which could be operationalized and tested. Do young men growing up in fatherless home have more adjustment problems than others? Are role models or mentor programs effective ways of keeping young men from getting into trouble? These are just two questions that could be explored. Critical inquiry could easily lead to the development of more.

A final area of research that could be advanced relates to undoing the negative effects of racism both in minority and majority populations. Research into how racism benefits majority populations and how it is sustained in a society which professes otherwise has potential merit. Similarly practical approaches to resolving conflict across racial and ethnic differences are needed. It is this researcher's contention that the constructivist model provides a high level of reciprocal benefits for the researcher and subject people by maintaining a power sharing perspective. As a result, the potential for diffusing barriers to transracial understanding and cooperation is enhanced.

Summary

The intent of this research has been to provide depth to the existing social work literature by focusing on current concerns about young black men as a population at risk. The contention is that many young black men are being squeezed out of mainstream participation in the American dream. This dream is one which promotes a vision of success and financial security, safety in one's own home and the love of a supportive family. We have seen through these case studies how in a variety of ways these aspirations are in doubt for many young African American males.

Not all young black men are endangered in the same way that Gibbs (1988) and others have described, but there are some serious concerns and they have been recognized. We have seen how they exist in the lives of real people on a variety of levels. Part of the problem however seems to be situated in the moral dilemma alluded to by Myrdal (1944) and never really resolved by the civil rights initiatives of the 1950's and 1960's. The American dilemma is that racism persists in American society and that very little in recent years has been done to improve the situation. Shelby Steele (1992) refers to racial vulnerability as a means of understanding emotional damage inflicted on black people as a result of ongoing social inequality. Cornel West (1993) refers to a truncated racial dialogue which he sees as being largely responsible for the inability of our nation to move toward the ideal of equality we espouse. Amos Wilson (1991) sees ongoing white racism and social injustice as the root cause of the urban violence we are experiencing in the 1990's.

Whether these writings comprise self evident truths or radical theories is not so important as the possibility that they rekindle a dialogue on race that has been ignored and neglected. Many of the sentiments offered by those interviewed at the three study sites can be found in the reflections of scholars. It is time for the dialogue to advance in new directions. It is time to explore new solutions rather than dwell on old pathologies. It is time for a new civil rights movement that challenges the old divisions and provides new opportunities for joint efforts to achieve a centuries old dream. The final intent in this work is to advance that dialogue in ways that inspire cooperation rather than conflict, instill hope rather than perpetuate despair, and restore justice as the centerpiece of the American dream.

Epilogue

The Iyeska and the Ronin

On numerous occasions, but especially in its initial stages of this research, as the author, I have been confronted with questions like "How can you, as a white man, do a study on black men," or the question may come in the form of "Why do you want to study this?" My answer has been similar each time but never exactly the same. The question has been similar each time but never exactly the same. Essentially it is a question of trust and fairness. "How can *we* trust *you* to be fair and why should we?"

The Lakota people have a term for someone who stands on the edges of two cultures. This person is an iyeska (Karol and Rozman 1974; J. Stands, personal communication, June 1991). He or she is betwixt and between, a person with a foot in two worlds who serves to bridge the gap and act as an interpreter between the two. It is not always a positive term. Sometimes it is derogatory. Sometimes it is used to identify people who live on the edge of the reservation, people who are not white and are not Indian. These are people who are not committed to traditional values but who are not fully accepted, nor fully comfortable with the values and ways of the dominant culture either. It could be a racial slur but having visited and talked with many Lakota people, I believe it is more a question of lifestyle than of physical characteristics.

In America, of all places, we need iyeskas. We are a nation of people caught betwixt and between. We are a nation of people with one foot in the old country and another foot in the new world. We are a nation of people living in different cultural, racial and ethnic enclaves. We need more people who are willing to stand on the edges, to exist in the margins between tribes and people of differing backgrounds, traditions or experiences. We need people who are willing to take a few shots, learn a few things about themselves and others, and bring back a few messages to their own group.

The point is not to go native. The point is not to become a member because then you have just changed sides. You cannot bridge the gap of understanding between different peoples if you just change sides. The point is to become an iyeska! The point is to live life on the margins, never forgetting who you are or where you come from, never forgetting that you *do not* represent the other side but are merely a link between the two realities. If one can remember that he or she is only a link, a conduit through which information flows and understanding grows, then there is a place for the iyeska in social research. If one forgets this and follows his own agenda and attempts to persuade, dissuade or invade, then he becomes either a spy or a traitor. In either case he will have then earned for himself the derision that so often accompanies the term. I hope to remain on the positive side of the equation.

In Japanese there is another term which refers to a samurai who pledges no allegiance to a single master. These people were referred to in feudal times as ronin (Musashi 1974). One of the greatest swordsmen of all times was a ronin who lived in the 16th century. His name was Miyamoto Musashi. He has been referred to as the sword saint and even today people still honor his legacy by reading his*Book of Five Rings*. To be a samurai with no master was not viewed as an admirable thing in feudal Japan. Traditional honor was linked to service to one's liege lord. To be a samurai with no master was not viewed as an entirely trustworthy and honorable situation.

Yet, for Americans this is a somewhat attractive notion. In America, to be in service to another is to enslave oneself, to lose that sense of freedom and independence we cherish so dearly. The idea of a ronin, a man steeped in bushido sense of courage, bravery and duty, without being tied to the whims and fancies of another, is the personification of individualistic freedom (Funakoshi 1975; Reid and Croucher 1983). For Americans the ideal ronin is likened to a romantic western hero, who straps on his guns, one last time, to answer the call from a helpless child or brutalized victim.

In the context of this study I envision the ronin as someone who has attempted to lift the oppressive yoke of group interests from his or her shoulders and to enter the field with no obligation, no political agenda except to serve the truth as depicted by the people encountered in the journey. The realization of the ronin is that a man or woman must be the master of his or her own fate. There are no liege lords worthy of the title, save the traditions themselves, for he never truly escapes being a samurai. He merely discards one layer of armor to find that he is still yet a warrior. He knows that he could strip naked and there would still be a warrior within. Therefore he cannot give up being a samurai. He can only give up allegiance to a false god.

America is a nation of ronin. We honor the warrior spirit while abhorring blind commitment to the will of another. Perhaps it is because our faith in the system is less than our faith in ourselves. Because of this, and in spite of this, we have collectively accomplished great things. As a white researcher studying issues affecting the black community, or any minority community, I hope to be seen as both iyeska and ronin. I hope to act as an interpreter in the best sense by presenting a clear and undistorted message between peoples. As a ronin I seek to pledge no allegiance to one particular point of view, I pay tribute to no master save the honor of my own integrity to provide an honest and fair representation of the issues in the best way I can. Whether I earn the title of sword saint or become an object of derision is for the reader to decide.

Appendix 1

Coding Procedure and Guidelines

Preliminary Coding

1. Identification of key phrases in fieldnotes and interviews.
"Key phrases" are defined as......
nouns, adjectives or factual statements representing
concepts which depict meaningful images or points of view.

2. Record common themes of discussion either through
Ethnograph or manually, with index cards.
"Common themes" defined as.....
frequent points of discussion or observation such as programs,
education, community organization, or other descriptive data.

3. Identify text segments as they relate to common themes.

4. Use self explanatory labels whenever possible given
reasonable labeling limits. Avoid labels that do not convey a
hint of meaning at a glance.

Coding Procedures

1. Text segments are defined as portions of the text deriving
from transcribed interviews or expanded field notes that
convey significant meaning relating to different aspects of the
research questions. A text segment should require a

minimum of supportive or qualifying information to represent a complete idea.

2. Select text segments for coding based upon consistency with identified themes

3. Group preliminary codes into logically linked groups based on common themes

4. Define with coding rules. Record and enter subsequent codes according to criteria established by coding rules.

5. If a text segment does not easily fit into a previous code label, create a new code and define the minimum criteria for identifying that label. Coding rules should be clear, concise and broad enough to include diverse comments on a single theme.

Coding Levels

Initial Coding - taking preliminary codes and standardize them using a frequently identified preliminary code to group as a basis to group other less frequently used preliminary codes to form groups of related statements. These are literal codes drawn directly from the text.

Code Groups - The continuation of coding into meaningful groups that can be linked together under one heading. These groups could be identified by a program name, a philosophical theme, or a commonly mentioned problem or issue. This step requires the grouping of literal codes into common themes and involves a higher level of abstraction than the initial coding.

Categorical Codes - Categorical codes consist of a broad based grouping of generalizable codes. This is the final level of abstraction where code groups are joined , or subsumed, under a large scale or broad conceptual framework.

Appendix 2

Code Rules and Definitions

I. Rules

 A. Code labels were selected from words and conceptual themes identified as words directly from interviews or field notes.

 B. Once a code label was established this label was assigned to other text segments that reflected common meaning based on identified conceptual themes.

 C. Code labels were designed to convey the maximum amount of meaning with a minimum amount of interpretation for the reader.

 D. When ten letters or characters were insufficient to reflect conceptual themes contained in the interviews or field notes, an acronym designed to convey the intended meaning in the text segment or data unit will be used.

 E. Acronyms were created with an effort to convey meaning at a glance.

 F. Codes and related acronyms that do not have obvious intended meaning will be included in the list of code definitions.

 G. Code group labels were chosen based on common themes identified from the master code lists at each research site.

 H. Code categories were established according to the original research questions reflecting an interest in issues, philosophies, and program.

II. Code Definitions

Activity(ies) - a singular event designed to meet program goals or
       objectives
Ad Coord - job title, administratvie coordinator
Adultleadr - comments having to do with adult leadership or leaders
Afamamalsw - African American male social worker
Aspiration - comment having to do with personal goals
Blackhstry - Black History, program name
Bldg Rel - building relationships
Blk celebs - black celebrities
Blk contrib - black contributions, to history, literature, science etc.
Blk males - black males
Blk Philan - black philanthropy
Blkpols - black politicians
BM/WM Rel - black male/white male relations
Brdn Horiz - broadening horizons
Brg Fruit - bearing fruit
Bridgelife - Bridge to Life, program name
Child negl - child neglect
Church Aff - comments depicting the relationship between the agency
       or program and a particular church or religion, abbreviation for
       church affiliation
Class Behav - classroom behavior in school
Community - joining together of several groups of people into a united
       effort; refers to people living or working together in close
       proximity such as in a neighborhood; statements relating to a
       philosophical or political sense of belonging or commonality
       among people
Com Health - community health concerns
Comm Org - community organization
Commu Mtgs - community meetings
Com Orient - community oriented
Comm Pride - community pride
Communicat - communication
Complitrcy - computer literacy
Comprehens - comprehensive

Concerncom - concern committee
Concriticis - constructive criticism
Conflctres - conflict resolution
Coop learn - cooperative learning
Court Inv - court involved, someone who is involved with the criminal
    justice system
Creaming - the practice of working with the youth who have the
    greatest potential for success in a program while
    simultaneously screening out those who are thought to be at
    high risk for failure
Descriptin - desrciption or descriptive information
Descriptve - description or descriptive information
Devlp Comm - developing community
Diversity - comments about differences in people
Dlg w Rage - dealing with rage
DRC - motto, Deiscipline Respect and Caring
Educere - latin verb to teach
Effects - comments reflecting the effects of program on people or
    community
Entrepenur - entrpeneurship, idea of becoming your own boss, owning
    a business
Energy con - energy conservation
Evaluation - assessments made by participants, staff or researcher
    regarding positive or negative outcomes of programs or
    activities
Evaluation - statements reflecting program success or failure
Ex Comm - executive committee
Expectatns - expectations
Failure - reflections or comments on strategies that don't appear to
    achieve desired ends
Fam Atmos - family atmosphere
Fam Inv - family involvement
Fam plang - family planning
Family Rel - family relationships
Fam skills - family skills
Giving Bk - giving back, philosophy of community service
Globalknow - global knowledge

Goals - recognized and desired outcomes of programs or personal
     aspirations
Goalsetopp- goal setting opportunity
Grp counsl - group counseling
Grpsession - group session, program activity
Hvg Effect - having an effect
Housing - comments about where people live and the physical
     structures in which they live
Hsg Projct - housing project(s)
Info sys - information system
Intake int - intake interview
Interdisci - interdisciplinary
Issues - factors and concepts that are described by interviewees as being
     of primary importance to understanding a problem, situation
     or observed behavior.
ITP - individual treatment plan
Job traing - job training
Job Trng - job training
JTPA - Job Training Partnership Act
Ki - philosphy of martial arts having to do with inner force
Law Enforc - law enforcement
Lrnd Behav - learned behavior
Mangmnt co - management company
Management - mangement company
Managmntco - management company
Med clinic - medical clinic
Mentalhlth - mental health
Mentheal - mental health
Membership - comments relating to belonging to the center or being a
member of a group at one of the sites
Metaemploy - meta employment skills, having to do with job related as
     opposed to job specific skills such as interviewing, writing
     resumes, money management, entrepneurship etc
MH Coord - mental health coordinator
Min Male - minority male
Mngful Alt - meaningful alternatives
Most trbld - most troubled youth

Movg Frwrd - moving forward
Multi-jobs - multiple jobs
Multi resp - multiple responsiblities
Negmessage - negative messages
Negmssg - negative message
Neighborhd - statements about immediate locality
Nondiscrim - nondiscrimination
Objectives - recognized and desired outcomes of activities or specific
    strategies
Other Ctrs - other centers
Ord Minstr - ordained minister
Outrch Ctr - Outreach Center
Parentalin - parental involvement in center activities
Part solut - quote "If you're not part of the solution you're part of the
    problem."
Peerpressr - peer pressure
Philosophy(ies) - belief or guiding principle usually relating to global
    themes or political ideology, closely related to values
Physical Description - any statement depicting or characterizing a
    physical conditions of a setting, person place or thing.
Pos Focus - principle of maintaining a positive focus
Postv Mind - positive mind, philosphy of positve thinking
Prim couns - primary counselor
Principle - belief or guiding principle usually relating to program design
    or methods can include goal and objectives
Pro Status - professional status
Program - an organized effort that is regularly scheduled and consists of
    a series of activities over time to accomplish an established
    purpose (includes subcategory of program identifier names
    such as *Rites of Passage, Girl Talk* etc.)
Quote - statements selected as particularly vivid expressions of an idea,
    event, person or thing, that supports the idea in such a way as
    to promote a better understanding of the emic meaning of the
    subject.
Rite o Psg - rite of passage
Reglaryth - regular youth who attend the winter program at CYSC

Relationsh - (relationships) any discussion of family or peers or where a
    third party is described as a meaningful influence on another
    person (usually   a youth/participant)

Rlv Stress - relieve stress

Serving - statements indicating the activity or philosophy of providing
    service

Somthnmore - something more

Speakgwell - speaking well

Specializd - specialized

Spritualty - abbreviation for spirituality, relating to comments having to
    do with spiritual or religious themes

Sportsprog - sports program

Strategy(ies) - the basic rationale behind an activity or program which
    guides the behavior of the participant

Sub Abuse - substance abuse

Success - reflections or comments on strategies that achieve desired
    ends

SW Educ - social work education

SW skills - social work skills

SYEP - summer youth employment program

Tenn Assoc - tennants association

Trust bldg - trust building

Values - statements relating to values, attitudes or pertaining to right
    or wrong, good/bad, should/shouldn't

Weatherize - Weatherizatin program

Wkg Poor - working poor

Wombtograv - womb to grave

Word of da - Word of the Day , a program activity name

Worktogthr - working together, philosophy of cooperation

3W's - work, worth, will / criteria for board mwmbership at CYSC

Appendix 3

Diamond Hill Development Center
Code Category Lists - Issues

Relationships
family
babies
belonging
boys
fatherhood
membership
parental involvment
peer pressure
relationships
race relations
parenthood
boyfriends
grand parent
admire
help from
stars
help
everyday
sttention
possessive
friends
fathers
familiy relations
fighting
jealousy
male/female
manipulation
respect
rolemodel
spanking
responsibility
leadership
heroes
n=33

Values
motivation
pride
religion
needs caring
manhood
kindness
love
hope
self identity
anger
jealousy
manipulation
appearance
respect
self esteem
leadership
truth
strength
character
manners
heroes
discipline
n=22

Crime
crime
at risk
abuse
dscrmnatn
crimnl just
rock throwr
police offcr
gang o' 7
conflict
childnglect
anger
beating
drugs
fighting
violence
stealin'
spanking
murders
n=19

Race Rel.
Black Hist
race relatn
police
black aware
dscrmnatn
niggerword
black comm
white folks
racism
n=9

235

Community
jobs
opportunity
healthcare
culture
black community
AIDS
concerns
home
housing
violence
poverty
needs
homeowners
environment
n=14

Education
black history
computers
college
labeling
school work
sports
scholarship
n=7

Health
healthcare
murders
AIDS
drugs
pregnancy
n=5

Diamond Hill Development Center
Code Category Lists - Philosophies

Philosophies	*Principles*	*Values*
philosophy	giving back	balance
produce life	guiding	buying in
holistic	one on one	potential
needspirit	mental ret	values
spirituality	development	serving vol
ownership	change	ownership
philosophies	patience	fatalism
n=7	serving	attitudes
	trouble	caring
	preparation	values
	flexibility	*n=10*
	community	
	alternative	
	principles	
	n=14	

Diamond Hill Development Center
Code Category Lists - Program

Activities	*Strategies*	*Evaluation*
activities	alternative	failure
boardgames	attendance	attendance
black history	force feeding	goals
conflict resolution	one on one	buying in
cooking	reaching	outcome
educational	goals	trust
friday trips	gettin' away	growth
homework	counselors	*n=7*
on the van	buyin' in	
play'n ball	diversity	
bible study	evaluation	
circus	function	
schoolwork	labeling	
sports	outcome	
youth program	trust	
the van	verbal	
sunday school	volunteers	
girltalk	work	
prayer	pushing	
rites of passage	help from	
n=20	growth	
	funding	
	consistency	
	prayer	
	learn	
	job description	
	serving	
	n=27	

Appendix 4

Bunker Hill Young Marines
Code Category Lists - Issues

Relationships
admire
admiremost
aunts
care for
cousin
family rel
fatherhood
fathers
fighting
friends
frienda
girls
grandfather
grandparen
helrpfrom
influence
intimate
m/f rel
mother
mother/son
mothers
parent
parentalin
parents
peer fear
peer suppr
peer prssr
peerprssur
peers

Relationships (cont)
peersupport
relationsh
rolemodels
single
sister
sportstars
teasing
uncle
ythleadrs
masculinity
$n=39$

Education
college
labeling
school
schoolwork
heritage
history
education
$n=7$

Other
food
sponsorship
$n=2$

Dreams
aspiration
aspiratios
big house
building
businessma
business
computers
goals
sports
sportstar
success
sucess
tech engine
writer
reputation
respect
$n=16$

Character
self esteem
maturity
frustrated
fun
getting up
language
pride
spritualty
$n=8$

239

Community Concerns
belonging
blackmen
com org
com ser
comm leadr
comm org
comm pride
change
caring
courts
culture
disadvantg
discipline
drugdealr
drugs
fear
feelin safe
financial
gangs
guns
homicide
housing
idleness
jobs
labeling
media
money
needs

Community Concerns (cont)

off street
order
police
publicity
residence
streets
trouble
vandalism
violence
leadership
influence
empowermnt
n=40

Bunker Hill Young Marines
Philosophies and Guiding Principles

Philosophies
biblical
caring
dedicated
discipline
faith
fatalism
God
holistic
Jesus
leadership
learning
led by spirit
living
linking
loving
love
reaching
materialism
mission
nihilism
philosophy
positive focus
positive things
positive mind
positive
prayer
pride
purpose
religious

Philo (cont)

respect
sharing
spiritual
structure
spirituality
trust
values
teaching
working together
work ethic
community oriented
helping
instruction
n=42

Guiding Principles	*Values*
church affiliated	caring
citizenship	biblical
commitment	dedication
constructive criticism	discipline
do something	learning
fun	love
giving back	materialism
goals	postive focus
hardworkin'	purpose
peer support	respect
looking good	sharing
motto	trust
positive focus	work ethic
responsibility	community oriented
self esteem	helping
small groups	citizenship
study the word	giving back
trust building	hardworkin'
values	looking good
working together	responsibility
work ethic	self esteem
n=21	working together
	motto
	do something
	spirituality
	n=25

Bunker Hill Young Marines
Code Category Lists - Program

Activities
activity
activities
activty
actvity
aftercare
basketball
bible study
black history
bootcamp
cleanup
boy scouts
bridge to life
cheerleaders
community service
concern com
cook out
homework help
infor & referral
cimm policing
dance
real men
recycling
sports program
survey
trips
tutoring
word of the day
young marines

Activities (cont)
PTA
playroom
partners
n=31

Y. M. Activities
basketball
black history
bootcamp
community cleanup
boy scouts
cheerleaders
concern committee
cook outs
homework help
real men
recycling
sports program
trips
tutoring
word of the day
partners
meetings
n=17

Program Design
attendance
back in
bring to community
boys & girls
all male
build leaders
channeling
constructive criticism
develop model
flexibility
growth
holistic
linking
instruct
instill
membership
mentors
network
peer support
principle
reaching
stand by
encourage
self help
effects
evaluation
prayer
sponsorship
volunteers
n=29

Strategies
classes
dues
folders
follow rules
how helps
why come
job description
meetings
meeting times
mottos
officers
committees
rules
n=13

Appendix 5

Comprehensive Youth Services Center
Code Category Lists - Issues

Relationships
rolemodels
communicat
relationsh
family
role model
afamalsw
big bro
blk celebs
rapstars
belonging
black men
fathers
fam support
family inv
children
male/male
parenthood
households
influences
support
home envir
the tribe
wm/bm rel
stars
fam skills
fam issues
concerns
females

Relationships (cont)
losing tch
fatherhood
family
father/son
testing
barriers
peers
bonding
abandonment
personal
family inv
single par
male/female
parenting
breakdown
n=43

Character
self esteem
anger
self hate
claim t'fam
direction
damage
atten span
acting out
pride
ability
excuses
failure
high risk
individual
identity
genius
trauma
talent
most trbld
self destr.
attention
behavior
devlpment
anger
rage
socializatn
grooming
status
n=28

Needs	*Crime and Violence*	
needs	violence	
employment	subs abuse	
anxieties	drugs	*Crime & Vio(cont)*
basic	court inv.	crime
feeling	alcohol	rage
self esteem	chil abuse	anger
power	doin harm	self defens
stress	blk on blk	threats
growth	drug prob	*n=33*
high risk	fighting	
loss	cursing	*Employment*
obstacles	court	poverty
skills	destructiv	big bsinss
need	prevention	economic
love	police	career
at risk	profanity	opportunity
exposure	neg options	hardwork
n=17	gangs	haves
	juv arrests	have nots
	jail time	investment
	womb t'grave	job
	law enforce	workforce
	subs abuse	success
	fights	work
	fear	*n=13*
	pain	
	drugs	
	guns	

Race and Ethnicity
race rel
domination
bm/wm rel
white domin
yng b men
nonminority
white
stereotype
oppress
ethnicity
diversity
false assmp
n=12

Other
masses
patterns
gay
unresolved
underused
yng males
problems
differences
n=8

Media
pos message
neg message
bombard
movies
neg mssg
n=5

Health
AIDS
alcoholism
nutrition
health
health related
men health
STD
n=7

Education
education
academic
ed skills
acad level
college
ed system
accents
deficits
schools
writing
labeling
ignorance
dropouts
reading
school exp
school sys
n=16

Comprehensive Youth Services Center
Code Category Lists - Philosophy

Philosophy
proactive
leadership
capitalist
commercialism
conspiracy
bearing fruit
Eurocentric
oppression
materialism
mov'g forward
giving back
inclusive
Afrocentric
entrepeneurship
theory
empowerment
coming back
wisdom
excellence
caring
concern
educere
serving
ki
ownership
holistic
God
religious
n=28

Principles
membership
for profit
principles
acessible
remotivate
pos change
proactive
dedication
self help
focus
consistency
coping
expectations
flexibility
encourage
serving
hands on
entrepeneurship
foundation
discipline
mission
inclusion
interdisciplinary
give it a try
use head
anger
control
mngful alt

Princ.(cont)
structure
innovation
comprehensive
goal
free entrprise
sense of hope
make way
lrnd behavior
understand
another way
lend a hand
be yourself
we there
caring
pos. focus
for profit
take low
wombtograve
belonging
serve needs
harvesting
meet needs
warehouse
prevention
male focus
lrn frm past
bldg. conf.
alternative

Princ.(cont)
raise up
serve
profit
creatvitiy
bldg relationonships
tangibles
nonprofit
goal settin opp
responsibility
n=65

Values
dedication
market value
nonviolent
tokenism
sense hope
leadership
discipline
hopelessness
emotional
patience
hopes
enthusiasm
hope
determination
want it now
helping
pride
trust
realness
kindness
caring
morals
devotion
confidence

Values (cont)
frustration
love
motivation
control
values
cultural
achievement
black pride
commitment
hardwork
style
multicultural
injustice
survival
relevance
neg prestige
spiritual
expectations
manhood
n=44

Comprehensive Youth Services Center
Code Category Lists - Program

Strategies
what works
strategy
coordinator
intern
policy
multi resp
design
agencies
staff
grants
activity
objectives
sw skills
guest speaker
tutoring
future plan
recruiting
child care
social work
job duties
job descrip
salaries
director
fees
billing
instructor
prof history
conflict res
fine tune

Strat. (cont)
hugs
listening
inspire
manipulate
daily living
computers
knuckle push ups
Af Am male SW
development
group
multi jobs
m/f groups
tutor
licensed
activity
many hats
workshop
LSW
staff mtg
assist
prof. credentials
social workers
multi agency
coalition
what I do
group session
classes
structured prog
funders

Strat. (cont)
referral
brd membership
services
activities
prof esper.
prim counselor
retreat
counselor
consortium
male group
adm coordinator
job benefits
prof status
planning
info system
resources
life skill
grp counselor
paperwork
rites of passage
selection
group mtg
social history
blk history
guidelines
warehousing
mentoring
family planning
bldg confidence
non resident
structured program

Strat. (cont)
ex-director
daily check in
goal setting opp
standing comm
prof identity
direct
dialogue
diffuse
community group
combination
committees
serving males
site supervisor
family skills
probation
female group
executive comm
private agency
placement
early intervention
prog development
funding
prob solving
finance
basic program
daycare
designs
crews
combined
goal
clear goal

Strat. (cont)
compliment
prof status
imagery
unstructured
specialized
youth services
supporting
ongoing
childcare
orientation
ad hoc committees
serving males
3 w's
long term
ITP
groups
drug testing
counseling
steps
intake
install
sr. coordinator
donations
fam atmos
ego boost
encourage
n=146

Education
GED
summer school
tutoring
blk history
enrichment
BSW degree
educational
drug educ.
SW educ
Proj 2000
tutor
summer youth
instruction
cooperative learning
Nelson test
Basic skills
computer literacy
school
in school
educate
ecuc supervisor
careers
curriculum
n=23

Employment
JTPA
voc skills
weatherization
training
job training
SYEP
summer
employment
building trades
worksite
energy conservation
meta employment
job benefits
equipment
management training
lighting
summer youth
job
inventory
hands on
repairs
world o' work
own tools
basic skills
contract
pre employment
career
careers
boiler repair
building skills
construction
n= 31

Membership
in school
males
black males
minority males
regular
enrollment
age limits
attendance
all male
caseload
90% Af Am
students
regualr youth
young kids
male attendance
participants
retaining
regual attendance
profile attrition
membership
n=19

Recreational
martial arts
self defense
aikido
recreation
relieve stress
commercialism
coaching
hug effect
n=8

Health & MH
mental health
assessment
drug treatment
health related
drug education
out patient
MH coordinator
medical exam
medical
clinic
n=9

Other
church
government
court
overview
pre-existing
federal government
5 yrs
social
building
n=9

Evaluation
what works
best thing
worst thing
fit people
assessment
standards
why come
buying in
creaming
fit
effects
performance
numbers
missing it
opening up
effects on
measuring
see results
rewards
fluctuate
hug effect
growth
change
success
criteria
n=25

Comprehensive Youth Service Center
Code Category Lists - Program Strategies

Design & Development
board membership
rules
job benifits
planning
development
multiple jobs
many hats
multi agency
coalition
consortium
structured program
funders
guideline
ongoing
long term
3 W's
nonresident
standing committee
committees
executive committee
private agency
program development
funding
finance
designs
crews
donations
ad hoc committes
n=19

Services
information system
resources
supporting
daily living
primary counselor
tutor
services
combination
serving males
probation
placement
early intervention
basic program
daycare
combined
family planning
counseling
orientation
childcare
life skills
ongoing
n=21

Staff
prof. experience
volunteer
ad. coordinator
prof. status
licensed
LSW
staff mtg
prof. credentials
social workers
sr. coordinator
group counselor
executive director
prof. identity
recruiting
program director
site supervisor
coordinator
staff
n=18

Activities
counseling
referral
activities
black history
retreat
black college trip
community meeting
consoritum
male group
computers
knuckle push ups
group
m/f groups
activity
workshop
group sessions
classes
intake
rites of passage
warehousing
mentoring
family planning
ongoing
daily check in
community group
class
 family skills
female group
n=28

What I do
what I do
listening
inspire
manipulate
assist
install
paperwork
build conf
direct
dialogue
diffuse
hugs
n=12

References

Allen, W. R. 1981. Moms, dads, and boys: Race and sex differences in the socialization of male children. In *Black men*, edited by L.E. Gary. Beverly Hills, Ca.: Sage.

Andersen, M. L. 1993. Studying across difference: Race, class and gender in qualitative research. In *Race and Ethnicity in Research Methods*, edited by J. H. Stanfield and R. M. Dennis. Newbury Park, Ca.: Sage.

Asante, M. K. 1991. The Afrocentric idea in education. *Journal of Negro Education* 60, 2: 170-180.

Asante, M. K. 1987. *The Afrocentric idea.* Philadelphia: Temple University.

--------- 1980. *Afrocentricity: The theory of social change.* Buffalo, N.Y.: Amulefi.

Ascher, C. 1992. School programs for African American males.....and females. *Phi Delta Kappan* 73: 777-782, June.

Auletta, K. 1983. *The Underclass.* New York: Vintage Books.

Bandura, A. 1969. Social learning theory of identificatory processes. In *Handbook of socialization theory and research*, edited by D. A. Goslin. Beverly Hills, Ca.: Russell Sage.

Baruth, L. G. and M. L. Manning. 1991. *Multicultural counseling and psychotherapy: A lifespan perspective.* N. Y.: MacMillan.

Bem, S. L. 1974. The measurement of psychological androgyny. *Journal of Consulting Clinical Psychology* 42, 2: 155-162.

Bierm, J. A. 1990. The effect of television sports media on black male youth. *Sociological Inquiry* 60: 413 - 427.

Bloom, M. 1990. *The drama of social work.* Itasca, N. Y.: F. E. Peacock.

Bogdan, R. and S. J. Taylor. 1984. *Introduction to qualitative research methods: The search for meaning.* N. Y.: John Wiley & Sons.

Bowser, B. P. 1990. *Black male adolescents: Parenting and education in the community context.* Lanham, Md.: University Press of America.

Boykin, A. W. 1984. Reading achievement and the sociocultural frame of reference of Afro-American children. *Journal of Negro Education* 53, 4: 464-473.

Carmichael, S. 1970. Power and racism. In *From a black perspective: Contemporary black essays,* edited by D. A. Hughes. N.Y.: Holt Rinehart & Winston.

Carnegie Corporation 1984. Education and economic progress toward a national education policy: The federal role. *Journal of Children in Contemporary Society* 16, 3: 3-9.

Carter, B. and M. McGoldrick. (1988). *The changing family life cycle.* N. Y.: Gardner Press.

Cazenave, N. A. and R. Smith. (1990). Gender differences in the perception of   Black male-female relationships and stereotypes. In *Black families,* edited by H. E. Cheatham and J. B. Stewart. New Brunswick: Transaction Publishers.

Chambers, D. E., K. R. Wedel, and M. K. Rodwell. 1992. *Evaluating social programs.* Boston: Allyn & Bacon.

Chiles, N. 1991. 'A' is for ashanti, 'b' is for black. *Newsweek*: 45-48, 26 September.

Childrens Defense Fund 1987. *The health of America's children.* Washington, D.C.: Childrens Defense Fund.

Clark, K. B. and M. P. Clark. 1947. Racial identification and preference in Negro children. In *Readings in social psychology,* edited by T. M. Newcomb and E. L. Hartley. N. Y.: Holt, Rinehart and Winston.

Clatterbaugh, K. C. 1990. *Contemporary perspectives on masculinity.* Boulder: Westview Press.

Collison, M. 1991. Black male schools. *Black Enterprise*: 18, February.

Cooley, C. H. 1902. *Human nature and the social order.* N. Y.: Charles Scribner and Sons.

Cronbach, L. J. 1975. Beyond the two disciplines of scientific psychology. *American Psychologist* 30: 113-127.

Cross, W. E. Jr. 1991. *Shades of black diversity in African American identity.* Phildelphia: Temple University Press.

Curran, D. J. and C. M. Renzetti. 1990. *Social problems: Society in crisis.* Boston: Allyn and Bacon.

Dennis R. M. 1993. Participant Observations. In *Race and ethnicity in research methods*, edited by J. H. Stanfield II and R. M. Dennis. Newbury Park: Sage.

De Vore, W. and E. Schlesinger. 1987. *Ethnic sensitive social work practice* (2nd Ed.) Columbus, Oh.: Merrill.

Dillard, J. L. 1975. A sketch of the history of Black English. In *Black American English: Its background and usage in schools and literature*, edited by P. Stoller: N. Y.: Dell.

Dubois, W. E. B. 1903. *The souls of black folk.* New York: The New American Library.

------- 1939. *Black folk then and now.* New York: H. Holt & Co.

Dodson, J. E. 1983. *An Afrocentric educational manual: Toward a non-deficit perpsective in services to families and children.* Knoxville: University of Tennessee School of Social Work.

Durkheim, E. 1952. *Suicide.* New York: Free Press.

Eisner, E. 1979. *The educational imagination.* New York: Macmillan.

Ellison, R. 1989. *Invisible man.* New York: Vintage Books.

Erikson, E. 1964. *Childhood and society.* New York: Norton.

Falck, H. S. 1988. *Social work: The membership perspective.* N. Y.: Springer.

Farley, J. E 1992. *Sociology.* Englewood Cliffs: Prentice Hall.

Federal Bureau of Investigation 1990. *Crime in America.* Washington, D.C.: U.S. Government Printing Office.

Federal Bureau of Investigation 1989. *Crime in America.* Washington, D.C.: U.S. Government Printing Office.

Federal Bureau of Investigation 1988. *Crime in America.* Washington, D.C.: U.S. Government Printing Office.

Fordham, S. 1988. Racelessness as a factor in black students' school success. *Harvard Educational Review* 58, 1: 54-84.

Fordham, S. and Ogbu, J. U. 1986. Black students, school success. *Urban Review* 18, 3: 176-206.

Franklin, C. W. 1984. *The changing definition of masculinity.* N.Y.: Plenum Press.

-------- 1986. Conceptual and logical issues in theory and research related to Black masculinity. *The Western Journal of Black Studies* 10, 4: 161-166.

Franklin, A .J. 1992. Therapy and African American men. *Families and Society*, 73: 350 -355.

Frazier, E. F. 1939. *The Negro family in the United States.* Chicago: University of Chicago Press.

Freire, P. 1973. *Pedagogy of the oppressed.* New York: Seabury Press.

Freilich, M. 1989. *Relevance of culture.* New York: Bergin & Garvey.

Freud, S. 1930. *Civilization and its discontents.* Reprint N.Y.: Norton, 1962.

Frye, H. D. 1990. Changing the inner city: Black urban reorganization. In *Black Male Adolescents: Parenting and Education in the Community Context* edited by B. P. Bowser. Lanham, Md.: University Press of America.

Funakoshi, G. 1975. *Karate-Do my way of life.* Tokyo: Kodansha International.

Gary, L. E. 1990. *The Status of African American Males: A Background Paper.* Washington, D.C.: Institute for Urban Affairs and Research.

------- 1986. Drinking, homicide and the Black male. *Journal of Black Studies* 17, 1: 15 -31.

------- Ed., 1981. *Black men.* Beverly Hills, Ca.: Sage Publications.

------- 1978. *Support systems in black communities: Implications for mental health services for children and youth.* Washington, D. C.: Howard University.

Gary, L. E. and W. E. Pullman. 1993. *Black males' perceptions of racial discrimination: Implications for social work education.* Paper presented at the Conference for Social Work Education , N.Y.: 01/93.

Gates, H. L. 1991. Beware of new pharoahs. *Newsweek* 118: 47.

Geertz, C. 1973. *The interpretation of culture.* New York: Basic Books.

Gibbs, J. T. (1990). Black adolescents and youth; An update on an endangered species. In *Black adolescents* edited by R. L. Jones. Berkeley, Ca.: Cobb & Henry.

Gibbs, J. T. 1988. *Young black and male in America: An endangered species.* Dover, Ma.: Auburn House.

Gilligan, C. 1982. *In a different voice.* Cambridge, Ma: Harvard University Press.

Glaser, B. and A. Strauss. 1967. *The discovery of grounded theory.* Chicago: Aldine.

Gordon, M. M. (1978). *Human nature, class and ethnicity.* N.Y.: Oxford University Press.

Goslin, D. A. (1969). *Handbook of socialization theory and research.* Beverly Hills, Ca.: Russell Sage.

Gouldner, H. 1978. *Teachers pet, troublemakers and nobodies; Black children in elementary school.* Westport, Ct.: Greenood Press.

Guba, E. G. 1985. *Perspectives on public policy: What can happen as a result of a policy?* June 1, 1985 unpublished paper.

------- 1990. *The paradigm dialog.* Newbury Park, Ca.: Sage.

Guba, E. G. and Y. S. Lincoln. 1981. *Effective evaluation.* San Francisco; Josey-Bass.

------- 1989. *Fourth generation evaluation.* Newbury Park, Ca.: Sage.

Hale-Bebson, J. E. 1986. *Black children: Their roots culture and learning style.* Baltimore: Johns Hopkins University Press.

Haley, A. 1964. *The autobiography of Malcolm X as told to Alex Haley.* N.Y.: Ballantine Books.

Hall, L. E. 1981. Support systems and coping patterns. In *Black men,* edited by L. E. Gary. Beverly Hills, Ca.: Sage.

Hare, B. R. 1979. *Black girls: A comparative anlysis of self perception and achievement by race, sex and socioeconomic background; Report no. 271.* Baltimore: Johns Hopkins University Press.

------- 1985. Stability and change in self-perception and achievement among black adolescents: A longitudinal study. *The Journal of Black Psychology* 11, 2: 29-42.

------- 1970. Brainwashing of black men's minds. In *From a black perspective; Contemporary black essays* edited by D. A. Hughes. N. Y.: Holt Rinehart & Winston.

Hare, N. and J. Hare. 1985. *Bringing the black boy to manhood. The passage.* San Francisco: The Black Think Tank.

Harrington, M. 1962. *The other America: Poverty in the United States.* N.Y.: Holt Rinehart and Winston.

Hawkins, D.F. 1985. Black homicide: The adequacy of existing research for devising prevention strategies. *Crime and Delinquency* 31,1:83-103.

Herskovitz, M. J. 1958. *The myth of the negro past.* Boston: Beacon.

Heffernan, J., G. Shuttlesworth, and R. Ambrosino. 1992. *Social work and social welfare.* St. Paul, Mi.: West Publishing.

Hendricks, L. E. 1981. Black unwed adolescent fathers. In *Black Men,* edited by L. E. Gary. Beverly Hills: Sage.

Holloway, J. E. 1993. *Africanisms in American Culture.* Bloomington: Indiana University Press.

Holloway, J. E. and W. K. Vass. 1993. *The African heritage of American English.* Bloomington: Indiana University Press.

Hudson, R. J. 1991. Black male adolescent development deviating from the past: Challenges for the future. In *Black male adolescents: Parenting and education in community context,* edited by B. P. Bowser. Lanham, Md.: University Press of America.

Hughes, D. A. 1970. *From a black perspective: Contemporary black essays.* N. Y.: Holt, Rinehart & Winston.

Hyams, J. 1982. *Zen in the martial arts.* Toronto: Bantam Books.

Irvine, J. J. 1990. *Black studies and school failure: Policies, practices and prescriptions.* New York: Greenwood Press.

Jeter, J. 1993. Their brother's keeper. *The Washington Post,* 1, 2 May.

Johnson, L. C. 1992. *Social work practice: A generalist approach.* Boston, Ma: Allyn & Bacon.

Karenga, R. 1977. *Kwanzaa: Origins, concepts, practice.* Los Angeles: Kwaida Publications.

Karol, J. S. and S. L. Rozman. 1974. *Everyday Lakota: An English - Sioux dictionary for beginners.* St. Francis Mission, S.D.: Rosebud Educational Society.

Katz, P. A. and D.A. Taylor. 1988. *Eliminating racism.* N.Y.: Plenum.

Kilson, M. and R. Rotberg. 1976. *The African diaspora: Interpretive essays.* Cambridge, Ma: Harvard University Press.

Kimmel, M. S. 1987. *Changing Men.* Newbury Park, Ca.: Sage.

King, M. L., Jr. 1959. *The Measure of a Man.* Phildelphia: Fortress.

King, P.M. and J.A. Taylor. 1989. Factors influencing intellectual development and academic achievement of black college students.

Final report submitted to the Counseling and Human Development Foundation.

Kenyatta, J. 1938. *Facing Mount Kenya.* Nairobi: Heinemann Kenya Ltd.

Kohlberg, L. 1969. Stage and sequence: The cognitive development approach to socialization. In *Handbook of socialization theory and research*, edited by D. A. Goslin. Chicago: Rand McNally.

Kotlowitz, A. 1991. *There are no children here.* New York: Doubleday.

Kornblum, W. and J. Julian. 1992. *Social problems.* Englewood Cliffs, N.J.: Prentice Hall.

Kuhn, T. 1970. *The structure of scientific revolutions.* Chicago: University of Chicago Press.

Kunjufu, J. 1983. *Countering the conspiracy to destroy black boys: Vol. 1.* Chicago: African American Images.

------- 1984. *Developing positive self images and discipline in black children.* Chicago: African American Immages.

------- 1986. *Countering the conspiracy to destroy black boys; Vol. 2.* Chicago: African American Images.

------- 1988. *To be popular or smart: The black peer group.* Chicago: African American Images.

------- 1993. The importance of an Afrocentric multicultural curriculum, *Phi Delta Kappa,* 74, 490-491.

Leacock, E. B. 1971. *Culture of poverty: A critique.* New York: Simon and Schuster.

Leake, D. and B. Leake. 1992. African American immersion schools in Milwaukee: A view from the inside. *Phi Delta Kappan,* 73: 783-785, June.

Leashore, B., S. Toliver, R. Taylor. 1988. An assessment of the provider role as perceived by black males. *Family Relations,* 37: 426-431.

Lee, C. 1987. Black manhood training: Group counseling for male blacks in grades 7-12. *Journal of Specialists in Group Work* 12, 1: 18-25.

Lefever, H.G. 1981. Playing the dozens: A mechanism for social control. *Phylon* 42, 1: 73-85.

Leibow, E. 1967. *Talley's corner.* Boston: Little and Brown.

Levi-Strauss, C. 1963. *Structural Anthropology.* N.Y.: Basic Books.

Lewis, M. 1982. Adolescent psychic structure and societal influences: A bio psycho social model. *Adolescent Psychiatry* 10: 125-139.

Lewis, O. 1961a. *The children of Sanchez*. New York: Random House.

------- 1961b. The culture of poverty. *Scientific American* 215, 4: 19-25.

Lincoln, Y.S. and E.G. Guba. 1985. *Naturalistic inquiry*. Beverly Hills, Ca.: Sage.

Little, C.B. 1989. *Deviance and control: Theory, research and social policy*. Itasca, Il.: F. E. Peacock Publishers.

Luelsdorff, P.A. 1975. *A segmental phonology of Black English*. Paris: Mouton.

Lum, D. 1986. *Social work practice and people of color*. Monterey, Ca: Brooks/Cole.

Madhubuti, H.R. 1990. *Black men: Obsolete, single and dangerous?* Chicago: Third World Press

Majchrzak, A. 1984. *Methods for policy research*. Newbury Park, Ca: Sage.

Majors, R. and J.M. Billson. 1991. *Cool pose: The dilemmas of black manhood in America*. New York: Lexington Books.

Manis, J. G. and B. N. Meltzer. 1972. *Symbolic interaction: A reader in social psychology*. Boston: Allyn & Bacon.

Mead, G.H. 1934. *Mind self and society.* Chicago: University of Chicago Press.

Merton, R. 1968. *Social Theory and social Structure*. N.Y.: MacMillan.

McAdoo, J. L. 1981. Black child and father interactions. In *Black men*, edited by L. E. Gary. Beverly Hills: Sage.

------- 1993. The roles of African American fathers: An ecological perspective *Families in Society* 75: 28-35.

McGhee, J. D. 1984. *Running the gauntlet: Black men in America*. Washington, D.C.: New Urban League.

McNeil, E. B. 1969. *Human Socialization*. Belmont, Ca: Brooks/Cole.

Miles, M. B. and A. M. Huberman. 1984. *Qualitative data analysis: A sourcebook on methods.* Beverly Hills: Sage.

Miller, W. B. 1958. Lower class culture as a generative melieu of gang delinquency. *Journal of Social Issues* 14: 15-19.

Mintz, S. W. and R. Price. 1976. *The birth of African American culture.* Boston: Beacon Press.

Mishine, J. M. 1986. *Clinical work with adolescents.* N. Y.: The Free Press.

Mitchell, L. 1990. We are the children of everybody: Community co-parenting-A biographic note. In *Black male adolescents: Parenting and education in community context.* Edited by B. P. Bowser, 160-182. Lanham, Md.: University Press of America.

Monte, C. F. 1987. *Beneath the mask: An introduction to theories of personality.* Fort Worth, Texas: Holt, Rinehart & Winston.

Moses, W. J. 1991. Eurocentrism, Afrocentrism, and William H. Ferris' *The African Abroad. Journal of Education* 173: 76-90.

Moynihan, D. P. 1965. *The negro family: The case for national action.* Washington, D.C.: Dept. of Labor.

Musashi, M. 1974. *A book of five rings.* Translated by V. Harris. Woodstock, N.Y.: Overlook Press.

Myrdal, G. 1944. *An American dilemma: The negro problem and modern democracy.* New York: Harper.

National Commission on Children (1991). *Beyond rhetoric: A new American agenda for children and families. Final Report of the National Commission on Children.* Washington, D.C.: U.S. Government Printing Office.

Nichols-Casebolt, A. M. 1988. Black families headed by single mothers: Growing numbers and increasing poverty.*Social Work* 33, 4: 306- 313.

Nobles, W.W. 1974a. Africanity: Its role in black families. *Black Scholar* 5, 9: 10-17.

------- 1974b. African roots and African fruit: The black family.*Journal of Social and Behavioral Sciences* 20, 2.

------- 1980. Extended self: Rethinking the so-called Negro self concept. In *Black Psychology.* Edited by R. L. Jones. New York: Harper and Row.

Oakes, J. 1985. *Keeping track: How schools structure inequality.* New Haven, Ct.: Yale University Press.

Ogbu, J. U. and M. A. Gibson. 1991.*Minority status and schooling: A comparative study of immigrant and involuntary minorities.* N.Y.: Garland.

Oliver, W. 1989. Black males and social problems: Prevention through afrocentric socialization. *Journal of Black Studies* 20, 1: 5 -39.

Orr, E. W. 1987. *Twice as less: Black English and the performance of black students in math and science.* New York: W. W. Norton.

Parsons, T. 1951. *The social system.* New York: The Free Press.

Parsons, T. and F. Bales. 1955. *Family socialization and interaction process.* N. Y.: Free Press.

Patton, J. M. 1981. The black male's struggle for an education. In *Black Men*, edited by L. E. Gary. Beverly Hills, Ca.: Sage.

------- 1993. Psychoeducational assessment of gifted and talented African Americans. In *Race and ethnicity in research methods*, edited by J. H. Stanfield, II and R. M. Dennis. Newbury Park, Ca.: Sage.

Patton, M. Q. 1980. *Qualitative evaluation methods.* Beverly Hills: Sage.

------- 1987. *How to use qualitative methods in evaluation.* Beverly Hills: Sage.

Pearce, D. M. 1983. The feminization of ghetto poverty. *Society*: November/December: 70-74.

Peters, M. F. 1974. The black family perpetuating the myths: An analysis of the family sociology textbook treatment of black families. *Family Coordinator* 23, 4: 349-356.

Petrie, P. 1991. Afrocentrism in a multicultural democracy. *American Visions*, August: 20-26

Pettigrew, T. F. 1988. Integration and pluralism.. In *Eliminating racism*, edited by P. A. Katz and D. A.Taylor. N. Y.: Plenum.

Pfohl, S. J. (1985). *Images of deviance and social control; A sociological history.* N. Y.: McGraw-Hill .

Phinney, J. S. (1988). *The development of ethnic identity in adolescents.* Paper presented at the United States University Workshop on Identity Formation: Theoretical and Empirical Issues. Logan,Ut.: 6/88.

------- 1991. Ethnic identity and self esteem: A review and integration. *Hispanic Journal of Behavioral Sciences* 13, 2: 193-208.

Phinney, J. S. and J. Rotheram. 1986. *Children's ethnic socialization: Pluralism and development.* Newbury Park, Ca.: Sage.

Piaget, J. 1954. *The construction of reality in the child.* N.Y.: Basic Books. (Original work published 1932)

Piaget, J. and B. Inhelder. 1969. *The psychology of the child.* N.Y.: Basic Books.

Pinderhughes, E. 1988. *Understanding race ethnicity and power.* N.Y.: Free Press.

Polyani, M. 1966. *The tacit dimension.* Garden City: Doubleday.

Popenoe, D. 1993. *Sociology.* Englewood Cliffs: Prentice Hall.

Pullman, W. E. 1993. *The Indian Child Welfare Act: A brief policy analysis.* Unpublished paper.

Radin, N. 1972. Father-child interactionand the intellectual function of four year old boys. *Developmental Psychology* 6: 353-361

Reid, H., and M. Croucher. 1983. *The fighting arts.* N.Y.: Simon and Schuster.

Reuter, E. B. 1927. *The American race problem.* N. Y.: Thomas Y. Crowell.

Richman, C. L. 1984. *General and specific self esteem in late adolescent students: Race x gender x SES effects.* Paper presented at the Annual Meeting of the Southeastern Psychological Association, New Orleans, La: March 38-31, 1984.

Rodwell, M. K. 1989. *Policy implications of the multiple meanings of neglect: A naturalistic study of child neglect.* Ann Arbor, Michigan: UMI Dissertation Services.

Rodwell, M. K. and W. E. Pullman. 1991. *The research productivity of social work doctoral graduate: 1960-1988; Qualitative summary and evaluation of open-ended question.* Report to the NIMH Task Force on Social Work Research, Richmond, Va.: Virginia Commonwealth University.

Ryan, W. 1971. *Blaming the victim.* N. Y.: Random House.

Schaefer, R. J. 1990. *Racial and ethnic groups.* N. Y.: Harper Collins.

Schumacher, E. F. 1973. *Small is beautiful: Economics as if people mattered.* N. Y.: Harper and Row.

Schwandt, T. S. and E. S. Halpern. 1988. *Linking auditing and metaevaluation: Enhancing quality in applied inquiry.* Beverly Hills, Ca.: Sage.

Seelye, H. N. 1988. *Teaching culture: Strategies for intercultural communication.* Lincolnwood, Ill.: National Textbook Company.

African American Men in Crisis

Seidel, J. V., R. Kjolseth, and E. Seymour. 1988. *The ethnograph user's guide*. Corvallis, Or.: Qualis Research Associates.

Siegel, E. 1993. Listening to young black men. *Baltimore Sun*, May 8.

Sigel, R. S. and Hoskin, M. 1991. *Education and democratic citizenship: A challenge for multi ethnic societies*. Hillsdale, N.J.: Erlbaum Associates.

Shade, B. J. 1983. The social success of black youth: The impact of significant others. *Journal of Black Studies* 14, 2: 137-150.

Shannon, B. 1973. The impact of racism on personality development. *Social Casework*: 519-525.

Sheal, B. M. 1976. *Schooling and its antecedants: Substantive methodological issues in the status attainment process*. Review of Educational Research 46, 4: 463-526.

Skritic, T. M. 1985. Doing naturalistic research in educational organizations. In Y. S. Lincoln (Ed.) *Organizational theory and inquiry the paradigm revolution*, edited by Y. S. Lincoln. Beverly Hills, Ca.: Sage.

Slaughter-Defoe, D. T. 1992. African-American, Anglo-American Grade 4 Children's concepts of old people and extended families. *International Journal of Aging and Human Development* 35, 3: 161-178.

------- 1991. Parental educational choice: Some African American dilemmas. *Journal of Negro Education* 60, 3:354-360.

Slaughter, D. T. and E. G. Epps. 1987. The home environment and academic achievement of African American chiildren and youth: An overview. *Journal of Negro Education,* 86,1: 3-20.

Smitherman, G. 1986. *Talkin and testifyin: The language of Black America*. Detroit: Wayne State University.

Snyder, T. D. 1987. *Digest of Education Statistics*. Washington, D.C.: U.S. Government Printing Office.

So, A. Y. 1992. The black schools. *Journal of Black Studies* 22, 4: 523-531.

Spencer, M.B., B. Dobbs, and D.P. Swanson. 1988. African American adolescents and socioeconomic diversity in behavioural outcomes. *Journal of Adolescence* 11: 117-137.

Spencer, M. B. 1982. Personal and group identity of black children: An alternative synthesis. *Genetic Psychology Monographs* 106: 59-84.

-------- 1985. *The social and affective development of black children.* Hillsdale, N.J.: L. Erlbaum.

Spradley, J. P. 1979. *The ethnographic interview.* N.Y.: Holt, Rinehart & Winston.

Spurlock, J. 1986. The development of self-concept in Afro-American children. *Hospital and Community Psychiatry* 37, 1: 66-70.

Stanfield, J.H. and R.M. Dennis. 1993. *Race and ethnicity in research methods.* Newbury Park: Sage Publications.

Staples, R. 1982. *Black masculinity: The black male's role in American society.* San Francisco: Black Scholar Press.

-------- 1985. Changes in the black family structure: The conflict between family ideology and structural conditions. *Journal of Marriage and Family* 47: 1005-1015.

-------- 1987. Black male genocide: A final solution to the race problem in America. *Black Scholar* 18, 3: 2-11

Staples, R. and L. B. Johnson. 1993. *Black families at the crossroads: Challenges and prospects.* San Francisco: Jossey Bass.

Steele, S. 1992. *The content of our character: A vision of race in America.* N. Y.: Harper Collins.

Stewart, J. and J. Scott. 1978. The institutional decimation of Black American males. *Western Journal of Black Studies* 2: 82-92.

Stoller, P. (Ed.). 1975. *Black American English: Its background and its usage in the schools and in literature.* New York: Dell.

Strauss, A.L. 1987. *Qualitative analysis for social scientists.* Cambridge: Cambridge University Press.

Taylor, K. J. 1978. A black perspective on the melting pot. *Social Policy* 8, 5: 31-37.

Taylor, M.C. and G.A. Foster. 1986. Bad boys and school suspensions: Public policy implications for black males. *Journal of Black Studies* 20, 1:15-39.

Taylor, R. J., B. R. Leashore, and S. Toliver. 1988. An assessment of the provider role as perceived by black males. *Family Relations* 37, 4: 426-431.

Taylor, R. L. 1976. Black youth and psychosocial development: A conceptual framework. *Journal of Black Studies* 6: 353-372.

-------- 1981. Psychological Modes of Adaptation. In *Black men* edited by L. E. Gary. Beverly Hills, Ca.: Sage.

------- 1989. Black youth, role models and the social construction of identity. In *Black Adolescents* edited by R. L. Jones. Berkely: Cobb & Henry.

Taylor, S. J. and R. Bogdan. 1984. *Introduction to qualitative research methods: The search for meaning.* N. Y.: John Wiley & Sons.

Tesch, R. 1990. *Qualitative research: Analysis types and software tools.* N. Y.: Falmer Press.

Toch, T. 1991. Fighting a racist legacy; Afrocentric schools. *U.S. News & World Report* 111, 74, 12/9/91.

United States Department of Education 1988. *Digest of Educations Statistics, 1988.* T.D. Snyder (Project Director) Washington, D.C.: National Center of Education Statistics.

United States Department of Education 1993. *Digest of Education Statistics, 1993.* T.D. Snyder (Project Director) Washington, D.C.: National Center of Education Statistics.

United States National Advisory Committee on Criminal Justice Standards and Goals. Task Force on Juvenile Justice and Delinquency Prevention. 1976. *Juvenile justice and delinquency prevention.* Washington, D.C: U. S. Government Printing Office.

Uomoto, J.M. 1986. Examination of psychological distress in ethnic minorities from a learned helplessness framework, *Professional Psychology: Reseach and Practice* 17, 5: 448-453.

Valentine, C. 1968. *Culture and Poverty.* Chicago: University of Chicago Press.

Van Dijk, T.A. 1993. Analyzing racism through discourse analysis. In *Race and Ethnicity in Researchs Methods* edited by J. H Stanfield and R. M. Dennis. Newbury Park: Sage Publications.

Vangelisti, A.L. 1988. Adolescent socialization into the workplace: A synthesis and critique of current literature. *Youth and Society* 19: 460-484.

Vizedom, M. 1976. *Rites and relationships: Rites of passage and contemporary anthropology.* Beverly Hills: Sage.

Wacker, R.F. 1983. *Ethnicity, pluralism and race; Race relations theory in America before Myrdal.* Westport, Ct.: Greenwood Press.

Wallace, W. 1972. *Sociological Theory.* Chicago: Aldine Atherton.

Warfield-Coppock, N. 1990. *Afrocentric theory and applications. Volume 1: Adolescent rites of passage.* Washington, D. C.: Boabab Associates.

Webb, E.J., D.T. Campbell, R.D. Schwartz, and L. Sechrest 1965. *Unobtrusive measures.* Chicago: University of Chicago Press.

Weis, L. 1985. Without dependence on welfare for life: Black women in the community college. *Urban Review* 17, 4: 233-255.

West, C. 1993. *Race Matters.* Boston: Beacon Press.

White, L. 1975. *The concept of cultural systems: A key to understanding tribes and nations.* N. Y.: Columbia University.

Williams, D.H. 1986. The epidemiology of mental illness in Afro-Americans. *Hospital and Community Psychiatry* 37, 1: 42-49.

Wilson, A. 1991. *Understanding adolescent black male violence.* N. Y.: Afrikan World InfoSystems.

Wilson, W.J. 1978. *The declining significance of race.* Chicago: University of Chicago Press

------- 1993. *The ghetto underclass: Social science perspectives.* Newbury Park: Sage.

------- 1987. *The truly disadvantaged: The inner city the underclass and public policy.* Chicago: University of Chicago Press.

Woodson, C. 1933. *The mis-education of the negro.* Washington, D.C.: Associated Publishers

Young, D. R. 1969. The socialization of American minority people. In *Handbook of socialization theory and research,* edited by D. G. Goslin. Chicago: Rand McNally.

Index